"I Have Called You Friends . . ."

"I HAVE CALLED YOU FRIENDS..."

Sacramental, Theological and Existential Aspects of Priestly Fraternity

Carlo Bertola

ALBA · HOUSE   NEW · YORK
SOCIETY OF ST. PAUL, 2187 VICTORY BLVD., STATEN ISLAND, NEW YORK 10314

Library of Congress Cataloging-in-Publication Data

Bertola, Carlo.
  I have called you friends.

    Translation of: Fraternità sacerdotale.
    Includes bibliographies.
    1. Catholic Church—Clergy—Religious life.
  I. Title.
  BX1912.5.B4513   1989   262'.142   88-26251
  ISBN 0-8189-0542-5

Designed, printed and bound in the United States of
America by the Fathers and Brothers of the
Society of St. Paul, 2187 Victory Boulevard,
Staten Island, New York 10314, as part of their
communications apostolate.

© *Copyright 1989 by the Society of St. Paul*

Printing Information:

Current Printing - first digit   1   2   3   4   5   6   7   8   9   10   11   12   13   14   15   16   17   18   19   20

Year of Current Printing - first year shown
            1989   1990   1991   1992   1993   1994   1995   1996   1997   1998   1999

An Opening Statement

The Church has always reminded its ministers of the many bonds uniting them in charity through sacred ordination, but it has been especially since Vatican II that their fraternity has been defined as "sacramental" (*cf*. PO 8a).

The ontological bond intimately uniting each of them not only to Christ but also to all other priests is a realization, in a full and special way, of that communion which God willed to bring about in the world by means of the Incarnation of his Son, the image of the perfect communion existing among the three divine persons.

This "intimate" and "sacramental" brotherhood which exists in the priesthood does not arise, therefore, from some kind of functional or psychological necessity. It has a solid basis in the Word of God and in sacramental theology where it is fully covered in the themes on charity and communion.

In our work we shall try to clarify the concept of priestly fraternity in all its richness and power and then seek to thoroughly examine its consequences in the priest's actual life, both at the personal and community levels, in the midst of the pilgrim People of God.

We shall attempt, by way of conclusion, to consider the effects of this brotherly relationship among priests on the formation of candidates to the priesthood and suggest an hypothesis of our own on the criteria of vocations.

Other aspects related to our topic will not be expressly developed but we will make reference to them for the sake of a more unified and comprehensive treatment of the subject. Thus, beginning with a consideration of the People of God as communion, a theme fully studied and generally accepted today, we shall proceed and refer also to the priesthood as a juridical organism, properly speaking, which must be a concrete and external manifestation of communion. We shall discuss the relationship between priests and their bishop, with whom they share a deep reciprocal communion by virtue of the sacrament of Orders (PO 7; *cf.* 2 LG 28), the multiple relationships between priests and the laity (PO 9), and the relationships of priests with religious (*cf.* the document *Mutuae Relationes* of May 14, 1978).

Without treating community life in itself, or the "common life" proper to religious or to institutes of consecrated life (yet taking these into account because communion with God, the Church, and one another is specific to them too), we shall indicate in broad outline the concrete ways in which fraternity among priests has been realized down the centuries and especially the impetus given since Vatican II, their development, and the opportunities they continue to provide priests who are seeking to live the gift they have received to its fullest.

Contents

An Opening Statement v
Introduction ix
   I. Foundations of Priestly Fraternity 3
      a) The Example of Christ .5
      b) The Apostolic College .9
      c) The Primitive Church .14
      d) Tradition and the Magisterium 20
      e) Common vocation, ordination and mission 23
  II. The Concept of Priestly Fraternity 33
      a) Vatican II 34
      b) One Thing Only ''in persona'' and ''sub
         auctoritate Christi Capitis'' 39
      c) True Friendship 43
      d) Fraternity and the Gift of Celibacy 48
      e) Fraternity as a Life Experience 54
 III. Consequences and Applications of
      Priestly Fraternity 65
      a) Human Maturation and Spiritual Progress 66
         In Search of one's identity 66
         Openness to others 68
         Means of Sanctification 71
      b) Difficulties and Risks .82
      c) Priests in the ''Diaspora'' 89
      d) Realized Fraternity 95
      e) Fraternity and the Criteria of Vocations 103
 IV. Conclusion 121

Introduction

The reign of God is made present in Christ Jesus ("*. . . the reign of God has overtaken you*" Mt 12:28; Lk 11:20; 17:21), in his ministry, his miracles, his words spoken "with authority" (*cf.* Mt 7:29; Mk 1:22; Lk 4:32), and in his gathering about himself a small group of disciples. They, for their part, acknowledged the reign of God as something of supreme value, the "precious pearl," "the hidden treasure" for which all else is worth sacrificing (*cf.* Mt 13:44).

While their faith encounter with the Lord may have required the abandonment and renunciation of family (Mt 10:37; 19:29; Lk 14:26; Mk 10:29), it also offered them a unique relationship to him and a share in a new reality: a life in community with the Divine Master in view of a common mission (Mk 3:14). This human community is of an absolutely new type, with a different but no less profound bond than the preceding.[1]

Sharing Jesus' mission means sharing the lot of others who are called to form with him a "family" of brothers who are reciprocally responsible in all fields of the apostolate. It also means to share one's personal spiritual life with them in a special way.

> "As the Father has loved me,
> so I have loved you.
> Live on in my love" (Jn 15:9).

> "This is my commandment:
> love one another
> as I have loved you" (Jn 15:12).

In order that the apostles might become a sign of unity, Jesus prays and offers himself for their sanctification. His love for all becomes distinct in a special way in his love for the apostles and constitutes the beginning and the source of their priestly communion and fraternity. His words about this are explicit:

> "I no longer speak of you as slaves,
> for a slave does not know what
> his master is about.
> Instead I call you friends,
> since I have made known to you
> all that I heard from my Father" (Jn 15:15).

If the Church is the "universal sacrament of salvation" (AG 1) and "the sign and the instrument of intimate union with God and of men among themselves" (LG 1), then the nature of its apostolic mission is that it be a "sacramental" sign by means of the communion among the apostles. It is by living in fraternal love that priests manifest Christ.

> "I have given them the glory you gave me
> that they may be one, as we are one —
> I living in them, you living in me —
> that their unity may be complete.
> So shall the world know that you sent me. . . ." (Jn 17:22-23).

INTRODUCTION

For this reason the Council has applied the concept of episcopal collegiality to priests, as can be noted in various places in its documents,[2] and has declared that the priesthood "has an essentially collegial structure, founded on sacramental fraternity."[3]

Fraternity, it would therefore seem, becomes a *necessary* requirement of the priestly life. The fraternal communion of priests, the Council says, by which they are bound to one another, manifests brotherly love in a sacramental way. It renders the communion which the Lord lived with the apostles visible in our modern world. It acts as a leaven in the communion of the Church and serves the unique role of building up the Kingdom of God here on earth.[4]

FOOTNOTES

1. Cf. T. Matura, *Celibato e communità*, Brescia, 1968, p. 50.
2. Cf. LG 28; SC 41; PO 7,8; AG 18-20; CD 11,15,28.
3. A. Massoleni, "The Common Life of the Priesthood of the Parochial Community," in *Presenza Pastorale* 3 (1970), p. 157.
4. M. Marini, "Celibacy and Priestly Fraternity," in *Sacerdozio e Celibato*, Milan, 1975, pp. 895ff.

COUNCIL DOCUMENT ABBREVIATIONS

AG	*Ad Gentes*
CD	*Christus Dominus*
DV	*Dei Verbum*
GS	*Gaudium et Spes*
LG	*Lumen Gentium*
NA	*Nostra Aetate*
OT	*Optatam Totius*
PO	*Presbyterorum Ordinis*
SC	*Sacrosanctum Concilium*
UR	*Unitatis Redintegratio*

Abbreviations

OLD TESTAMENT

Genesis	Gn	Nehemiah	Ne	Baruch	Ba
Exodus	Ex	Tobit	Tb	Ezekiel	Ezk
Leviticus	Lv	Judith	Jdt	Daniel	Dn
Numbers	Nb	Esther	Est	Hosea	Ho
Deuteronomy	Dt	1 Maccabees	1 M	Joel	Jl
Joshua	Jos	2 Maccabees	2 M	Amos	Am
Judges	Jg	Job	Jb	Obadiah	Ob
Ruth	Rt	Psalms	Ps	Jonah	Jon
1 Samuel	1 S	Proverbs	Pr	Micah	Mi
2 Samuel	2 S	Ecclesiastes	Ec	Nahum	Na
1 Kings	1 K	Song of Songs	Sg	Habakkuk	Hab
2 Kings	2 K	Wisdom	Ws	Zephaniah	Zp
1 Chronicles	1 Ch	Sirach	Si	Haggai	Hg
2 Chronicles	2 Ch	Isaiah	Is	Malachi	Ml
Ezra	Ezr	Jeremiah	Jr	Zechariah	Zc
		Lamentations	Lm		

NEW TESTAMENT

Matthew	Mt	Ephesians	Ep	Hebrews	Heb
Mark	Mk	Philippians	Ph	James	Jm
Luke	Lk	Colossians	Col	1 Peter	1 P
John	Jn	1 Thessalonians	1 Th	2 Peter	2 P
Acts	Ac	2 Thessalonians	2 Th	1 John	1 Jn
Romans	Rm	1 Timothy	1 Tm	2 John	2 Jn
1 Corinthians	1 Cor	2 Timothy	2 Tm	3 John	3 Jn
2 Corinthians	2 Cor	Titus	Tt	Jude	Jude
Galatians	Gal	Philemon	Phm	Revelation	Rv

"I Have Called You Friends . . ."

I.

Foundations of Priestly Fraternity

The law of solidarity present in the universe has its primary basis in the "mode of being" of God, who is himself a communion[1] of three divine persons.

The human creature, who by nature has a deep need for socializing (GS 25), has been called to an intimate communion with God himself, so much so that original sin has further whetted this insuppressible need.

The whole history of salvation with its fundamental structure, the Covenant, thus becomes the actualization of this communion from an historical and communitarian aspect, as *Presbyterorum Ordinis* continually stresses (*cf.*, for example, n. 16).

In the Old Testament the history of salvation becomes the story of the encounter, the communion, between God and men first in Abraham (Gn 17:4-7; 18:1-5), then in a people (Ex 19:4-5; 29:43-46; Dt 32:10-11; Hos 2:21-22, etc.), expressing itself in cult (Lv 3:1-5), in the Covenant (Ex 24:4-8), in the Law (Ps 119:1-2), in prayer (Ps 42:2-3; 65:5; 74:1-2), and in brotherly solidarity (Lv 19:17-18; Dt 6:5).

Through the descendants of Abraham, all the peoples of the earth have been called to communion with God (Ps 89:4-5; Is 49:3-6).

But it is especially in the New Testament that *Koinonia* expresses all its intensity of meaning in Christ, the Sacrament of communion between God and men and of men among themselves (Ep 2:19; Col 1:5; 3:3; Rm 5:2; 8:19-22). He is the favored Son who reveals to us the Father's true image (Jn 1:18; 14:9), the "image of God" (2 Cor 4:4), in communion with the Father in the Spirit (Jn 5:19; 7:16; 8:28; 12:49).

By means of the radical orientation of Christ to the Father, we find the solution to the most pressing of human problems — that of communion with God: "... *through him we both* [Jews and Gentiles alike] *have access in one Spirit to the Father*" (Ep 2:18). And the Father has blessed us, inundating us with his love (Ep 1:3-10), making us a single family of brothers and calling us "*to participate in his life and glory*" through the Church, the new People of God, "*the living sign and efficacious instrument of the love of God for man and for the world.*" He has made us a "saved" and "saving" community (See *Vocation and Mission of the Laity* . . . , 1986 Synod of Bishops, n. 14).

Baptized in the one Spirit to make up one body (*cf.* 1 Cor 12:13), participating — through the breaking of the Eucharistic bread — in the Body of the Lord, *"we have been elevated to communion with him and among ourselves."* Members of that Body (*cf.* 12:27), individually we are also *"members of one another"* (Rm 12:5). And even though not all have the same function (*cf.* Rm 12:5), nevertheless every Christian has to act in intimate and vital communion with the whole Church (See *Vocation . . . , ibid.,* nos. 15-21).

The same Lord, then, "so that the faithful might be united in one Body . . . , promoted some of them as ministers," marking them with a "special character" which likens them to him, "in such a way as to be able to act in the name of Christ, the Head of the Church" (*cf.* PO 2).

a) The Example of Christ

Participants in the one priesthood and ministry of Christ (*cf.* LG 10, 28; PO 2), and his collaborators (PO 2), to increase the growth of and build up his whole Body which is the Church (PO 12) and to reunite it into one family (LG 28; PO 5-6), his sacred ministers must unite themselves ever more to Christ "in the discovery of the Father's will and in self-giving for the flock entrusted to them" (PO 14), always penetrating more deeply into the mystery of his life and mission. Thus we discover that

Christ, the Son of God, by becoming man, wanted to live two realities, related to the life of the Trinity and to the apostolic community. Here we enter into the very heart of the mystery of the Godhead where the infinite and eternal communication of love among the three divine persons overflows into creation, finding a completely unique expression and realization through Christ's human experience with those who were *"his own."* He surrounds the apostolic community with superabundant attention because this community is to be the privileged locus and living image of that impetuous current of love which flows within the Trinity.

Thus we learn how the very life of our Lord, as it emerges from the pages of the Gospel, was not a life of solitude but of fellowship: *"He named twelve as his companions whom he would send to preach the good news"* (Mk 3:14).

Norms of behavior and rules regarding the common life, like that of making oneself *"the last and servant of all"* (Mk 9:35; *cf.* Lk 22:27), of looking first at one's own defects before pointing out those of another (Mt 7:3), of being *"at peace with one another"* (Mk 9:50) are also to be understood in the light of the Trinitarian concept of community.[2]

This little fraternity, this small group of men who believed in Jesus, received the gift of the Father's love through a moving experience of communion which made them feel that they were indeed sons and, for that reason, radically related as brothers one to another irrespective of any possible social or family barriers. Referring above all to them, the Lord affirms:

> "These are my mother and my brothers. Whoever does the will of God is brother and sister and mother to me" (Mk 3:34b-35).[3]

Little by little this unheralded communion proposed by our Divine Master opens the way. He calls some to him to share his very life and he will go so far as to make a complete gift of himself out of love (the paschal mystery) which will open the doors to that final banquet in the Father's house when the communion of all will be perfect and complete.[4]

We must also consider Christ's unique priesthood in whose mystery the principle of communion is better understood and defined. The "supreme and eternal Priest" guarantees his saving presence in the world through his revelation of the Father's love and through the sacrifice by which he glorified the Father (Heb 7:27; 9:26). Thus, *"by means of the blood of Christ"* (Heb 10:19), we find ourselves immersed in God with him. But he also prolongs his loving and life-giving presence in time by means of his priesthood which he shares with men through the sacrament of Orders. This sacrament, while expressing the richness of God's gifts and mirroring the different mansions of the spiritual life, is always and only at the service of unity and the principle of communion.[5]

Fraternity, then, does not come about through spontaneous generation. We are brothers in Christ because we are children of the same Father, by means of the same Spirit whom Christ has given to us. Through the mediation of Christ, we are united to the Father who enables us to live as brothers one to another, welcoming together the gift of the Spirit. Sharing the same Spirit of Christ, we cannot but be brothers of the Lord and brothers to one another.[6] For this reason, apart from different gifts and services, the little apostolic fraternity is also a charismatic fraternity. And the communion lived therein is, in the last analysis, a gift of the Spirit. The invitation that Jesus extended to some in particular to follow him is at the same time a call to an experience of fraternity before being able to dedicate oneself to a mission (*cf.* Lk 14:26). His word is a word of fraternity; it is a "call" to live the faith in the context of brotherly love:

> "His commandment is this:
> We are to believe in the name
> of his son, Jesus Christ,
> and are to love one another
> as he commanded us" (1 Jn 3:23; cf. 1 P 1:22).

Fidelity to him from those who participate in his priesthood must be based on mutual love (as *Sacerdotalis Coelibatus* recalls, n. 59, where Jn 13:13, 34-35 is also cited).

The primitive gospel experience, that is, the experience of Christ with his life companions, is presented to us as a precise proposal which makes its acceptance the measure itself of fidelity to him.

Unlike his contemporaries (for example, the community of Qumran) who placed an ideal before their disciples — even a great one like that of God or the Law, Christ put forth his very person.[7]

b) The Apostolic College

Christ reunites *"the dispersed children of God"* (Jn 11:52) throughout the world, beginning to bind some to himself with the power of the Spirit, forming a family of brothers with them so as to bring them into communion with the Father (Jn 17:21). Through them, this love is to reach the world (Jn 17:23). They call him *rabbi* (Mt 9:11; 17:24; 23:8; 26:18), but he is above all a prophet who announces the Kingdom of God. And for this purpose he calls together a group of brothers to share closely in this mission. He has called them (Mk 10:21) and they have loved him in return (Jn 1:35-51).[8]

> " 'Come and see,' he answered.
> So they went to see where he was lodged,
> and stayed with him that day" (Jn 1:39).

> " 'We have found the Messiah!'
> (This term means the Anointed.)
> He brought him to Jesus . . ." (Jn 1:41-42).

> "He said to them:
> 'Come after me and I will make you
> fishers of men.'
> They immediately abandoned their nets
> and became his followers" (Mt 4:19-20).

> " 'Follow me.'
> Levi got up
> and became his follower" (Mk 2:14).

It is Christ and his mission which united them. What established the group was an "undeniable call": "Come! Follow me!" "And in this one act, the Twelve experienced both conversion and call; they perceived their vocation as the concrete expression of their adherence to Christ. The apostolic life was the specific way in which the Gospel was presented to them; they took the *kerygma* seriously and agreed to become its messengers."[9]

It is from among the most faithful that Christ chose a small group comprising a significant number, twelve, representing the twelve tribes of Israel.

> "He summoned the men he himself had decided upon,
> who came and joined him.
> He named twelve as his companions
> whom he would send
> to preach the good news..." (Mk 3:13).

> "At daybreak he ... selected twelve of them
> to be his apostles" (Lk 6:13).

They became apostles solely on the basis of a precise vocation: "*It was not you who chose me; it was I who chose you*" (Jn 15:16). And this vocation, this "undeniable call," came from God. It was the object of a colloquy within the bosom of the Trinity, and the reason Christ passed the night in prayer before selecting the apostles (Lk 6:12-13). It is also the reason that he was able to affirm at the moment of his departure from them: *"These men you gave me were yours"* (Jn 17:6).

An "undeniable call" must be answered by an equally energetic and irrevocable response, an immediate execution. Not even the most sacred duties can be allowed to prevail (Lk 9:59-61), nor is there time for farewells. What is being asked for is more than a simply "generous" life. Such an intimate relationship with Jesus unifies apostolic existence to such an extent that "function" and "life" become one. Apart from unreserved dedication, a proven perseverance in an irrevocable lifestyle that permits no second thoughts is likewise required:

> "Whoever puts his hand to the plow
> but keeps looking back
> is unfit for the reign of God" (Lk 9:62).[10]

Here we are already given an indication of the fact that the life which the apostles embraced was the prototype of a lifestyle which would later become normative. Ministry and apostolic life were one and the same for them; "following Christ" and "living in perfect community" were but two sides of the same coin. Fraternity was not a concession or an added extra; it didn't have a functional aspect for them, but rather delineated something of the essence itself of the priesthood. Further still, Christ chose to live with the apostles in order to bring home to them the fact that in fraternity the mystery of the Trinity present in the world in his own person was made visible:

> " 'Lord,' Philip said to him,
> 'show us the Father
> and that will be enough for us.'
> 'Philip,' Jesus replied, 'after I have been with you
> all this time, you still do not know me?
> Whoever has seen me has seen the Father . . .' " (Jn 14:8-9a).

That is why "the apostles, in following Jesus and renouncing their former lives and jobs, treasured the Absolute in his Person; they demonstrated for future centuries that 'to believe would be to follow, the truth would be a society.' "[11]

Christ, therefore, engages the apostles full time. To form a perfect community with them he exacts an intimacy that includes total conformity of heart and life. Only in this way will they be able to enjoy with him the confidences reserved for friends (Lk 12:3) and come to know clearly the mystery of the Kingdom of God (Mk 4:11). Each of the apostles then becomes a living profession of faith in Jesus Christ. And the college of the Twelve becomes truly apostolic, thus beginning "that common life among persons who help each other to believe in order to witness to Jesus before the world, and who show towards one another the same concern that they have for all humanity . . ."[12] In this context, how significant are the Lord's words: "*Where two or three are gathered* in my name, *there am I in the midst of them*" (Mt 18:20)!

The fraternity brought about by their common life required their disengagement from both their family of birth as well as from their own proper families inasmuch as Christ, calling them to himself, absolved them of all preceding bonds in order to create for himself a new "family" (Mk 3:35). He is the foundation upon which an absolutely new and much wider fellowship would be built (Mk 10:28-31). The same thing is to be said of the fraternity of the apostolate, when the disciples are sent out *"two by two"* (Mk 6:7; Mt 10:1; Lk 9:1; Mk 3:14-15) not so much so that they can be of mutual help to one another and still less so that they can keep an eye on one another, but precisely so that what they proclaim can be made visible, for the people need to "see" in order to believe. And nothing is more "visible" than love. "Heart knowledge" is much richer and more productive than the adherence of the mind.

This new reality, this communion of life with Christ, cannot but produce in them a joy which has little of the human and much of the divine. It is a "theological joy" because it comes from knowing that they are loved by the Father: *"The Father himself loves you, because you have loved me and have come to believe that I came from God"* (Jn 16:27). Their joy is great because it presupposes an equally great interior freedom, a refusal to set conditions in order to belong totally and solely to the Father and completely available for mission.

Above all, this "theological fellowship" is to be lived in shared service: *"The Son of Man has not come to be served but to serve . . ."* (Mk 10:45). Such service is made up of practical deeds and concrete gestures. It is a challenging school for whoever cultivates dreams of power. It goes so far as the paradigmatic gesture of the washing of feet as the reference point of the whole mission of Christ.[13] Making oneself *"the last of all and the servant of the rest"* (Mk 9:35) is the best guarantee of fraternity. With no time for theoretical discussions and exercises in one-upmanship, practical and concrete service favors sticking together, mutually giving and accepting aid in a spirit of charity.

Interior freedom generates that availability which leads the apostle to *"take up his cross"* (Mk 8:34). Indeed, "his communion in the cross of Jesus, right up to bearing the signs of it in his flesh, is his whole life" (*cf.* Gal 6:7).[14] Only in this way can one truly be "reborn," have a new identity in a new "family," and live in anticipation of that definitive and perfect one in heaven.

c) The Primitive Church

The love of the Father, the example of Christ, and the grace of the Holy Spirit worked the wonder of the transformation of the apostles in such a way that each of them could say, with St. John, that he proclaimed what he had seen and touched:

> ". . . so that you may share life with us.
> This fellowship of ours is with the Father
> and with his Son, Jesus Christ" (1 Jn 1:3).

Their proclamation of the good news was the communication of an experience which was absolutely life-determining for them:

> "This is what we proclaim to you:
> what was from the beginning,
> what we have heard,
> what we have seen with our eyes,
> what we have looked upon
> and our hands have touched —
> we speak of the word of life" (1 Jn 1:1-3).

The apostle's communication was "all that more personal one might think because it attempted to share with someone else an event that had turned his whole life around . . . Communion is above all an encounter with concrete persons who know one another, who speak to one another, and who communicate to one another their experience of Christ and who thus come to possess in common that which for each of them is the most important thing in life; that is, his or her personal encounter with the Lord . . . Only the one who knows from personal experience what it is to have communicated to others his own living of Christ and to have received from them in return their experience of the Lord knows what the word Church means."[15]

This is what happened to the primitive Church which was born of such a proclamation, namely the interpersonal communication of this experience of Christ. "The communion of which the Acts of the Apostles (2:42) and the First Letter of John (1:3, 6, 7) speak, that togetherness (Ac 1:14; 2:46; 4:34; 5:12; 15:25) so characteristic of those first communities, is a gift of God; it is the new mode of being that comes from above. It is a participation that God grants us of his mysterious "being together" in the Trinity. It is our sharing, through grace, in the togetherness which bound Jesus to his first disciples whom he called to be his companions (Mk 3:14).[16]

Through baptism, God made a gift to the early Church of the communion characteristic of his own Trinitarian life, just as each one of us has had an experience of interpersonal communion within the Church. "Apostolic life" was inseparable from "apostolic ministry" in the newly founded Church, almost as if the latter could not produce all the fruits of conversion and of the following of Christ without the former."[17]

We are speaking here of the communion which originated, as it were, and established the Church: *"God is faithful; and it was he who called you to fellowship with his Son, Jesus Christ our Lord"* (1 Cor 1:9). It is a communion brought about by Christ through his paschal sacrifice in which he gave us all his love and united us to one another as brothers (Ac 2:23; 3:13ff.; 10:39; 13:26ff.). It is a communion effected by him when he raised us up to share in the loving and eternal embrace between him and the Father and poured forth his love *"into our hearts by the Spirit who has been given to us"* (Rm 5:5). It is a "society" of Jesus which lives by his love, which is charged with the service

FOUNDATIONS OF PRIESTLY FRATERNITY

of the Word but which especially forms around his table: *"They devoted themselves to . . . communal life . . . [and] the breaking of bread." "They broke bread in their homes"* (Ac 2:42-46).[18]

The point of departure is always the table where Jesus breaks bread with them. He himself chose the supper as the visible sign of the invisible and anticipated gift of the Kingdom (1 Cor 11:17-34). The supper always has reference to him: the supper is *"the supper of the Lord"* (1 Cor 11:20); the chalice is *"the cup of the Lord"* (1 Cor 10:21; 11:27). It is *"through Christ"* that communion is offered to us by the Father so that we might live our fellowship in oneness of heart and mind.[19]

The Acts of the Apostles underscores the characteristics of the first Christian communities which were held in common with the apostolic fraternity: "the undeniable call," "the irrevocable response," total involvement, unreserved service, unconditional following, and radical renunciation for the sake of an equally unlimited dedication to the cause of the Kingdom. The early Christian communities were, therefore, a prefiguring, an example, a point of reference for the whole Church. The fraternity they practiced was the *"bit of yeast"* which increased faith, hope and love to the edification of all, thus *"winning the approval of all the people"* (Ac 2:47).

There is no lack of evidence regarding the life of these first budding communities, such as that of Jerusalem (Ac 1:12-14; 2:41-47) or others even (Heb 13:1-2, 16; Rm 12:10) where this kind of fraternity was practiced. And we're not dealing here with a generic kind of fraternity which united all believers, even if in a very lively way, but rather of a new, very intensive kind of fellowship which constituted a very strict bond between the newly converted and was expressed in a community life, much like that of a close knit team, and which was considered normal for one who had given up his or her own family for the sake of the Gospel. Particular expressions of Paul in reference to his closest collaborators, such as Timothy, Titus, Luke and others, show this clearly (*cf.* Ph 2:19ff.; 1 Tm 1:2; 2 Tm 1:2; Ti 1:4; Phm 1).[20]

Whoever left on a mission (a couple, a group, or an individual alone) could thus count on the help, support and hospitality of many brothers and sisters, realizing also in this way the Lord's word to the one who has left everything for his sake and that of the Gospel, namely that they should receive a hundredfold in this life: houses and brothers and sisters and mothers and children, etc. (Mk 10:29-30). On this point, the example of Paul, which we have already cited, is enlightening. He formed around himself a group of collaborators who, based on their sharing of the ideals of Christ, were convinced that by his resurrection Christ was for the Church the living and present Lord in such a way that "the more real and profound their communion with Him, that much more alive and real would be their communion with one another in the Church: *'thus we, though many, are one body in Christ and individually members of one another'* (Rm 12:5)."[21]

The apostle's "unmarried" condition (*agamos*; see 1 Cor 7:7), along with his constant preoccupation about the various churches (*cf.* 2 Cor 11:28; Ph 2:20) to which he is united with bonds of great affection, permits him to enter into "personal relationships, deep friendships with certain persons, and above all with his closest collaborators: Timothy, first of all, and then Titus, Silvanus, Luke and others."[22]

Of this Pauline fraternity we have more than one piece of evidence (Ac 13:1-3; 15:39-40; 16:1-3; 18:5; 1 Cor 9:6). And little by little we see the names of Barnabas, Mark, Silas, Timothy and others appearing with the new foundations, new missions, new apostolic activities and even with the inevitable difficulties attached to them. Silvanus and Timothy, Titus and many others especially will be called, from time to time, "my brother," "my beloved brother," "our dear companion," "collaborator," "companion in work and conflict" for the purpose of establishing Paul's fraternal relationship with them in view of the spreading of the Kingdom.

If the apostle is the bearer of communion and fraternity, he is also their guarantee. As "ambassador of Christ," when the communion is broken and the fraternity is threatened, Paul's presence becomes one of reconciliation (*cf.* 2 Cor 5:18-21) because he does not look to his personal prestige but to the good of the community so that it may quickly regain peace in the integrity of communion (*cf.* 2 Cor 7).[23]

d) Tradition and the Magisterium

The witnesses of the patristic era, while carrying on the practice and the teaching of the apostolic college and that of the early Christian communities, stress the spiritual and apostolic life which priests must lead in union with the bishop and the people. And they do so more from a pastoral and ascetical than from a theological point of view.

In this respect we can name St. Ephrem, St. Gregory Nazianzen, St. Basil, St. John Chrysostom, St. Augustine, St. Jerome, and St. Ambrose.[24]

With time even the meaning of the word "apostolic" will change, not without some distortion. Talk will be of common life, continence, sharing of goods, etc. Pachomius, Basil, Cassian and Benedict[25] will curiously claim for themselves the "superior way of the apostles."

Significant figures in the union of ministry and apostolic life are St. Eusebius of Vercelli with the clergy of his diocese, St. Augustine with his *Rule*, and Crodegang of Metz with the clerics of his cathedral. Later St. Peter Damian and Hildebrand seek to revive the *apostolic form of life* at a time when the condition of the clergy left much to be desired. Other attempts to overcome the division between the apostolic life and the ministry are to be found among the Premonstratensians, the Dominican Order of Preachers, the Friars Minor of St. Francis of Assisi, St. Ignatius' Society of Jesus[27] and the like.

Among the theologians of the scholastic period, we limit ourselves to noting that St. Anselm and St. Thomas Aquinas especially are among those who insist on a sense of fraternity among priests.[28]

The Church and its magisterium has always insisted on the bond of charity which must unite her ministers, both for mutual support and for efficacious witness. We may recall, for example, the admonitions of Pope Siricius († 399),[28] the *Apostolic Constitutions* (400),[29] the Council of Nicea (352),[30] Pope St. Gregory the Great († 1604),[31] and the Council of Rome (826).[32] The Council of Trent (1545-63)[33] develops a theology of the priesthood which "becomes operative by virtue of the sacrament; whose apostolic activity requires union; the discipline of the clergy, even when it seems to be in decline juridically, finds its foundation in the asceticism proposed by the Fathers, in the imitation of Christ and in conformity to the life of the apostles."[34]

More recently we find the specific recommendations of the Supreme Pontiffs, such as the Exhortation of St. Pius X, *Haerent animo* of August 4, 1908,[35] the encyclical of Pius XI, *Ad catholici sacerdotii* of December 20, 1935,[36] and the Apostolic Exhortation of Pius XII *Menti nostrae* of September 23, 1950.[37]

After Vatican II, Pope Paul VI, in his encyclical *Sacerdotalis Coelibatus* of June 24, 1967, established an explicit connection between "sacramental fraternity" and celibacy. And at n. 79 he affirmed that "Priestly chastity is increased, protected and defended by a lifestyle, an ambience, and an activity which is becoming to the minister of God for whom it is necessary to foster to the utmost that 'intimate sacramental fraternity' (PO 8) which all priests enjoy by virtue of their sacred ordination."[38]

The theme regarding priests in ecclesial communion and in particular their relations among themselves, with an explicit reference to Vatican II (PO 8), is taken up again by the Third Synod of Bishops (held between September 30 and November 6, 1971) in the document entitled *The Ministerial Priesthood.*[39]

Pope John Paul II, on more than one occasion, has reminded priests of the many ties which, in a certain sense, must make visible their fraternity both in their daily life and in the ministry that the Synod called "essentially communitarian." On November 9, 1978, for example, he said to the clergy of Rome: "The communion of priests among themselves and with the bishop is the fundamental condition of union among the People of God. This constitutes their unity in plurality and in Christian solidarity. The union of priests and bishop must become the wellspring of the reciprocal union of priests among themselves and of groups of priests."[40]

In the "Letter of John Paul II to All Priests of the Church on the Occasion of Holy Thursday, 1979," the principal points of the doctrine of Vatican II contained in the Constitution *Lumen Gentium* and in the Decrees *Presbyterorum Ordinis* and *Ad Gentes* regarding our theme are recalled quite often. The letter says, among other things, at n. 1, par. 3: "Vatican Council II which, in a very explicit way, underscored the collegiality of the episcopacy in the Church, also gave a new form to the life of priestly communities, bound among themselves by a special tie of brotherhood and united to the bishop of each particular Church . . ." And further along he quotes St. Ignatius of Antioch: "We are eager to fulfill all things with that harmony which is pleasing to God, under the presidency of the bishop who represents God, and with the priests who represent the apostolic college, and with the deacons, most dear to me, to whom has been entrusted Jesus Christ's role of service."[41] In his address to the German Episcopal Conference at Fulda on November 17, 1980, he expressed himself in these words: "Many priests are consumed by work but they become loners and lose their bearings. It is much more important that the unity of the priesthood become lived and felt. Support everything that strengthens priests in their encounter with one another and in their mutual help in living the Word and the Spirit of the Lord."[42]

e) Common vocation, ordination and mission

Now we are better able to define the bases of priestly fraternity. In fact, to be more precise, we can even speak of the "sacramental fraternity" of priests. Thus, using strict logic, we will be talking about the "remote" basis, which is the vocation itself, of an "ontological" basis, the sacramental foundation of holy Orders, and of a "teleological" basis which has to do with the mission which priests share of announcing the salvation which they celebrate sacramentally.[43]

It is clear that what we tend to separate for the sake of attentive analysis is, in fact, all one. Vocation, consecration and mission are three aspects or three phases of the one process. If God calls someone, a consecration follows his appeal and both are made in view of a mission. Christ himself, who affirmatively answered the Father's call ("Here I am, Lord; I come to do your will," Heb 10:7), is the supreme and eternal Priest "whom the Father has consecrated and sent into the world" (Jn 10:36) "to give witness to the truth" (Jn 18:37). How can one forget that passage of Isaiah (61:1-2) which Christ makes his own in the synagogue at Nazareth?

> " 'The Spirit of the Lord is upon me;
> therefore he has anointed me.
> He has sent me to bring glad tidings
> to the poor. . .' " (Lk 4:18-19).

Christ, on his part, commissions the apostles: "*As you have sent me into the world, so also have I sent them into the world*" (Jn 17:18) and the apostles are aware of being the continuators of Christ because, like him, they, too, have been called, consecrated and sent to announce the Kingdom, but always united among themselves in charity:

> "Father, protect them with your name
> which you have given me
> that they may be one,
> even as we are one" (Jn 17:11).

In the dogmatic Constitution *Lumen gentium*, at n. 28c, the Second Vatican Council affirms that "in virtue of their common sacred ordination and mission, priests are bound among themselves by an intimate fraternity." This indicates clearly that priestly fraternity does not arise out of sentiment or any other human motive, even though these may have their importance. It is rather founded on profound and solid theological bases. The gift of vocation, the grace of ordination, the patterning on Christ in participating in his mission are what constitute the objective reasons for priestly communion or fraternity. These presuppositions of a theological and spiritual nature precede every other aspect of a psychological, pastoral or practical kind.[44]

This theological unity among priests "constituted in the order of the priesthood through the laying on of hands" is such that their fraternity may be correctly defined as "sacramental" thus confirming that theirs is an ontological bond deeply rooted in their very personality, transforming and structuring their existence. It is not something that can be reduced simply to the also profound bond arising from baptism.[45] This fraternity "is realized through the grace typical of the sacrament of Orders and by the imposition of the hands of the bishop which makes priests 'servants of communion' to the point of becoming 'experts of communion.' "[46]

Deserving of emphasis here is the deep meaning of the rite of the imposition of hands on the heads of newly ordained priests, of which we have various testimonies from the third century to the present.[47] This liturgical tradition of the imposition of hands on the part of the "bishop who ordains" is symbolic of the essential link between episcopal priesthood and presbyterial priesthood. And that imposition which is performed by the priests who are present at the sacred ordination of their confreres manifests, with striking evidence, the bonds of the brotherhood of the "one priesthood," all of which is significantly crowned by a eucharistic concelebration.

All this unfolds in a well-defined community, the local Church, where the priestly fraternity finds its concrete ecclesial dimension, defined by both time and space.

The bond of consecration, whose author is Christ himself — a deep sacramental bond which reaches far beyond any possible juridical aspects — is strictly tied in with the upbuilding of the Body of Christ. This is its theological basis. All priests, "intimately united among themselves by this priestly fraternity," forming the "one presbyterate," contribute to the "one same work" notwithstanding its multiplicity of functions and new adaptations (PO 8). For that reason, just as there exists one priesthood, so, too, there exists just one goal for priestly mission.[48]

"As the Father has sent me, so I send you" (Jn 20:21), Christ told the apostles when he confided to them the mission which he had received from the Father and promised the assistance of the Holy Spirit. The apostles, for their part, transmitted this mission to their successors, bishops and priests. And this mission is what, ontologically speaking, makes the priest "function" just as sacred

Orders makes him "be." The real Body of Christ (the Eucharist) requires the mystical Body of Christ (the Church). We, therefore, find a true *koinonia* between bishop and priest, bishop and presbyterial college, and every priest with all other priests: one priesthood, one ministry.[49]

Presbyterial communion, a communion of faith and life, is also a communion of "proclamation" and more than ever "a particular manifestation of the Spirit for the common good" (1 Cor 12:7).

The whole reality is given marvelous sign value when the salvation event is sacramentally celebrated. The celebration of the Eucharist is the culminating moment of priestly ministry — the most intense moment of sacramental communication — because there the priest is involved with all his being and existence in the dynamism of sacramental self-giving, when Christ makes a total gift of himself under the humble signs of bread and wine. In the "invitation to fraternal communion" (GS 38), from the intimacy that Christ wants to have with each one of his priests (Gal 2:20), it is much easier for priests to move to intimacy with one another: *"Because the loaf of bread is one, we, many though we are, are one body, for we all partake of the one loaf"* (1 Cor 10:17).[50]

Meeting around the altar to celebrate the Eucharist with unanimity of sentiment, together with their own bishop, priests manifest the unity of the Church, the unity of the priesthood, the unity of the presbyterate (*cf.* SC 57; PO 7, 8). Sharing together in the Bread of life and drinking from the Chalice of salvation, they remain united to one another and with the Lord because the Eucharist is the font, the principle, and the "bond of charity," the humble yet powerful sign of unity, the center of communion shown forth even visibly.

We can therefore conclude that "the fraternal bond which unites priests in a singular way runs all through the mystery of Christ the Priest. It is a bond which carries the seal of God's initiative in calling and sending them as priests into the Church with the task of announcing the word and celebrating the Eucharist so that the community may grow in faith and love. It is a question, then, of a profound fraternity, inscribed in the very secret of one's being by the hidden power of the Spirit, who marks forever the one whom he calls and admits to the community of the Church with this specific sacramental qualification. The fraternity of priests arises, therefore, from the sacrament, and in the sacrament it finds its first expression and the roots of its nourishment.[51]

FOOTNOTES

1. In Greek, *koinonia*, which in the New Testament indicates participation in the same life or grace; hence, also an intimate and vital relation between God and the Christian and among Christians themselves in Christ. In theological language, generally it is the term "relation" that is used when referring to God.
2. Cf. C.M. Martini, *General Introduction to the Synoptic Gospels*, in *Il Messaggio della salvezza*, Vol. 6, Turin, 1979, pp. 81ff. D. Marzotto, commenting on n. 59 of the encyclical *Sacerdotalis Coelibatus* of Paul VI, writes: ". . . Christ did not find himself in the condition of solitude (*solus fuit*) except during his passion (*tristissimis in rerum adiunctis* . . .). On the contrary, in the beginning Christ organized a type of existence which, while not contemplating conjugal life, nevertheless was not meant to be a life of solitude but of companionship and this by means of the choice of those whom he wanted as witnesses and companions (*socios*) for life and whom he loved to the end, to the limits of his strength [See Jn 13:1]." Cf. his article "On the Nature of Priestly Celibacy," in *La Scuola Cattolica*, 6 (1979), p. 605.
3. Cf. M. Legido, "Jesus' Apostolic Fraternity," in *De dos en dos. Apuntos sobre la fraternidad apostolica*, Salamanca, 1980, p. 86.
4. This is what the document of the Italian Episcopal Conference [hereafter CEI], *Comunione e comunita*, 1981, n. 25, means when it affirms that Christ lived a "relationship of intimate friendship with the Twelve he had chosen *because they remained with him* [See Mk 3:14], sharing confidences with them as with friends (cf. Jn 15:16), calling them to participate in his mission of evangelization (cf. Mk 6:7), and sharing with them his moments of prayer and trials (cf. Lk 22:39; Mt 26:40, etc.). And before dying, he left the best and mysterious sign of communion, the Eucharist, as a witness to his life given for them and for all (cf. Lk 22:14-20; Mt 26:26-29; Mk 14:22-25; 1 Cor 11:23-25)" (cf. *Comunione e comunita*, in *Pastoral Letters 1980-81*, Verona, 1983, col. 632).
5. Cf. A. Ballestrero, *In Comunione con Cristo. Meditazioni teologiche sul sacerdozio*, Rome, 1977, opp. 65f. For a more in-depth study of Christ's priesthood, see J. Galot, *Pretre au nom de Christ*, Martini-A. Vanhoye, *Bibbia e vocazione*, Brescia, 1983 (2); A. Vanhoye, *Pretres anciens, pretre nouveau selon le nouveau testament*, Paris, 1980.
6. Cf. M. Legido, *op. cit.*, p. 106.
7. "To be more precise, from the historical-existential point of view, the experience which Jesus proposed can be described in these terms: the person called renounces some very precise family relationships to dedicate himself principally to service and friendship with, the heeding of and living with, another historically determined person: Jesus, the Divine Master from Nazareth. And in placing himself at the service of this Master, the person called simultaneously encounters other disciples with whom he must form deep and constant relationships" (D. Marzotto, "The Celibate in the New Testament," in *La Scuola Cattolica*, 110 1982, p. 341).
8. Cf. M. Legido, *op. cit.*, pp. 114ff.
9. "Thus their 'accepted' vocation coincided with their act of personal faith; the shape that their life was to take begins to appear, from the moment of their conversion, as the palpable expression of their call; their vocation becomes the

concrete expression of what they would have chosen anyway given a sincere faith and a love disposed to every eventuality" (A. Manaranche, *Come gli apostoli*, Brescia, 1971, p. 83).
10. *Ibid.*, pp. 90ff.
11. *Ibid.*, pp. 86-87.
12. *Ibid.*, pp. 101-111. "It is something quite different from a 'rescue squad' for lonely hearts."
13. *Ibid.*, p. 90f.
14. *Ibid.*, p. 113.
15. S. Dianich, *La Chiesa mistero di comunione*, Turin, 1975, pp. 57-58.
16. Cf. C. M. Martini, "Our Priestly Communion," in *La Parola nella citta*, Bologna, 1982, p. 51.
17. "It (the new born Church) considered it all the more indispensable in so far as, after the Ascension of Jesus to the Father, the preaching of the faith had a great need of being confirmed by that eloquent manner of living which was evident proof that the Jesus who had died was indeed alive (AC 25:19)." Cf. A. Manaranche, *op. cit.*, p. 120.
18. Cf. M. Legido, *op. cit.*, pp. 101-105.
19. *Ibid.*, p. 106.
20. Cf. D. Marzotto, *op. cit.*, pp. 352-353.
21. S. Dianich, *op. cit.*, p. 61.
22. "Even more. From this point of view it can be said that St. Paul almost always worked as part of a team in his apostolate, with a solidarity that was very close knit as is evidenced in particular by the greetings of his letters where he associates his collaborators with him." Cf. D. Marzotto, *art. cit.*, p. 347, where in a note he also mentions P. Ternant, "The Common Life of the Apostles and their Collaborators According to the New Testament," in *Spiritus*, 41 (1970), 154-166.
23. Cf. G. Marcandalli, *I segni del vero apostolo nella seconda ai Corinzi*, Milan, 1982, pp. 73-87.
24. St Ephrem, "Sermo de sacerdotio," in *Opera Omnia*, III, cols. 1-6; St. Gregory Nazianzen, *Tract on his Flight*, PG 35, 407-514; St. Basil, in *Enchiridion Asceticum*, 264-265 and 271-272; St. John Chrysostom, *Tract on the Priesthood*, PG 48, 623-692; *Enchiridion Asceticum*, 347; St. Augustine, in *Enchiridion Asceticum*, 611-698, and in *Letters*; St. Jerome, *Letter to Nepotianus*, PL 22, 527-540; St. Ambrose, *De Officiis*, PL 16:9ff.
25. Cf. St. Benedict, *Rule* 72, 1-11, where a vivid sense of fraternity among priests and their confreres is expressed.
26. Cf. A. Manaranche, *op.cit.*, pp. 121 ff.
27. Cf. the *Letters* of St. Anselm of Aosta, in *Opera Omnia*, ed. F. S. Schmitt, London-Paris, 1946-1961; St. Thomas Aquinas, *Summa Theologiae*, III, questions 22, 71 and 82; *Supplementum*, questions 18-20 and 34-40.
28. Cf. *Enchiridion Clericorum*, pp. 15ff.
29. Cf. *Enchiridion fontium historiae ecclesiasticae antiquae*, pp. 679-680, 690.
30. Cf. *Seminaria Ecclesiae Catholicae*, pp.31 ff.
31. Cf. *Enchiridion Clericorum*, pp.63 ff.
32. Cf. *Ibid.*, pp. 76ff.
33. Cf. the Decree *De Reformatione*, Session XXII, can. 1, XXIV-XXV.
34. Cf. G. Genacchi, "The Priest and the Other Priests," in *Il prete per gli uomini d'oggi*, Rome, 1975, p. 579.

FOUNDATIONS OF PRIESTLY FRATERNITY 31

35. For the complete document: P. Veuillot, *Il nostro Sacerdozio*, Vol. I, Milan 1956, pp. 119ff.
36. For the complete document, see AAS, 28 (1935), pp. 5-53.
37. Cf. AAS, 42 (1950), pp. 657ff., in particular, p. 693: "We approve and strongly recommend in as much as it is already the wishes of the Church that the custom of the common life among priests of the same parish and of neighboring parishes be introduced and extended. If this practice of common life involves some sacrifice, there can be no doubt that great advantages will nevertheless come from it: above all else, it daily nourishes zeal and the spirit of charity among priests; it then gives a marvelous example to the faithful of the detachment of God's ministers from their own interests and family; and finally it gives witness to the scrupulous care with which they protect priestly chastity."
38. Cf. also nn. 80, 81 in *Ench. Vat.*, Vol. II (1976 10), p. 1243. And speaking to the clergy of Rome on February 9, 1970, he said: "Ecclesial communion exists; but does this always equal a perfect communion of spirits, intentions, works? Are we sometimes loners in the midst of a multitude which should comprise brothers and constitute one family? Do we not prefer at times to be isolated, to be ourselves, distinct, and even separated, or perhaps even disassociated, and finally antagonists, in the midst of our ecclesiastical assembly? Do we really feel we are ministers united in the same ministry of Christ? Is brotherly affirmation, which makes us concerned about and joyful over the welfare of our confreres, always alive among us?" Cf. *Teachings of Paul VI*, Vol. VIII (1980), p. 119.
39. Cf. part II, II, in *Ench. Vat.*, Vol. IV (1978 10), pp. 750ff.
40. Cf. *Teachings of John Paul II*, Vol. I (1978), p. 115.
41. Cf. *Ench. Vat.*, Vol. VI (1980), pp. 900ff.
42. Cf. *L'Osservatore Romano*, November 17, 1980.
43. Cf. G. Cristaldi, "Fraternity and Priestly Friendship," in *Rivista del Clero Italiano*, 55 (1974), p. 681.
44. Cf. G. Cenacchi, "Priestly Fraternity," in I Sacerdoti nello spirito del Vaticano II, ed. A. Favale, Torino-Leumann 1968, pp. 643ff.; A. Favale - G. Gozzelino, *Il ministro presbiterale*, Torino-Leumann, 1972, p. 214.
45. Cf. C. M. Martini, "Celibacy and Priestly Fraternity," in *Sacerdozio e celibato*, ed. J. Coppens, Milan 1975, pp. 895-916.
46. C. M. Martini, "Our Priestly Communion," *loc. cit.*, p. 52.
47. Cf. *Traditio Apostolica* of Hippolytus of Rome; *Ordre* in ThC, col. 1254; the various sacramentaries — Leonine, Gregorian, Gelasian, etc. For a study of these themes in great depth, see J. Lecuyer, *Le sacrement de l'Ordination. Recherche historique et theologique*, Paris 1983, p. 281.
48. Cf. M. Caprioli, *Sacerdozio e Santita. Temi di Spiritualita Sacerdotale*, Rome 1983, 3, pp. 132ff.
49. Cf. G. Cenacchi, *op. cit.*, pp. 576ff.
50. Cf. A. Favale, *Dissenso cattolico e comunione ecclesiale*, Torino-Leumann 1975, pp. 94ff.
51. G. Cristaldi, *art. cit.*, p. 678.

II.

The Concept of Priestly Fraternity

Up to now we have been studying the gift of communion offered to us by the Father, the example of the life of Christ himself who lived two realities as man and as God, and the lifestyle of the apostles who had an uncommon experience of communion with Christ the God-man and one another, thus becoming the proto-types of the disciples of Christ in general and of priests and bishops in particular.

We have also briefly considered the witness of the early Church and of the small communities which faithfully received the message which was conveyed by the type of earthly existence that our Lord Jesus led, the incentives proposed by the Church's two-thousand-year experience and by the authoritative interventions of the magisterium, and, finally, the appeal of sacramental theology with its evident ontological rationale.

All this has enabled us to glimpse something of the strength of the deep bond which exists between priests, a bond which unites them in the whole of their lives and in their every relationship, a bond greater than that flowing from baptism and which gives rise to duties of mutual concern which must be addressed day after day.

Into this tradition of the priestly fraternity willed by Christ, lived by the apostles and always insisted upon, enters Vatican II which defined in an excellent way the minister of the People of God (PO 6-8) and described in an outstanding manner his "apostolic" existence (*ibid.*, 15-17), from the days of the churches described in Acts (*ibid.*, 17 and 21), addressing itself to all priests indiscriminately because by reason "of Orders and ministry all priests, both diocesan and religious, are associated with the episcopal body and, according to their vocation and grace, serve the good of all the Church" (LG 28b; *cf.* PO 1; OT, preface).

a) Vatican II

Despite all that has been said and even though there were theological and historical assumptions involved, one can say that only with Vatican II was priestly fraternity stressed in such an explicit way, revealing new and unusual aspects. Scanning the various documents rapidly, we notice that *Lumen gentium* calls this fraternity "intimate," to be lived "spontaneously and freely" (LG 28c);

Presbyterorum Ordinis says that priests live "in the midst of men like brothers among brothers," leading them with "goodness, sincerity, firmness of spirit and constancy" (PO 3); "they bring the family of God together like a fraternity animated by unity" (PO 6a); "they find themselves in the midst of the laity to lead all to the unity of charity 'loving one another with brotherly love' . . . " (Rm 12:10; PO 9c), guarding and re-enforcing "the necessary unity with their brothers in the ministry" (PO 15b) because — as the Decree *Christus Dominus* recalls — they constitute "but one family" (CD 28a). Examining the documents more in detail, we notice especially that the Council explicitly asserts that priestly communion finds its motivation in sacred ordination and mission, developing a theology based on Christ, the One sent by the Father, who in turn sends the apostles who in turn send others who make up the one presbyterate with the bishop (LG 28).

> "In virtue of their common sacred ordination
> and mission, all priests are bound among themselves
> by an intimate fraternity, which must
> spontaneously and freely manifest itself in mutual help
> — spiritual and material, pastoral and personal —
> in the conventions and communion of
> life, work, and charity" (LG 28a).[1]

The Decree on the Pastoral Office of Bishops in the Church, *Christus Dominus*, affirms in the same place (n. 28):

> "All priests, both diocesan and religious,
> in union with the bishop, participate in the one
> priesthood of Christ . . . they constitute a single
> presbyterate and family. . . .
> Moreover, all
> diocesan priests are united among themselves. . . ."

The Constitution on the Sacred liturgy, *Sacrosanctum Concilium*, had in fact already provided the bases for a clearer and deeper doctrine on the unity among priests. This course of treatment, followed in the documents already cited, reaches its highest point in the definitive text of the Decree, *Presbyterorum Ordinis*, with its addition of the word "sacramental" in reference to priestly fraternity, an absolutely new element which emerged in the discussion of means[2]:

> "Priests,
> constituted in the order of the presbyterate through ordination,
> are all united among themselves
> by intimate sacramental fraternity;
> but, in a special way, they form one presbyterate
> in the diocese to whose service they are assigned
> under their proper bishop. . . .
> Therefore, each is united to the other members
> of the presbyterate
> by particular bonds of apostolic charity, ministry and fraternity. . .
> Each of the priests, therefore,
> is bound to his confreres
> by the bond of charity, prayer, and every kind of collaboration,
> thus showing that unity with which Christ wished his own
> to be made perfectly one
> so that the world might know that the Son
> had been sent by the Father (cf. Jn 17:23)" (PO 8a).

The same paragraph then specifies even further the concrete contents and manifestations of this fraternity, speaking of the harmony between generations of old and young priests, of hospitality, sharing of goods, of the care of priests with problems, of brotherly encounters, of spiritual, intellectual and pastoral help, of common life, of associations, of understanding toward those who might have fallen into some deficiency, showing themselves "on each occasion as true brothers and friends." We shall have reason to return to all these points further on. In the Decree on Priestly Formation, *Optatam totius*, at n. 2, after having recalled that "the duty to foster priestly vocations falls on the whole Christian community," the Council Fathers speak thus of the contributions of families and educators, but they especially remind the presbyterate that:

> "All priests should show their apostolic zeal
> most of all in favoring vocations —
> and by their humble, industrious life,
> lived with interior joy,
> as well as by the example of their mutual priestly charity
> and their brotherly cooperation
> they should attract toward the priesthood
> the spirit of adolescents" (OT 2a).

These conciliar texts which, together with others we could mention, emphasize some very important concepts: If the Church exists to realize communion with God, she — like the body of Christ which lives in the presence of the Spirit — knows that access to the Father is made possible by her Head. But she also knows that there are those who act *in persona Christi* — because "in virtue of the sacrament of Orders, the image of Christ, supreme and eternal Priest (*cf.* Heb 5:1-10; 7:24; 9:11-28), they are consecrated to preach the Gospel, tend the faithful, and celebrate the divine cult" (LG 28a) — those who must offer the concrete example to the People of God of "a fraternity animated by the spirit of unity" (*ibid.*). Thus, "having generously become models of the flock" even in fraternity and "combining their zeal and their work," it will be easier to suppress "every cause of dispersion so that all the human race may be drawn once again to the unity of the family of God" (LG 28d, e).

This fraternity certainly does not come about spontaneously nor from human good will. It is rather a gift from on high, the fruit of God's choosing, directed to the communication in turn of the gift of salvation. The fraternity thus assumes its value as a "sign of that communion which shapes the interior and profound visage of the Church."[3]

Besides, as Father Congar says, "ministries cannot be recognized except as a structuring within a community which is Christianly qualified and alive. Ministry does not create community as though from the outside or from above. Ministry is placed within a community by the Lord so as to stir and build it up."[4] The presbyterial fraternity cannot, therefore, remain in the indeterminateness and elusiveness of a kind of mystical happening. But, as it has become so delineated by the steps the Council took, it must continually verify its authenticity, viewing itself interiorly, in fidelity to the word spoken by its Founder and especially in imitation of the life he led.

b) One Thing Only "in persona" and "sub auctoritate Christi Capitis"

With brief but bold strokes, the Council delineated the concept of the priestly brotherhood of those who act *in persona Christi Capitis* (LG 28a; PO 2c). We shall now attempt to examine this concept thoroughly starting with this fact: In the fulfillment of his ministry, the priest cannot prescind from divine initiative. It is not he who decides, but he is called and sent by Christ to bring salvation to his brothers (*"You have not chosen me, but I have chosen you . . . "* [Jn 15:16]). In his special role within the Mystical Body, he works in the name and person of Christ, the Head. His is a qualified service, therefore, which he exercises in virtue of a special grace which enables him to enter into a most personal ontological-sacramental relationship with Christ who thus prolongs his mission in time and space.

This total immersion in Christ, besides being a participation in his love for all, is such that every priest occupies a privileged place in the heart of the Lord: *"I no longer speak of you as slaves . . . Instead, I call you friends"* (Jn 15:15). It also becomes a total immersion in charity: service of the Church and universal love which implies and supposes in the first place a kind of "unity in love" with one's confreres in the priesthood. Pope Paul VI mentions this in his encyclical *Sacerdotalis Coelibatus*, nos. 59 and 79, where he often speaks of the example of Christ and his "commandment of love, renewed especially in conjunction with the institution of the priesthood, as if to say that fidelity to him, in particular on the part of those who participate in his priesthood, must be given form especially in mutual love (Jn 13:15, 34-35 is cited)."[5]

The brotherhood of priests is, then, nothing other than a full and meaningful realization of the Lord's commandment: *"Love one another"* (Jn 13:34; 15:12; 17). If the document on *The Ministerial Priesthood* affirms that the priest is "at the service of communion" (Part I, n. 6) and that "his ministry tends always toward the unity of the whole Church . . . ," "then even the priestly ministry itself is essentially communitarian" (*ibid.*) and the whole life and activity of the priest must be inspired by this fundamental principle.[6]

There is, therefore, a very strict relationship between the sacrament of Orders and fraternity (this is why the priesthood is referred to as a "sacramental fraternity"). If the sacrament of Orders is, so to speak, the "objective gift" of grace which recalls in its ontological root the priesthood of Christ, then the fraternity among priests is the "subjective given" of assimilation, the logical outcome of the communion-like rapport among those who are called to share in the same sacramental service to the Church.

The ontological-sacramental relationship just referred to between Christ and the priest is operative at the most intimate level in the person of the minister. And, while completely respecting his personal freedom and integrity, it works in such a profound way that he may truly conform himself to Christ, experience the feelings of Christ, imitate his example, and make Christ's priesthood efficacious and real to the extent that the priest truly becomes an *alter Christus* who can say with the apostle Paul, *"The life I live now is not my own; Christ is living in me"* (Gal 2:20).

It is precisely this profound experience of personal communion with Christ and of intimacy with him that produces an intimate communion among priests, because communion with the Divine Master cannot be separated from a fraternal relationship with the other disciples whom he many times referred to as "friends" (*cf.* Mt 10:40; Lk 12:4f; Jn 15:14) and "brothers" (Jn 20:17).[7]

This interpersonal communion, therefore, goes far beyond one's personal efforts at collaboration or the desire for friendship or other psychological realities because it is founded on theological realities, beginning with the priest's participation in the mysterious "togetherness" of Christ with his apostles. It is a matter of saying:

> "Of his fullness
> we have all had a share" (Jn 1:16).

In order to be "signs and builders of unity" among the People of God (See *The Ministerial Priesthood*, 1971 Synod of Bishops), priests must feel and have a strong awareness of their unity, rendering their priestly fraternity visible in their daily life and ministry. They should carefully cultivate communion with the Pope, the successor of Peter and the visible head of the universal Church, the principle and foundation of the unity of faith and communion of the whole People of God (*cf.* LG 8b; 23a, etc.). They should feel themselves united to their bishops "by priestly honor" (LG 28b). Their relationship must bring to mind the intense love of Christ and his apostles (*Sacerdotalis Coelibatus*, n. 92). In their "role as sharers in the episcopal order" (PO 12a), priests must perceive their resonance with the hierarchy as a matter of consistency if not of identity. The bond uniting them with their proper bishops is, according to the Council, an essential part of their very life and ministry.

This awareness of their unity must then be translated into a communion with one another in the work of salvation (*"As the Father has sent me . . ."* Jn 20:21, etc.) and be of spiritual value to their sanctification, something which becomes ever more authentic because it is felt within and lived without.[8]

The "one thing only" of priests is, therefore, the bond of supernatural love which makes priests "intimates of Christ" and "intimates of one another." Priestly life and existence are understood and developed under the sign of communion and fraternity. And priestly fraternity itself is seen as the efficacious sign of the union of priests in the light of the theology of "signs" and "Church-Sacrament" in which the Second Vatican Council positions it.

If priests, by means of ordination, "are elevated to the condition of living instruments of Christ the eternal priest" (PO 12a), they become for that very reason living moments of communion by way of their assimilation-incorporation in Christ. Grace and a free personal response will facilitate the attainment of that unity of life in which personal life and ministry have the same basis and flow into each other, manifesting themselves "in a lifestyle collegially lived at the level of internal charity and, within the limits possible for each one, even in unity of action, thus developing the communitarian dimension of their spiritual life."[9]

c) True Friendship

Finding themselves in a "de facto" situation — the ontological *status* of fraternity with such an intense bond (as the theological vision just elaborated has shown us) — priests are not exempt from the danger of limiting themselves to vague and ultimately arid exhortations to "charity" towards their fellow brothers in the priesthood. This is true even though, originally, their relationship was a matter of personal choice. It is necessary to go beyond the factual ontological situation to reach a friendship which "expresses a '*willed*' bond and, as such, one nourished with care which goes beyond constancy even to the point of intensity."[10] Fraternity tends, therefore, to translate itself into and emerge as friendship: in its turn "proceeding from fraternity, friendship returns to fraternity with that typical enrichment proper to friendly communication. Born of communion, communication returns to communion."[11]

For a reason, therefore, that is more than just serious and noble, namely, in order to enjoy a truly effective means of sanctification, priests must seek at all costs that which, in an almost untranslatable but effective expression, is called in Spanish *"una vivencia de amor de amistad"* ("a lifestyle of loving friendship").

St. Thomas defines friendship as "a reciprocal love of benevolence with some communication of goods."[12] Applying this definition to our own case, priests must move well beyond the reciprocal love based on the law of universal charity.

"Every priest, in fact, because he is one, participates in that special love of Jesus Christ which produces the priestly vocation and brings it to completion. Occupying the same privileged place in the heart of Jesus Christ, all priests can only feel very close to one another; and thus the preaching of the Lord produces a deep bond of supernatural love among them . . . Is it possible to stand worthily in the circle of the Lord's intimates without also being supernaturally intimate with all those who stand within the same circle? Never has the French axiom been better applied: 'The friends of my friend are my friends.' "[13]

As Aristotle said early on, friendship either finds men equal or makes them equal. This is the true reason why the priest is the picture of Christ: *Sacerdos alter Christus*. And Christ lived in friendship with others. He chose friendship as his mode of expressing human love. He died for friendship. In fact, he consumed his life in friendship[14] to show that

> "There is no greater love than this:
> to lay down one's life for one's friends" (Jn 15:13).

In effect, within the rich typology of human relations, Christ only put special emphasis on two of them, and interestingly enough they were relationships of parity, namely, the conjugal union and the union of friendship (or fraternity). Both of them he raised to the "rank" of a sacrament (Matrimony and Holy Orders). "Thus the typical dynamic of Orders and its spirituality is the evolution in a sacramental context of the basic human relationship that we call fraternity or friendship."[15]

Moreover, as the Angelic Doctor already noted, it is the goal of every other human relationship. Without it the others fail, while it can exist alone. And on the existential plane, as Lacordaire recalled, it is the purest, freest, and most virginal of all human relationships . . . As regards friendship, one can observe how it is the typical structure used by Christ in the encounter with, the preparation, establishment and mission of the apostles and the one which lasted as their form of human relationship (Jn 13:35; 15:15f; Lk 12:4)."[16]

Friendship, human and spiritual in value at the same time, was actually restored by Christ with his initial coming into this world such that, living it in the first person, he purified it of every material and egoistic concern, restoring it to the "pure love of benevolence" and "authentic cordial giving," founding it on supernatural charity and manifesting it exteriorly in gestures which were always marked by his total self-giving.[17]

In this light the richness of Christ's humanity is better understood when we see that its fullness contemplates and even embraces the predilection of friendship. How could we not recall here the special fondness — the model for the spiritual life of the priest — that Jesus had for John (*cf.* Jn 21:20), the apostle who, more than any other, could say from personal experience: *"We have come to know and to believe in the love that God has for us"* (1 Jn 4:16)?

If friendship is the natural outlet for the dynamic of fraternity, priestly fraternity cannot nourish itself solely on an intense life of prayer but must also translate itself into an authentic experience of friendship with all the human virtues that accompany it.

> Priests must truly live as "brothers,
> sharing joys and sufferings, united in an open spirit,
> without secrets,
> banded together by the same apostolic sentiments
> because they are friends."[18]

This is behind the Council's thought when, referring to Christ who calls his disciples not slaves but friends (*cf.* LG 28), it purposely combines the words "brothers and friends" (PO 7b), for only in the profound experience of true friendship can brothers be signs of joy and Christian hope.

Some intensity of communication is needed to entertain the possibility of friendly relations, to keep them up and to develop them. Distance and time can cause even a sincere and genuine friendship to cool if there is not some regularity in this area of communications. "The fact that friendships are suspended by the thread of good communications accounts for the fragility and risk inherent in every friendship, even those born of a chosen and desired fraternity."[19] Therefore, since the stakes are so high precisely where the communications involved in friendship seem so difficult, the charity that comes from communion and perennially tends toward communion will always be capable of creating and inventing new gestures of benevolence that build up confidence and hope.

One's personal duty will then be that of assuring authenticity in friendship because only in authenticity can friendship fully measure up to the dignity of the human person and positively increase priestly fraternity. How much more could be said about this. How much further there is yet to go in order to purify some relationships where artificial mannerisms, formalities, conventions, and fantasies are still so widespread and because of which fraternity is inevitably compromised!

Authentic human friendship which arises from the friendly thrust of priestly fraternity will certainly not end up being exclusive because it carries within itself a brotherly vocation which is fulfilled in giving and in openness, where even things which belong to the realm of the senses are understood as a sign of the profound spiritual and supernatural gift of self.[20] A priest friend — by really consenting to share, in depth, experiences and difficulties, along with gifts of nature and grace with his confreres — precisely because his friendship springs from a sense of brotherliness which is also sacramental, will know how to make himself available, seek various ways in which to get together, to dialogue, and to overcome eventual polarizations and the inevitable tensions which are present in the priesthood.

Friendship is one aspect of the encounter between the human and the divine in the priest, between nature and the grace of the sacrament. And, as we shall see, it is also one of the greatest aids to the interior sanctification of the priest's spiritual life and existence.

d) Fraternity and the Gift of Celibacy

Reflection on the theme of friendship has reminded us of the importance of interpersonal relationships for all people, emphasizing the need for profound, reciprocal and joint human relations (today regarded as essential to a person's psychological balance). Does this need for friendship not create a conflict with the celibate choice of the priest in which some relationships would be missing and others could become dangerous?

Some consideration of the meaning of ecclesiastical celibacy seems called for here. Celibacy in our world is often regarded as an unnatural human state of life or a convenient choice, selected by those suspected of individualism or misogyny and who live on the fringes of society for almost exclusively selfish or functional reasons.

As an important premise, it should be remembered here that the choice of celibacy is a mature choice requiring emotional stability, weighty judgment, self-mastery, and especially a capacity to give oneself to others as indispensable presuppositions for a decision that also implies certain very real renunciations. Only with personal and affective maturity and the overcoming of the attractions which come from the flesh — along with the constant exercise of human and supernatural virtues — will it ever be possible to live in continuity and fidelity a love without distinction or restriction, open to all, like the love of Christ.[21]

We have already indicated how the experience of the Kingdom of God as an absolute value, was felt by his closest companions, following the example of Christ, as an "all-encompassing" experience which brings in its wake certain precise life-choices and concrete renunciations (Mt 19:11, 27; 1 Cor 7:1, 7; 8:32-34). Those who have *"left everything"* to follow him, who *"have made themselves eunuchs for the sake of the kingdom of heaven,"* who have renounced not only things and family but also themselves (Mt 16:14-25; Jn 12:25-26) have understood the radical nature of this pledge requested by Christ.

This invitation to leave all in order to follow him was made by the Lord to some women as well, confident that the apostles all understood well the meaning of the gift of celibacy, as well as the renunciation and dominion of self that it requires (*cf.* Lk 8:2; Ac 1:14). But at the same time, after the Master's example who "gave his celibate choice a special form, placing it in the context of a small group, the apostolic fraternity,"[22] they also understood the requirements of this new lifestyle established by Christ, the little fraternity or apostolic community where, besides the intuition of being able to direct one's personal life along the line of following Christ, there was also an awareness of the particular type of love with new, profound bonds which had to accompany it. "Celibacy, thus lived in fraternal communion, renders visible and ritualized the community of life lived by the Lord with his own, thus becoming a ferment for the communion of life which must animate the whole Church."[23]

The celibate priest, it bears repeating, is "he who above all else lives a gospel experience. He has left everything to follow Christ as a fisher of men; as a consequence, he is deeply situated in an apostolic communion, and is, therefore, in the world and in the Church, a witness in his way of the unlimited nature of the Kingdom and of friendship, a friendship that is personal and at the same time open to the most universal dimensions."[24]

We are thus drawn to a radical reflection on the meaning of celibacy at the level of theological anthropology explored so well by the encyclical *Sacerdotalis Coelibatus*. The reasons compelling some to share Christ's priestly mission are the same reasons which impel them to embrace a celibate lifestyle (n. 23). The apostolic challenge proceeds apace within the ambit of profoundly human relationships in a totality of self-giving (nos. 27 and 29), as the full and unique realization of the command:

> "You will, therefore, love the Lord your God with all your heart, with all your mind and with all your strength . . . And you will love your neighbor as yourself" (Mk 12:30-31).

Working backward in time, it seems that priestly celibacy, rather than arising from a codification of a spontaneous orientation of the clergy at the beginning of the fourth century, is of apostolic origin.[25]

And the same call of the first disciples which the Fourth Gospel presents to us would appear to constitute that first nucleus of followers of Christ who, like John the Baptist, were vowed to a life of celibacy.[26]

While it is presented to us as pertaining to the internal logic of a determined religious experience and of a precise witness of life, celibacy does not exclude the intersubjective dimension of one's own realization almost as if this were in concurrence with the exclusive and radical choice of God and the Kingdom. Were that true, we would find ourselves face to face with an obvious contradiction, namely a closing in on the self and an exclusion of every deeply human relationship precisely on the part of him who has made a "profession" of greater love.[27]

The priest's life is not, therefore, a following of Christ which prescinds from every other human relationship, but one which encourages other human relationships apart from the conjugal one. The priestly ministry lived in the first centuries of the Church in a collegial manner goes so far as to consider common life as necessary for those who have chosen evangelical celibacy in this apostolic perspective.[28] Priests give up marriage to follow Christ in an apostolic community where "they can realize those deep and beneficial interpersonal relationships" that favor their deep openness to the love of Christ and make them a typical sign of that communion which Christ wills to establish in the world,[29] without forgetting that the integration of brothers in the spirit of fraternal communion is itself part of one's integration into the total Christ.

Even though it envisions some renunciations, celibacy is a gift, even a "great" gift. However,

"Not all can accept this word,
but only those to whom that is granted" (Mt 19:11).

Far from diminishing or mortifying the human person with his or her need for intersubjectivity and communication, thus endangering the person's psychological balance, "consecrated celibacy is completely founded on love; it is a life of love. And only in the climate of genuine, great, and natural love is it possible to live celibacy with joy and enthusiasm. We are definitely at the opposite end of egoism here."[30]

This great richness of celibacy which contemplates the interhuman dimension, "the ordered insertion of the priest into an assemblage of social relations" (See *The Ministerial Priesthood*, n. 4d), and in particular into an abiding daily fraternal relationship with other priests and the bishop, "reminds everyone of the depth of fidelity in love and manifests the supreme significance of every single life" (n. 4b), which is "associated with Christ in a special way," and which "manifests ahead of time the freedom of the sons of God . . . " (*ibid.*).

Celibacy and fraternity, therefore, have a deep intrinsic rapport with one another because, as the Sacred Congregation for Catholic Education affirms in "Educative Orientations for Formation to Priestly Celibacy" (April 11, 1974): "Voluntary celibacy makes sense in the context of 'relationship': it is lived within a fraternal community that presupposes exchange and which allows one to reach others beyond the need one may have for them: and it is an initiation into 'nonpossessiveness.' The sign of a well-lived celibacy is the capacity to create and maintain valid interpersonal relations" (n. 49).

And for the attainment of the "priest's affective maturity," after having said that "a man can be judged mature who prefers living in community because he is open to the gift of himself to others" (n. 18), the document affirms that "the priest is capable of true and profound friendships, particularly as these are useful for his affective growth when they are developed within the priestly fraternity" (n. 30). They are words that ought to give us pause.

When we recall, as *Sacerdotalis Coelibatus* makes quite clear, that priestly fraternity strengthens chastity,[31] we can give assurance, at the same time, that whoever embraces the celibate priesthood can live a mature love, a love that is authentically oblatory.[32] "Love" is not "taking" but "giving," not "seeking" but "offering." It is the making of a continuous gift of oneself. And this requires a difficult renunciation of ourselves in an ongoing pledge to discover and eliminate from our own lives all that could offend that communion.

e) Fraternity as a Life Experience

The example of Christ is the basis of every priestly choice. For this reason all priests must become one with him in order to discover his original intention which is that of a ministry inseparable from their lives, apart from any successive specification and charism. Sacramental fraternity is also ministerial fraternity (*cf.* Jn 13:3-20) because the same Spirit that unites priests in communion unites them also in service (*cf.* LG 4).

Fraternal communion among priests implies communion on the plane of apostolic ministry as well as on the plane of apostolic life, even if, unfortunately, we have been accustomed for a long time to separate the two.[33]

The call to the priestly life is a call to live an interpersonal relationship of parity which precedes an efficient plan for the apostolate. It is the call to an experience of fraternity possibly in the common life, in order to place oneself at the service of the Kingdom.[34]

Fraternity in ministry and in life supposes a climate of living more than it does a juridical rule that must be respected. It presupposes an equality among brothers ahead of any hierarchical relationship, a sharing of choices more than obligations and laws that must be observed. It demands an availability which is at once enriching on both the human and the supernatural levels, and goes beyond attachment to one's own position or to the desire to do everything by oneself, condemning every form of individualism. As a gift from on high, with bonds of divine (and, therefore, universal) origin, sacramental fraternity is antecedent to the formation of every diocesan priesthood. At the same time, every presbytery — as a fraternal organization which unites all the priests of the diocese and their bishop — must become its more immediate and concrete expression in the spirit of universal communion (see *The Ministerial Priesthood*, Part I, n. 6).

Fraternity is formed of attachments which are the exact opposite of the segregation of persons or groups. It requires the harmonization of duties because — without an overload of work for some and a dangerous lack of involvement on the part of others — each priest, in his own place and with his own charisms, according to his own competencies, does something edifying for the common good. It facilitates the division of mansions, without the scramble for position on the one hand and the lack of challenge on the other, based on a criterion that goes beyond that of simply dividing up the pie. And it provides mutual help based on complementarity and understanding, convinced that the meeting of different minds will eliminate any kind of leveling process, depersonalization or the breakdown of personal balance. Like the Council (PO 8b) we, too, should devote a word to a delicate point in priestly relations — that between the young and the old.

> "The older should treat the younger as brothers,
> helping them in their initial activities
> and responsibilities in the ministry,
> making an effort even to understand their mentality,
> different though it may be,
> and viewing their efforts with sympathy."[35]

The above suggestions call for a very open attitude and keen psychological sensibility both of which presume a serious ascetical intent.

> "The young, for their part, should have respect
> for the age and the experience of the elderly;
> they should know how to join them
> in studying the problems affecting the care of souls
> and they should collaborate with them" (*Ibid.*).

Here, too, the expressions used in the Council text refer to an attitude which requires an ascetical effort made over a long period of time.[36]

Real fraternity has some very basic requirements: above all, reciprocal awareness which must not be limited to occasional get-togethers or, worse, to superficial and gossipy chattering. It should be fruitful and treasured, the kind of awareness expressed reciprocally in a personally enriching form of communication. Next, the desire for an encounter which helps first of all in the discovery and then in the appreciation of the human and spiritual wealth of each one who makes up the presbyterate, with his qualities of intuition, study, accomplishments, and experiences that help to tone down individualism and conquer discouragement. Finally, availability for dialogue in which everyone participates in the conviction that there is always something to correct or to learn from others, dialogue in which the contribution of each adds something and in which the confrontation of one's opinions with those of others obliges one to reflection, promotes self-criticism, and stimulates research in the awareness that harmony comes not only from an identity of views but rather from the serenity with which these are expressed.[37]

Nothing is more disturbing — and it would obviously be a counterwitness to the faithful — than a mind closed to new ideas, a hardening of one's positions, negative criticism, backbiting, willfulness or stubbornness in relationships among priests who are called to announce to the world the message of Christ's love.

If the encounter among priests, more than being an instrument geared to the apostolate, is an aid in bringing priests together at the level of communion, it must then also involve pastoral structures, starting with the diocesan presbyterate,[38] the Priests' Council, the diocese itself, including the diaconate, the pastoral region, the parishes and so forth. In particular:

> "The service of authority, on the one hand, and
> the exercise of obedience that's not merely passive on the other,
> must be carried out in a spirit of faith,
> with mutual charity, filial and friendly confidence,
> continual and patient dialogue

so that the collaboration and responsible cooperation
of priests and bishop may succeed in being
sincere, human, and, at the same time, supernatural''
(See LG 28; CD 15; PO 7; and
The Ministerial Priesthood, Part II, II, n. 1).

In this regard the Priests' Senate has an important role. "It is an institutionalized form of the fraternity existing among priests" (*ibid.*) to which it pertains in a special way "to help individuals and groups, to favor the spiritual life so that necessary unity may be achieved" (*ibid.*).

Fortunately, the system of honors seems to be disappearing. It was aligned more with the worldly spirit of classes, favors, and careers than to the gospel spirit of service (*cf.* Mk 10:42-45ff.), and created discrimination and distance precisely where an equal relationship and fraternity even in regard to individual duties should have prevailed.

The friendly and brotherly rapport between priests and their bishop would require separate treatment because the bishop is sometimes called "father" by the Council in virtue of sacramental generation and pastoral responsibility, and at times "brother" because he shares in the same priesthood within the maternity of the Church.[39]

In parallel fashion, priests in relation to the bishop are called "sons and friends" (LG 28; CD 16) and, at other times, "brothers and friends" (PO 7). It should not be forgotten that the reference point and the principle of unity in the presbyterate is the ordinary of the place (CD 15 and

16) within the one sacrament of Orders possessed by him in its fullest and by priests and deacons in a subordinate form. This tells us that "the priest is not fully a priest if he is not in communion with his bishop; and the bishop is not fully a bishop if he is not in communion with his priests and deacons."[40]

What has been said of diocesan priests applies, for the most part, also to religious priests who, even though they depend on their superiors by virtue of their specific charism, in the pastoral field, like every priest, have to act in communion with and in dependence on the bishop in whose diocese they exercise their apostolate.[41] Being at the service of a particular diocese, they will have to take into account the basic directions of the spirituality of the diocesan priest, integrating them with the characteristics of the spirituality of their own religious family and, at the same time, placing at the service of the local Church the riches of their personal charism.[42]

Another aspect of priestly fraternity in the Church's communion-in-unity regards the People of God as a whole because the priest is the "brother" of the faithful by virtue of the common priesthood all share in Christ through baptism. His relationship of fraternity with the laity, precisely because it is "typical" and flows through his intensive participation in the priestly office of Christ, makes him a sign and source of communion with and among the laity. He participates in Christ the Head, sent to gather, animate, guide and sanctify the Christian community, as the Good Shepherd who "gives his life for all," great and small, men and women, those near or far, "father and brother." The priest must, therefore, be a man of total dedication and pastoral charity, giving more attention to concrete persons than to organizations, allowing to resonate within himself the problems, tensions, joys and hopes of others, making himself "all things to all" (1 Cor 9:22) and thus bringing to fruition his own fulfillment and sanctification.[43]

Sacramental fraternity, then, challenges every priest to meditate often on the human and divine reality of his calling and to rediscover his own "roots" based on the example of the life of Christ with his "own." His reflection should culminate in a profound awareness of the fact that he participates in the priestly powers of the Lord. And it will likewise spur him on to acquire through fraternal sharing the full reward of those who make a total gift of themselves with a "full heart" like that of the Lord and Master.

FOOTNOTES

1. It's not necessary to remind the reader that as far as the Second Vatican Council's teaching on the nature and mission of the priesthood is concerned, there is an immense and easily found bibliography. Besides the more recent works referred to by us, one can recur, for ample bibliographical information, to A. Marranzini, "Informative and Bibliographical Notes on the Ministerial Priesthood," in *Presenza pastorale*, 11-12 (1971), pp. 1029-1037.
2. Cf. J. Rambaldi, "Sacramental Fraternity and the Presbyterate in the Decree '*Presbyterorum Ordinis*' n. 8," in *Periodica de re morali, canonica, liturgica*, 57 (1968), pp. 331-350; G. Visconti, "Unity Among Priests," in *Seminarium*, 31 (1979), pp. 505ff.
3. G. Cristaldi, *art. cit.*, p. 681.
4. Cf. Y. Congar, *Ministeres et communion ecclesiale*, Paris, 1971, p. 37.
5. C. M. Martini, "On the Nature of Priestly Celibacy," *art. cit.*, p. 607, where he adds: "The measure of Christ's presence in his own is thus posited in direct proportion to the presence of the love that is to be found among them — a love which must be understood as the Father's gift because it is the same love with which the Father, from all eternity, loves the Son."

6. The same n. 6 concludes: "According to Christ's example, priests should foster fraternity with their bishop and among themselves, a fraternity founded on ordination and unity of mission so that priestly witness may become more credible." Cf. *Ench. Vat.*, Vol. IV (1978 10), p. 771.
7. "The priest needs a priest to be a priest. In this sense, it is the priestly '*equipe*' team which makes itself the first need. The priesthood is by nature collegial. "I can no longer be a priest without living and working with other priests. The priest I am no longer recognizes in himself the idea he has been presented from the start of a priesthood which is functional above all and independent of other priests." Cf. M. Retif in *Etudes sur le sacrement de l'Ordre*, Paris, 1957, p. 427.
8. For a more elaborate reflection on the particular vocation of priests to holiness, cf. Molinari, "The Call of Priests to Perfection," in *I sacerdoti nello spirito di Vaticano II*, pp. 793-883.
9. Cf. A. Favale - G. Gozzelino, *op. cit.*, p. 215.
10. "It can be said that if the bond of fraternity is existential within a framework which is ontological, the bond of friendship is typically psychological, with the following connotations: spiritual consonance, decision of the will, intensity of communication, and constancy" (G. Cristaldi, *art. cit.*, p. 675).
11. *Ibid.*, p. 677.
12. Cf. *Summa Theologiae*, I-II, q. 65, a. 5. For a first-rate bibliography on friendship starting with patristic texts, cf. M. Marini, *loc. cit.*, p. 908, note 28.
13. J. Capmany, *La espiritualidad del sacerdote diocesano*, Barcelona 1962, p. 336.
14. It would help to reread what Paul VI said in his next-to-last Wednesday address (*L'Osservatore Romano*, July 26, 1978) on "that human and spiritual relation called 'friendship.'" And he added, citing Jn 17:21, that "having consumed itself in love, friendship breaks out into a mystical identity which is modeled on the inexpressible Trinitarian relationship between Father and Son in the Spirit" (*ibid.*).
15. Cf. M. Marini, *loc. cit.*, pp. 906-908.
16. *Ibid.*, p. 907.
17. Cf. J. Capmany, *op. cit.*, p. 336, where he says in his summation: "Jesus Christ effected this restoration of friendship, calling all men to fellowship with him, who is God in the flesh. But he did so in a special way by giving himself as a friend to his priests whom he called to collaborate in his work of reuniting all men to God in love and friendship."
18. G. Cenacchi, *loc. cit.*, p. 662.
19. G. Cristaldi, *loc. cit.*, p. 678.
20. Some of the most noble effects of brotherly friendship include: "The *joy* that makes us happy over the happiness of others; the *peace* which goes beyond simple agreement because it is acquired equilibrium and the patient expectation that the good seed will germinate after the sacrifice of consummation; and *mercy*, which is not to be confused with compassion or some kind of ephemeral sympathy, but gentleness which is greater and more noble than justice or strength alone" (G. Cenacchi, *loc. cit.*, p. 201). For the latter which are also "fruits of the Spirit," one can examine the volume by the same title of J. Janssens - M. Ledrus, Milan 1984, p. 231.
21. See the article by G. Cruchon, "Celibacy and Maturity. The Time of Choice," in *Sacerdozio e celibato, cit.*, pp. 801-833.
22. D. Marzotto, "Crisis of Vocations and Gospel Celibacy," in *L'Osservatore Romano*, November 7-8, 1983, p. 7.
23. M. Marini, "On the Discernment of a Priestly Vocation," in *Rivista di Vita Spirituale*, 30 (1976), p. 56.

24. D. Marzotto, in *L'Osservatore Romano, art. cit.*, p. 7, where he continues as follows: "The celibate priest who lives apostolic communion is a priest who has greater aids and stimuli to opening himself up to the problems of the community which he serves and to promoting universal solidarity, of which the solidarity of the diocesan priesthood is the first essential element. He is a priest obliged each day to face the requirements of fraternal relationship, to refine, therefore, his relational abilities, to be continually creative, personable and open to new solutions in his contact with others. Association with his confreres spurs him on to a closer union with God, to greater apostolic effort, and to an ever broader approach to his pastoral work."
25. Cf. C. Cochini, *Origines apostoliques du celibat sacerdotal*, Paris 1981.
26. Cf. Raymond E. Brown, *The Community of the Beloved Disciple*, New York 1979, p. 26; G. W. Buchanan, "Jesus and Other Monks of New Testament Times," in *Religious Life*, 48 (1979), pp. 136-242.
27. "Any exclusivity will have to be understood, as *Sacerdotalis Coelibatus*, n. 25, indicates, in the sense that the priest, in his every choice, will give impetus to a love which has Christ alone as its ultimate end and, as a consequence, the good of his Mystical Body, the Church" (See D. Marzotto, "On the Nature of Priestly Celibacy," *cit.*, p. 624).
28. Cf. A. Lemaire, "Priests in the Early Church," in *Il prete per gli uomini d'oggi, cit.*, pp. 79-97; E. Testa, "The Priests of the Mother-Church of Jerusalem," *ibid.*, pp. 99-117.
29. Cf. nos. 14, 46, 49, and 70 of "Educative Orientations for Formation to Priestly Celibacy," in *Ench. Vat.*, Vol. IV, pp. 188ff; also *Sacerdotalis Coelibatus*, nos. 79-80, *ibid.*, Vol. II, p. 1243.
30. S. Strano, *Celibato e solitudine del prete*, Rome 1981, p. 33.
31. "Priestly chastity is strengthened, protected and defended by a lifestyle, surroundings and activities suitable for a minister of God, for whom it is necessary to encourage to the fullest that *intimate sacramental fraternity* (PO 8) which all priests enjoy by virtue of their sacred ordination" (n. 79).
32. "And still on the subject of what Jesus did — *he loved his own and gave himself up for them* — the priest's friendship will take on different forms of oblation, which is the communication of love. Priestly celibacy thus acquires as well the meaning of a witness to friendship for one's brothers: the priest places at the service of the faithful, his brethren in Christ, that solitude of the flesh and heart which, in the tension of a total assimilation to Christ the Priest, has been consecrated to the Lord" (G. Cristaldi, *art. cit*, p. 677).
33. Cf. R. Castielli, "Called to Fraternity," in *Presbyteri*, 13 (1980), p. 109; Jerome Murphy-O'Connor, "Celibacy and Community," in *What Is Religious Life: A Critical Reappraisal*, Dublin 1977, pp. 53-69.
34. "If the gospel experience is not presented in its fullness, the person is exposed to living an existence lacking an adequate picture of its original context. He would be subjected then to problematic conditions from the psychic-affective point of view, precisely because he lacks those general conditions of balance which were present in the original proposal" (D. Marzotto, "The Celibate in the New Testament," *cit.*, p. 369).
35. "Besides the spiritual problem, there is a psychological one: the young priest often feels that he is surrounded by those who lack confidence in him and he risks feeling that he is alone and inexperienced, always at the level of the private who executes commands but is never given any responsibility. In this state of mind attitudes of rebelliousness and childishness — two equally harmful positions — can grow. In fact, one almost always acts childish when rebellious and vice versa. Such a vicious cycle

must, therefore, be completely broken" (G. Cenacchi, "Priestly Fraternity," in *I sacerdoti nello spirito . . .* , *cit.*, p. 650, note 54).
36. Here there can exist "the previous situation in reverse. Many elderly priests today feel that they have been bypassed by new methods and new philosophical and theological theories of recent coinage. Even for them there can be two mistaken approaches: extreme rigidity which renders them closed and incommunicative in their ideas and headstrong in their pastoral activities, or psychological despondency which robs them of confidence almost as if their past apostolic efforts were completely useless" (*ibid.*, n. 55).
37. "One should not distrust a friend, only a stranger. The dialogue among friends — always possible — is gentle in form, sensible in argumentation, open to accept the true reasons of the one who objects, and very effective for an encounter with the truth. On the contrary, violence, subtlties in desperate defense of one's own position, stubbornness, and finally confusion are characteristic of a dispute between persons in disagreement or cordially opposed to one another" (J. Campany, *op.cit.*, p. 339. Cf. also the characteristics of dialogue set forth in Pope Paul VI's encyclical, *Ecclesiam suam*, August 6, 1964, in AAS, 56 (1964), pp. 634f.
38. For an ample and updated bibliography on the diocesan priesthood, consult, for example, M. Caprioli, *Sacerdozio e Santita, cit., passim*; J. Esquerda Bifer, *El Sacerdocio Hoy*, Madrid 1983, pp. 617-624. There are also recent theses presented to the Pontifical Gregorian University.
39. Cf. Henri De Lubac, *Les Eglises particulieres dans l'Eglise universelle*, Paris, 1971, pp. 141 ff.
40. G. Marchandalli, *op. cit.*, pp. 76ff.
41. The decree *Christus Dominus*, at n. 46, is explicit in this regard: "By the fact that they participate in the care of souls and in the works of the apostolate under the authority of the sacred pastors, they are to be considered as appertaining to the diocesan clergy." Cf. the document *Mutuae Relationes*, already cited, in *Ench. Vat.*, Vol. VI, pp. 432ff.
42. Cf. *Per una presenza viva dei religiosi nella Chiesa e nel mondo*, ed. A. Favale, LDC, Torino-Leumann 1970.
43. Cf. G. Marchandalli, *op. cit.*, pp. 65ff.

III.

Consequences and Applications of Priestly Fraternity

If God himself willed to have everyone's cooperation in his plan of universal salvation (Mt 28:19; Mk 16:15; Lk 24:26; Jn 15:15), all the more reason why he has willed and does will to have the collaboration of the priest who is *"chosen from among men and made their representative before God"* (Heb 5:1), in imitation of Christ, the man-God. While the priest promotes communion around him, he also contributes to its fullness from the Christian humanist point of view. Human and divine in him cannot be in contradiction, just as humanity and divinity are not in contradiction in Christ.

Priestly fraternity, then, has nothing to do with psychological compensation but is the full and rich realization of the man-priest at the human, cultural, pastoral, spiritual, and other levels.[1]

a) Human Maturation and Spiritual Progress

In search of one's identity

In the life of the priest there is a very rich fabric of human relationships of every kind within the framework of his charitable ministry with both superiors and equals. Even granted the absence of conjugal experience, in reality the priest's "solitude" as a celibate is nevertheless well "inhabited," as Paul VI reminds us in *Sacerdotalis Coelibatus*, nos. 54-59.[2] His personality development is favored, even psychologically speaking, by his religious growth because the person, in the process of communion is encouraged to fulfill his humanity in an upward ascent, as the life of Christ — lived in virginity and yet incredibly rich in love — demonstrates so very well.

It should be emphasized that sacramental fraternity contributes a great deal to the search for one's priestly identity whenever there prevails an encounter with others on a one to one basis. In such a relationship between equals, the axiom, "I am not I if there is no you," assumes a deep meaning according to the universally accepted thesis of modern personalism.[3] If the person is a "being-in-relation," in the priestly fraternity the individual priest acquires, so to speak, a new awareness, an interchange of ideals, an interior synthesis and fusion of all his qualities.[4] And this is so true that one can say of him that his charism is radical and absolute relationality.

The Sacred Congregation for Catholic Education, in its document "Educative Orientations . . . ," cited already, in speaking of "apostolic communion in which profound and beneficial interpersonal relations can be realized" (n. 14), does no more than accent the intense life of interpersonal relationships which engages those who are called to the priesthood. For the rest, human relationships take on many forms. In marriage, as in every other relationship, it has its price and its limitations. The priest, in reality, is placed within the context of human relationships which range from family to parish co-workers to persons who live in the same household, with the risk that he may come under the influence of less meaningful relationships and not sufficiently develop the one which his state in life might justly require — the one alone which might permit him to communicate as an equal and in depth with another person and help him to manage other affections and human friendships in the best possible way.

This intersubjectivity and reciprocity, this enrichment of relationships produced by different ages, mentalities, charisms and the like, is fundamental to an authentic realization of the "I" and a great help in difficulties of every sort, inevitable in every state of life and from which not even the priest is immune. We are not speaking only of incommunicability, to which we shall return later, but also of the radical solitude of the man of every epoch and of the actual problem of isolation which causes so much suffering precisely in this era of "mass communications."[5]

Priestly fraternity favors a serene and productive maturation in view of an adult affectivity and is effective in overcoming not only solitude but also the risks taken by one who lives his affectivity in a repressed way which could lead to neurosis, aggressiveness, scruples, pseudo-asceticism, and the like — all evident signs of a little lived or enjoyed fraternity.[6]

Openness to others

Almost like the prolongation of one's own personality, the apostolic group provokes the emergence from isolation and stimulates individual efficiency, favoring in the meantime the conquest of egotism.[7] Complacent and sometimes pride-filled "listening to self" is replaced by listening to others, thus opening the way to communication, solidarity, mutual presence, participation, solicitude and the capacity for understanding.

It is a short step from this to availability in all senses, especially apostolic, to complete availability for the Word in order "to serve an unconditionally loved Christ the best way possible, betaking oneself wherever pastoral choices indicate a crucial need, a particularly urgent task."[8]

This openness is shown and cultivated, for example, even by rejoicing over the qualities of confreres and the prestige they enjoy, conscious of working and growing weary in a common undertaking where "*sower and reaper rejoice together*" (Jn 4:36). . . . One has "planted," another "irrigated," "*but it is God who gives the increase*" (*cf.* 1 Cor 3:6).

It is an openness which reaches an intimate sharing of goods, possibly even material ones, because even this is a visible sign of friendship and guarantee of the sincerity of one's ideals. The change is brought about not simply according to sociological models but after the very example of Jesus, the apostles, the Jerusalem community where, as Vatican II recalls (PO 21), "*everything was held in common*" (Ac 4:35), and "*was divided among them on the basis of each one's needs*" (Ac 4:35), in an attitude of voluntary poverty and in the spirit of true freedom (cf. PO 17), the sign of their redemption from the need of possession of things and the prophecy of the coming of the Kingdom.[9]

A brotherhood open to self-criticism helps in overcoming jealousies, diffidence and suspicion; in not judging and still less in not condemning; in not being so startled by defects but rather in being edified by virtues. It encourages its members to offer and to accept that kind of collaboration which makes for communion of life and work at every level. And how very necessary that is today, because in our day and age no priest "is in the condition of basically realizing his own mission if he acts alone and on his own account without uniting his forces to those of other priests" (PO 7). Staying together in a parish — in order to propose, program and decide in full responsibility with one's fellow priests and according to the diocesan pastoral plan — is a concrete form of achieving the spirit of unity in which the search for points in common, a proportionate distribution of work, solidarity in difficult moments, and reciprocal confidence offer the Spirit space to make the apostolate bear fruit. It also helps the priests involved to avoid a partial vision of things, and thus impedes the creation of closed groups or "islands" where the circulation of ideas and experiences may perhaps exist, but where there is, at the same time, a closing off of encounters with others.

Where there is a spirit of fraternity, differences in age, mentality and ideas which exist in the priesthood — as in every other institution — will not prevent the search for points of contact, the revision of concepts, the serene examination of activities and the evaluation of results. At the same time, differences in matters open to discussion and apostolic approach are inevitable in a world in continuous and rapid evolution. These may even be providential in so far as pastoral choices and the search for a better way to proceed together are concerned. The problem is actually one of how to integrate the differences with unity, of how to emphasize the complementarity of differing charisms, of how to combine the variety of gifts converging towards one end with the plurality of responsibilities and offices which are to be found harmoniously existing within the one ministerial priesthood.

> "If they proceed from this criterion,
> priests will find the unity of their own lives
> in the unity of the mission of the Church itself;
> and thus they will be united to their Lord
> and by means of him to the Father in the Spirit,
> and . . . be overwhelmed with consolation and joy" (PO 14c).

This openness within the priestly fraternity leads to greater openness also both within and outside the Church by the overcoming of a "caste mentality" as well as that attitude which is frequently referred to as "dogmatic" — a categorical and unappealing way of expressing oneself in areas which do not pertain to the faith — found at times in some priests. Rather than speaking of "flight" or "separation" from the world, one would have to talk rather of the priest's insertion into the world to animate it in the name of that universal fraternity (within which he lives a particular form) which has Christ, "*the firstborn among many brothers*" (Rm 9:29), as its head. Nor can we forget that by virtue of the communion of life with the Trinity initiated at baptism and confirmation, the priest is a brother among brothers even when he fulfills the service of president or guide of the community, united to it by close bonds of communion which supersede every distinction.[10]

Means of Sanctification

Without pretending to want to branch out into the area of priestly spirituality — something others with competence have done very well indeed[11] — it seems to me that we ought to offer some points made here and there to emphasize how lived fraternity can be a powerful means offered the priest for his progress on the road to spiritual maturity.

It is clear that the priest's spiritual growth is a requirement deriving not only from the universal call of all believers to holiness, but also from the theological foundations of his vocation, sacramental consecration, and mission through which he must seek within his special ministry his own path to sanctity. It is by sanctifying others that he sanctifies himself, just as by sanctifying himself he sanctifies others by virtue of his communion with them, his bishop and his confreres (*cf.* PO 12). In fact:

"The end toward which priests tend
with their ministry and life
is the glory of God the Father
which they must procure in Christ"
and while they "contribute to the increase of God's glory . . .
at the same time they help advance men in the divine life" (*ibid.* 2a).

His whole life and the model which his fraternity puts before him indicate a total giving to the Lord and to the Church. Renouncing some precise, intimate family relationships through certain specific acts of self-denial, he dedicates himself to the service, friendship, listening to, and living with the total Christ. His communion with the Lord and with his confreres is in the service of ecclesial communion and is its term of comparison, in the total gift of self without limit or reservation.[12]

Priests' lives in fraternity, besides what *Menti Nostrae*[13] has told us, is a testimony to their esteem of chastity because it situates the priest in a condition of greater adherence and conformity to Christ who, surrounded by the little community with which he lived, chose the state of absolute virginity in order to be totally available for the service of God and the people. In this participation in the dignity and mission of our Blessed

Lord, "the more perfect to the extent that the sacred minister is free of the bonds of flesh and blood" (*Sacerdotalis Coelibatus*, 21), chastity manifests the freedom of the sons of God. It has value as an escatological sign. It gives an indication of the priest's spiritual fruitfulness and offers a witness to the People of God which is all the more enriching when it is lived in a community as a gospel value and the manifestation of a conscious, total and irreversible gift.[14]

Over and above the spirit of "socialization," fraternity stirs up pastoral charity and apostolic zeal in pursuit of the primacy of that love which knows no measure in its giving. Such charity in the priesthood gives life to faith as a personal and communitarian journey, instills hope and confidence in self and others, inspires every effort imaginable, and promotes in the broadest possible way a community spirit whereby, with the collaboration of talented laypeople, a team pastoral approach can very easily make headway.

By being faithful to its origins, the sacrament, which makes use of humble and simple signs, will give value to the simple and the essential without losing anything of quality. Offering and accepting the example of detachment from personal interests in the spirit of the "voluntary poverty" recommended by the Lord who, "*though rich became poor for our sakes*" (2 Cor 8:9), every priest will find ways to a certain communion of things and economic goods which no ecclesiastical law could achieve if the law of charity and the gift of self did not precede it.

"A certain common use of things —
on the model of that community of goods
which is so praised
in the history of the early Church —
contributes in a most notable measure
to smoothing the way towards pastoral charity" (PO 17).

Despite all the advantages offered by fraternity, it can never lack a spirit of abnegation and renunciation because one can never attain ecclesial communion by skirting the truth or by closing one's eyes to reality.[15] The way of Christ is presented as the way of total renunciation, of the denial of one's very self in order to rediscover one's self in him:

"If anyone wishes to come after me,
let him deny himself, take up his cross, and follow me."
(Mt 16:24; Mk 9:34; Lk 9:23, and the like.)

"Whoever wishes to save his life will lose it . . ."
(Mt 16:25; Mk 9:34; Lk 17:33; Jn 12:25.)

Nights without sleeping, days without eating, hunger, thirst, dangers, insults and the like (*cf.* 2 Cor 11:23-28) form part of the disciple's life as they did the Master's:

"If they have persecuted me,
they will persecute you also" (Jn 15:20).

The little apostolic fraternity was formed precisely during Easter, that is, on the occasion of the Lord's passion, death and resurrection. Its unity was sealed by the outpouring of the Holy Spirit on Pentecost, and crowned by the "martyrdom" which proclaimed and gave yet more faithful witness to Christ who went on before it.[16]

There will be many occasions for humility for young and old alike because no one can pretend to have done or to do everything nor to know *a priori* the exact solution to every problem. Past experience alone does not suffice nor the awareness of the most recent and accepted theories.

> "Aware, therefore, of his own weakness,
> the true minister of Christ works with humility,
> seeking to know what is pleasing to God" (PO 15).

At the same time, aware that priestly ministry can be realized only in communion with the hierarchy,

> "priests working in this communion should,
> with obedience,
> make a gift of their own will
> in the service of God and their brothers" (*ibid.*).

Obedience implies availability which defends from rigidity and brings with it unconditioned dedication to the entire Church, either by perseverance in a burdensome duty or in the freedom of heart to take on another task on the occasion of a new appointment.[17] It "leads to a more mature freedom of the sons of God," is both "responsible and voluntary," and helps priests to entertain in themselves the sentiments which Christ had (Ph 2:7-8), as the same conciliar document reminds us (n. 15).

Deriving from the sacrament, priestly fraternity expresses itself in sacramental style, making reference especially to the Eucharist which "in its threefold dimension of Sacrifice, Communion, and Real Presence, should be at the center of our interests, our love, our ministry, our life. The Eucharist is the privileged seat of Communion with God in Christ."[18] As "the most perfect Sacrament of this union" (John Paul II, *Redemptor hominis*, n. 20), the Eucharist, besides being the font of "pastoral charity," will also be "the center and root of the priest's whole life, so that the priestly soul strives to mirror in itself what is made a reality on the altar" (PO 14b; *imitamini quod tractatis*).

Re-evaluating the experience had in eucharistic concelebration (*cf.* SC 57), the Council then even laid down the premises of a more profound doctrine on the unity of priests.[19] If Christians, "nourishing themselves with the body of Christ in Holy Communion, show concretely the unity of the People of God" (LG 11), how much more in concelebration does the sign of unity and love become for priests the font, principle, and bond of their fraternity and the privileged moment of reconciliation — provided that this does not remain an isolated, almost magical, gesture and that this "oneness of sentiments" (PO 8) "best expressed" (PO 7) by liturgical concelebration is strongly willed and manifested in their daily life.

The eucharistic liturgy and the exercise of sacramental ministry come together in prayer where, aware that everything is a gift, we better understand that fraternal communion is also the result of the petitions "thy

Kingdom come," "thy will be done," "give us this day our daily bread," "forgive us our trespasses," as it also is of the journeying together based on the Word of God.

The intense experience of prayer by priests (LG 42c) in all its forms (*cf.* PO 12-13): liturgical (SC 52-54), biblical (SC 90), communitarian (SC 7, 27-30, 33, 41, 99; UR 2, 8), and personal (SC 12, 90), united to the prayer of Christ and of the Church (SC 9) — where we include our concrete intentions (LG 41c) but especially the intention of Christ's own prayer "that all may be one" (Jn 17:21; *cf.* UR 2, 8; GS 24, 32) which finds its ultimate expression in the mystery of the Trinity, perfect unity in perfect communion — becomes a true spiritual sacrifice (*cf.* LG 34), a bond of union (*cf.* LG 13, 15), a sacrifice of praise (*cf.* LG 12), the increase of charity (*cf.*LG 42), and the school and example for the faithful (PO 5c).

"*Where two or three are gathered in my name, there I am in their midst*" (Mt 18:20). Across the peculiar modalities of the presence of the Savior among those who in virtue of the sacrament of Orders he has chosen as his ministers, priests — "anointed" by the Lord — achieve the fullest and most perfect modeling on Christ in his role as High Priest, which is the highest ideal of their priestly life.[20]

Efficacious Witness for the Christian People

Priestly fraternity has immediate ramifications for the Christian people because the priest, the man of communion with God, is also a man totally involved in the affairs of his people: the man-for-others, the man of service to the community, of pastoral dedication to the community where pastoral duty, rather than being an obstacle, becomes a powerful stimulus to journeying along with one's brothers and sisters. To them he brings his rich experience of communion and sharing, because fraternity begets fraternity. It is a way, a light. When this light glows from within the priestly fraternity, some "good news" is beamed to the men and women of today. "If the apostolic fraternities generate ecclesial fraternity, because they build up the Church as a fraternity of fraternities, their mission will not end there. They know that they must also imprint on the People of God such dynamism as may make possible the fraternity of peoples and nations."[21]

This is the task, the challenge, but also the result, the effect, of such fraternity:

"With power, the apostles bore witness
to the resurrection of the Lord Jesus
and great respect was paid to them all" (Ac 4:33).

"All who believed were together and had all things in common;
they would sell their property and possessions
and divide them among all according to each one's need . . .

Day by day, the Lord added to their number
those who had been saved" (Ac 2:44-48).

As *"models of the flock"* (1 P 5:3), already "established by Christ through a communion of life, love, and truth" (LG 9), priests may not exempt themselves from giving specific witness of fraternity because ecclesial communion is not optional but the very being of the Church ("... *to gather into one all the dispersed children of God*": Jn 11:52). And in the Church, the People of God, salvation is found and the freedom and unity of all humanity attained. The Church is the definitive "place" of the encounter between God and man and of men among themselves (*cf.* LG 1). The smaller fraternity exists for the sake of the larger fraternity of all the Church. It is where one finds the Lord who presides, who guides and who enlivens by means of his Spirit who creates communion. The Church, in its turn, is at the service of the reunion of all mankind journeying now and in the future in the Master's footsteps. It is the "transparency" of the Master's strong and humble "Servant" hands which helps brothers and sisters to come together, to share and to follow along behind him.[22] It is not a little church within the Church. Its identity lies in its apostolic mission, in its unity in spite of diversity. It serves as a mediator between God and his people and gives a positive sense of the immediateness of the Lord among his own, as a bit of "light" come into the world so that it will no longer remain in darkness (*cf.* Jn 12:46) and a bit of "leaven" that ferments the whole mass (*cf.* Mt 13:33; Lk 13:20-21; 1 Cor 5:6). All those who make up the smaller priestly fraternity have as their own mission and service the representation of Christ who calls his own to unite among themselves in a communion to the point of being but one body and one spirit (Ep 4:4), in an ecclesial witness offered without subterfuge: "*Whoever wishes to be the first among you will have to be the servant of all*" (Mk 10:14). For this purpose, as we have already noted, the Lord, in a special way, sent his disciples out "*two by two*" (Mk 6:7; Lk 10:1) for the fullness of witnessing, so that in their common proclamation, the "good news" might be presented with all its force. Through the demonstration of the Spirit and the power of God (*cf.* Ac 1:8; 4:32), the fraternity goes on to become the fulfillment of the presence of the Kingdom (Lk 17:21) where all can call God by the name of "Father" (Gal 4:6; Rm 8: 15-17), where all have been invited to seat themselves at a common table at which Christ repeats to us:

> "Blest are the eyes that see what you see.
> I tell you, many prophets and kings
> wished to see what you see, but did not see it;
> and to hear what you hear, but did not hear it" (Lk 10:23-24).

This presence of the Kingdom leaps up before the eyes of the brethren who fully bear witness to fraternal union (*"See how much they love one another!"*) because, according to the Lord's own words,

> "By this will all men know that you are my disciples,
> if you have love for one another" (Jn 13:35).

The presence of the fraternal community of priests in a Christian community will also be a testimony and concrete example of true freedom — that Christian freedom which raises the spirit despite the heaviness of one's own being, that freedom which encourages the right use of things and self-control in order to be better persons, freedom in vigilance and in readiness to seek always that which unites rather than that which divides. "The priest, as a brother among brothers, united in an apostolic fraternity, says to people that it is possible to be 'a brother among brothers.' His existence is changed into a prophetic canticle to universal brotherhood."[23]

The little fraternity, "courageous prophecy of a renewed society," is nothing other than the beginning of the great assembly of the house of the Father, a dot of light, a living reflection of the Lord, "the Light of the world" (Jn 8:12), come to enlighten the whole of humanity. It is the expression and the beginning of the escatological community, "the living sign of that future world, present already through faith and charity" (PO 16), of which priests experience the anticipation.

"Though marriage is indeed an eminently Christian value, it is destined to end while the value which will always remain is precisely the Christian fraternity of which priests desire to be an altogether particular living image."[24]

The participation of priests in apostolic communion, nourishing the desire to spend themselves always more and more in the service of their brothers in respect, compassion and attention to their problems and a sharing in their worries, besides increasing their pastoral charity (*cf.* "Educative Orientations," nos. 49, 51, 80), also increases the efficacy of their apostolate. The life of communion will be for the faithful a sign of profound giving, a stimulus to them to collaboration, and the occasion for arousing generous responses in them — according to each one's vocation and with respect for their personalities — in the upbuilding of the ecclesial community and the Kingdom of God. And for the priest, placed as he is at the heart of the mystery of the Church, it will be a moment of total communion in that fidelity to God and fidelity to man which is the mind of the Council itself.

b) Difficulties and Risks

All the good things that have been said about presbyterial fraternity should not cause us to forget the difficulties along the way and the risks that are faced. Just as with every other precious good, the more authentic it is, so much the more will be its demands. Often it is the crucial proof of the individual's human and Christian maturity that, here as in every other environment, he can accumulate so many daily burdens and nerve-wracking situations that at times can explode into verbal bouts, instances of intolerance and animosity, displays of insufferability and acrimony, or even provoke touchiness and resentment, the holding of grudges and a sense of indifference to the point of closing in on one's self.[25]

A sense of reality will not let us ignore our limits and those of others, the weaknesses and the miseries connected with human frailty which, despite the imposition of hands and the gift of the Spirit, never completely leave us, even indeed after years and years of priestly life. Besides, priestly fraternity is so exalted (and even indispensable) a gift which we cannot and must not give up in the face of any difficulty whatsoever. It is part of the logic of every gift that only by offering and accepting it does it truly enrich us. Otherwise, if we do not create communion, human isolation and spiritual impoverishment would make us prone to judgment and condemnation and we could be, perhaps, "pure as angels," but "proud as devils."

Among all the real needs, we cannot forget the hope for unity, today more than ever felt in all the areas of human life. More than ever before individuals feel within themselves not only the inability to know themselves with any kind of depth and to define themselves as persons, but also the difficulty of working in the face of ever accelerating specialization and of structures which rob the person of his or her own "space."

Unremoved from society, the Church "feels itself really and intimately one with the human race and its history" (GS 1). At the same time the priest, immersed in the times in which he lives, while manifesting traces of the influences of the historical-social climate and its crises, continually rediscovers with his confreres — aided by the word of God — that it is the Holy Spirit in the Church, the pilgrim People of God with its variety of charisms and vocations, that unifies and creates communion.

Apart from certain moments of dramatic solitude (something which is experienced in every state of life, marriage[26] not excepted), the causes of difficulties with communication can be various and both psychological and sociological in character. We can note the differences in temperament and character which can give rise to silence, reserve, diffidence, moroseness and the like. Even differences in social extraction, formation, culture, environment, and so on are all realities which shape the person and, in the long run, modify even his or her behavior and attitudes.

What is to be done in these cases? One must above all accept the other as he is and work toward the serene acceptance of differences, realistically taking the factual situation into account. Differences should not be exaggerated if we wish to preserve interior serenity and pursue sincere relationships.[27] There could even be limited cases of a break in communications for the purpose of saving fraternal communion. This will remain for some time as an ''intentional'' value in the expectation that the difficulties in communicating will be replaced by authentic communion.[28]

At times communion is lessened because of misunderstandings or a split on the affective level on account of the bishop's own words, words that provoke unfortunate or continual tension. If it is everyone's task to seek, cultivate and strengthen communion, then the bishop — an elder brother — ought to be the first to approach individuals and to suggest ways of doing so. He should be the last to rend his garments and to destroy confidence, mindful that, even in the most difficult situations, only true love knows how to invent new ways and unsuspected possibilities.

We all recall that even the apostolic fraternities of the early Church were not exempt from difficulties, tensions and conflicts such as those caused by the problem of the circumcision of the pagans (*cf.* Ac 11:15; Gal 2). Submission to the Spirit frequently provokes tension among those who enjoy power: political or ecclesiastical. But in the end, where there is mature reflection, serene dialog and confident prayer, the Spirit always finds a way, as happened in the assembly of Jerusalem (Ac 15:28). We should never forget this.

The Second Vatican Council delicately points out not only priests "who are suffering some difficulty," exhorting the bishop "to help them in time, even with a gentle admonition, when it should prove needed" by virtue of their joint "participation in the priesthood" (PO 8d), but it also speaks of those who make mistakes:

> "As regards those who may show some deficiency, let them be treated with fraternal charity and understanding, let prayers be said for them without ceasing, and let them show themselves on every occasion to be true brothers and friends" (*ibid.*).

Further comment would be superfluous.

Besides the difficulties already mentioned, we must speak at least briefly about the limits and risks of some expressions of priestly fraternity. Institutions that are too official and organized (the Priests Council, for example) tend to limit themselves to general themes or to promoting certain practical and showy programs of little depth, or which hardly touch upon the person's more vital needs. Other concrete realities are left alone to the individual's free spirit of initiative. Even though these individuals may excel in spontaneity, generosity, and mutual respect they are not exempt in the long run from the danger of fatigue, loss of quality, weakened ideals, group narrowness, and even criticism of others.

Very negative, indeed, is any falling back on one's own group in order to find especially a moral and affective support, in a sincere search perhaps for human acceptance, but with a practical cutting off of true ecclesial communion. The "group as refuge," the search for a fragile closeness based on some kind of sterile opposition to other groups or simply the concrete ignorance of their existence is the very denial of priestly fraternity, both ideal and real.

The sign of true fraternity is not to be found in some kind of flight in search of reward or a sense of belonging whose motives are of doubtful origin or in settling on less mature organizational forms, such as little groups that are closed in on themselves or dependent on strong personalities, "gurus."[29] It should surprise no one when compensations and surrogates are sought for a nonexistent or badly formed fraternity (one, for example, shaped for efficiency's sake more than for equal interpersonal relationships) when solutions are uncritically left more to chance than to reflection or a pondered and mature choice.[30]

Further, it must be well borne in mind that the dimension of communion and fraternal charity must begin with him who is closest (in the same rectory, community, zone, diocese, etc.), where old rancors and childish jealousies are most likely to be found. Is it not true that, all too often, we are masters of dialog, open, affable and ready to smile for the faithful and the distant but incapable of dialog, closed in on ourselves and suspicious with our confreres, our bishop and the members of our own community?[31]

In all these situations the important thing is to save communion and its authenticity even to the point of temporarily sacrificing communication, if that should occur. True *koinonia* — if there is a sincere and honest search — will not delay in taking the place of pseudo-friendship and in overcoming every egotistical thrust or artificial type of communication. We need a lot of patience for this, a tenacious patience which accepts periods of growth and takes into account the much longer times of fatigue and ennui.[32] When the dialog becomes difficult, we have to make a studied effort to understand the various existential aspects of that situation we are living through, clarifying our own ideas and rethinking our own positions,

> "but nothing will be able to supply the decision —
> the result only of a change of heart —
> of extending one's hand anew,
> of offering the result of one's own experience,
> welcoming the other's,
> agreeing to a meeting and a waiting,
> suffering the tension and the obscurity of the way,
> and extending a hand to the Spirit.
> And hoping against hope for the dawn."[33]

It is the Spirit in fact — as some new and original resources testify — who, rendering possible the free reception and the offer of one's own weakness to those who unite around the same table, infuses hope into them.[34]

We ministers of reconciliation must not ignore the fact that we are also witnesses of pardon.[35] Love is expressed also in fraternal correction, done in due ways and received with humility and gratitude. We thus love and go out to meet our brother, entrusting him in prayer, at least, to him who alone can change mind and heart.[36]

In confident expectation, with patience that does not run out and a hope that does not delude, we leave room for the boldness of a charity which always invents new gestures of friendship, starting with prayer and sacramental celebration, our strong moments. A small gesture is enough at times; on other occasions the deep communication "is already had in taking another seriously, in attention to a greeting, in a show of sympathy, and then it becomes — like confidence, friendship and love — always stronger, more significant, and more lasting."[37]

In the end, we must acknowledge that perhaps we are still afraid to go beyond ourselves and to entrust ourselves to the Lord. Our capacity to trust and dare is still insufficient. Perhaps we still lack some dose of healthful humor which allows us to laugh a bit at ourselves and our "seriousness."[38] Perhaps we still do not know how to accept difficulties without blowing them all out of proportion, forgetting that the "gift" received in our vessels of clay (2 Cor 4:7) is so great that we could never make it smaller. Maybe we should still learn from the Lord something of the liberating force of humor[39] and especially a little more humility from him who "like his brothers in all things" is "the merciful and faithful high priest":

"... therefore he had to become like his brothers in every way,
that he might be a merciful and faithful high priest
before God on their behalf,
to expiate the sins of the people.
Since he was himself tested through what he suffered,
he is able to help those who are tempted" (Heb 2:17-18).

c) Priests in the "Diaspora"

We have examined some of the difficulties that can arise in the priestly life and the risks that are associated with it, whether these are connected with human frailty and weakness which priests have in common with other men or are moments of tension and crisis from which nothing and no one can guarantee them immunity.

It would be worthwhile now to look at another type of problem where perhaps the personal responsibility of the individual is not so much a factor; where the concrete environment or circumstances themselves determine particular situations more than personal choices or modes of being do. They are objective difficulties, nevertheless, which must be borne in mind.

We are speaking, for example, of those priests described above by us as "in the diaspora," who live isolated lives, indeed in places that are impervious, miles and miles from other priests, weighed down with work, alone in the midst of a multitude of people (we are thinking of some missionaries, or of places where the clergy is very scarce), or even dispersed in a secularized world.[40]

We cannot ignore the psychological danger of personal frustration inherent in these difficult situations, which can give rise to outbursts of aggressiveness or to dangerous repression.

True, the Council recommends:

> "As far as possible,
> priests should not be sent alone into a new region . . . ;
> it is better that they go as groups of at least two or three,
> like the Lord's own disciples (cf. Lk 10:1),
> so as to help one another.
> It is also important that care be taken
> of their spiritual life
> and their physical and mental health . . ." (PO 10c).

It can also happen that more attention is given to programs than to persons, or that — objectively and subjectively — one remains overburdened with work to the point of not having "a moment for relaxation and rest" (PO 8c).

Another objective difficulty can be noticed in those who — while disposed to the possibility of encounters with and openness towards others — are heirs to a particular kind of priestly formation, not infrequent in the past, in which priestly fraternity was little practiced or spoken about. This lack can provoke or carry with it a kind of "material and spiritual solipsism." But this "interior emptiness, which could have a mystical value and, in different historical circumstances, made the priest a segregated person worthy of respect and capable of exercising authority in the midst of the faithful, would today transform itself into something purely negative which produces alienation and an inability to dialog with God or the People of God."[41]

What is to be done in all these cases? How can these difficulties be avoided?

Above all, frequent reference must be made both in prayer and in personal reflection to the very nature of Sacred Orders with its special qualities and requirements — not the least of which that of ontological and sacramental fraternity which, even though deprived of external and visible manifestations, stands nevertheless as the basis of every accomplishment since the priesthood is not only a personal event but one having an eminently communitarian dimension with a collegial style within an ecclesial communion.

It is certainly not easy to be nurtured by fraternity when it is not or cannot be lived in reality. But just as in married life the radiant day of the wedding can be followed by many others in which are felt *"the burden of the day and its heat"* (Mt 20:12), so too priests who have taken into account the difficulties that await them also know how to refer to that radiant day on which they experienced it to be true of themselves that *"the life I live now is not my own; Christ is living in me"* (Gal 2:20) and thus obtain light and strength for the present darker moment. And the things they feel inside, the charge they get as soon as they recall their priestly ordination day!

Another source of strength and renewed enthusiasm is to relive happy experiences of communion with Christ (who never fades away) and with one's confreres, starting with those years in the seminary and the first years in the priesthood. This is certainly not enough to overcome the dullness one may be feeling, but is it not perhaps true that thinking about rich and positive experiences can help one feel again their beneficial effect even in the present?

Surely, the "diaspora" is not the ideal, even if it seems at times inevitable. It should not last a lifetime and one is conscience-bound to do all that is possible to leave it. And if, because of an act of God, a priest should have to live in isolation, he can and must at least create around him, as a community of collaborators, observant laypeople who are sensitive to a sharing of pastoral duties, making a gift to them (and certainly receiving it in exchange) of that charity of Christ which must burn in his heart.[42]

There are also many other means which, if they are not the cure-all of the situation, nevertheless very much reduce the risks and the negative consequences of a life set apart and sometimes in disarray.

It is necessary to create the occasions for frequent periodic meetings, both programmed and spontaneous, at various levels which could assume from time to time the form of prayer, debate, reflection, experiences, and the like, in order to avoid priests' being isolated, without friends. Further, their human, cultural and spiritual situation must be the heartfelt concern of all, starting with the bishop and including every other priest, all equally "responsible for those who are suffering some difficulty" (PO 8d). Short conferences, study and updating days should also be organized at which attendance is requested for the sake of a spirituality of communion.[43]

Besides retreats, days dedicated to spirituality or spiritual exercises at which one prays with and for confreres beyond priestly "functions" or those prayers which are, so to speak, "obligatory," there is a precious aid, even though not much sought after today (and perhaps little offered). It is the help of spiritual direction which can go by a different name without prejudice to its need or urgency (*cf.* PO 18b).

In our day ongoing formation has assumed greater importance, and rightly so. It is all the more urgent today because we are so often caught up in different and sometimes baffling situations. Bringing one's experience of life to where it can be interpreted in a group of priests in the light of God's word is to provide a real service to personal faith and that of the Christ in people while increasing communion. At the same time, the continuity of the dialog with a human being in transformation is promoted and the listening capacity needed to read God's signs in time and space is increased (*cf.* PO 7a, 19; OT 22).[44]

Letter-writing can still be a great help, especially when the voice of God calls one to serve in different posts or in disparate situations where distance and separation make themselves felt. It will then fall to those who are closest and most benefited by brotherly communion especially to allow echoes of solidarity, brotherly concern, and apostolic efforts to reach the furthest and most isolated confreres. The latter, then, whatever their future condition, will never feel themselves alone but because of the spiritual presence and material help of others, will remember that they are a vital part of the presbytery.

Last of all, we should not forget the value and the importance of those moments of encounter for recreation, togetherness, and just sitting around the same table, which are characteristic of friendship. These moments are useful in rediscovering oneself, in breaking out of one's shell, in moving away a bit from demanding projects and fixed routines — moments which perhaps a misunderstood asceticism has caused to be ignored for some time. While they enable one to come down from his pedestal and make another feel acknowledged and well-received, brotherly agapes fill all with a greater joy. Joining divine wisdom and human richness, the Council expresses itself in this regard with much wisdom and humanity:

> "It is good also that priests freely gather
> to pass together in joy a moment of relaxation and rest,
> recalling the words with which the Lord himself invited the Apostles,
> exhausted by work: 'Come by yourselves to an out-of-the-way place
> and rest a little' (Mk 6:31)" (PO 8c).

And, to conclude, while we recall the obligation of all to create and foster fraternity — a requirement and not a luxury — and the intensity which one should feel in seeking it even in difficult situations, without leaving anyone outside the flow of his love, we must emphasize at the same time both personal responsibility and that of competent authority.

> "Bishops, considering priests as 'brothers and friends,'
> are always to have 'at heart, in every way possible,
> their material and especially their spiritual welfare'
> because on them 'befalls in the first place
> the grave responsibility of the sanctification
> of their priests' (cf. PO 7a),
> in which fraternity occupies a significant place.
>
> Priests, on their part,
> on occasions in which 'they find themselves in such conditions
> in which it is easy to lose themselves in so many different things,'
> should seek insistently unity of life and activity in Christ
> who remains 'its principle and font'
> and should work with that 'pastoral charity' which requires
> 'if they do not wish to run in vain,
> that they work always in strict union
> with the bishop
> and their other brothers in the priesthood'' (PO 14).

d) Realized Fraternity

We have already stated how fraternity must not be limited to affirmations of principle, even solemn and established ones, but must translate itself into an experience of a lived life and realize itself in a concrete situation (*cf.* Chap. II, e). We now want to look at various modes and forms of fraternity, indicating how it was achieved in the past and how it can be realized today. Even though it strongly underlined the importance of intimate sacramental fraternity and insisted on the contents of the same, which go from mutual help to communion of life and work, the Council, in speaking of common life, did not get down to ironclad specifics but adopted the criterion of adaptability, both to respect the experiments that were going on and to leave room for new ones:

>"In order that priests may find mutual assistance
>in the development of their spiritual and intellectual lives,
>that they may be able to cooperate more effectively in their ministry
>and be saved from the dangers which may arise from loneliness,
>let there be fostered among them some kind or other
>of community life.
>Such a life can take on several forms
>according to various personal and pastoral needs:
>for instance, a shared roof where this is feasible,
>or a common table,
>or at least frequent and regular gatherings'' (PO 8c).

Sacerdotalis Coelibatus (n. 80) takes the same line as does the Synod of Bishops (*The Ministerial Priesthood*, Part II, II, 2), which limits itself to a formulation of a general character:

>"Some community of life or some type of living together,
>which can take various forms, even non-institutional ones,
>should be promoted among them and should even be foreseen
>by the law with opportune norms,
>renewing pastoral structures or finding new forms of them."[45]

... APPLICATIONS OF PRIESTLY FRATERNITY

Some general directions can be derived from these indications, as, for example, the usefulness of a presbyterial fraternity in parishes which cover a vast territory granting more collegial responsibility to the figure of the pastor himself; the promotion of a team approach with each priest placing his talents and specific preparation at the disposition of the area; the replacement of the concept of the autonomous parish with its own pastor by a larger pastoral entity in which priests even share the same rectory, etc.

Let us examine a little more in detail the forms or levels on which such fraternity might be realized.

"Animated by the fraternal spirit, priests should not neglect hospitality" (PO 8c). This simplest form is expressed by a spirit of openness and welcome towards confreres who, for pastoral, cultural, health, or even recreational motives, must travel to different cities or nations. It is true that there are any number of clergy residences or boarding schools run by religious or diocesan institutions. But it is also true that at times, apart from human prudence, indifference or suspicion which can hide egotistical or smug attitudes can prevail in the rectory which speaks of anything but hospitality. If we do not help one another as priests, how can we preach charity to others or teach young Christian couples to have an "open" house?

A second level of fraternity might entail living together. "It can take the form of a shared roof, where this is possible, or a common table" (PO 8c). It is up to those concerned to agree on the type of life to which each can pledge himself. There can be enormous advantages to this important manifestation and realization of the spirit of fraternity which go from freeing up time for prayer to the exchange of ideas and experiences, to help in moments of difficulty and crisis, to a wider availability for ministry (without worry over such things as the preparation of meals, etc.). Even if this level is not reached, the minimum of a common table, of periodic reunions and gatherings guarantees more freedom and serenity, which are the first steps towards communion and a more deepened awareness of sacramental fraternity.

A third mode is "common life" properly so called in which, uniting the previous two levels of hospitality and mutual sharing on a regular basis, daily living and pastoral goals are joined together, and the same spiritual benefits are even enjoyed. There are difficulties and roadblocks en route in all of this, but when there is some give and take and we don't allow ourselves to get frozen into hard and fixed mental attitudes little apt for the mission of the diocesan priest (whose theological presuppositions and ascetical motivations differ from those of religious), the result will not be long in coming. The important thing is to fix on the community spirit, helping one another and verifying one's choices by the light of gospel love. Only thus can common life become an authentic value.[46]

The ideal that must always be striven for is the creation of a real community, that is, a community of life which — though it may take a strong initial dose of realism and afterwards prove difficult to sustain — truly constitutes an efficacious sign of the Lord's presence, both in the area of sanctification and of apostolic action. In effect, in this community of life,

> "priests are called, with their words and works,
> to make themselves a sign and instrument before all
> of the mystery they bear within themselves.
> The hidden mystery, then, is revealed
> in their interpersonal relations
> marked by faith, hope and love.
> The richness and the good of each
> are placed at the disposition of all,
> in the reciprocal gift which exalts fraternity,
> in which one is necessary to the other;
> what one has completes what the other lacks
> and each participates in the community growth which involves all
> and gives worth to the contribution of all."[47]

History gives us different examples of realized fraternity both in the form of famous friendships among the saints themselves — it is enough to recall St. Augustine and Possidius who lived together for many years, or Sts. Cyril and Methodius — and in the various forms of common life in general, or even in forms of priestly community almost always tied to the search for and increase of the spirituality of the diocesan priest.

We thus have a long series of rich and varied experiences which comprise, just to give some examples, the "Brethren of the Common Life" of Geert Groote, the "Oblates of St. Ambrose" of St. Charles Borromeo, the "Congregation of the Oratory" of St. Philip Neri, the "Priests of the Mission" of St. Vincent de Paul, the "Congregation of the Oratory of Jesus" of Cardinal Pierre de Berulle, the foundation of Bartholomew Holzhauser, the "Company of St. Sulpice" of Jean-Jacques Olier, etc.[48]

The "communion of life, work and charity" (LG 28c) seems to express the priestly vocation much better. This is a vocation to brotherly love and to friendship in the fruitfulness of celibacy. On the basis of the Gospel, it will be necessary to rediscover all the richness of this calling to fraternity which seems to postulate a kind of common life in a precise group or community for its better realization. There is among priests in general a sincere understanding of and a strong desire to live by mutual assistance and in fraternal community with God and their brothers. But in the hour of truth, the affirmations of principle are not always followed by a consonant response by all, a response which would overcome the difficulties and obstacles in the way of the construction of an authentic community.

We admit that some of the initial enthusiasm for this after the Council has diminished a bit but a re-attempt with a little more flexibility, imagination and especially much good will, will not indeed be time lost.[49] The Apostle's exhortation to re-clothe ourselves applies to us too; that is, *"as God's elect, holy and beloved, clothe yourselves with heartfelt mercy, with kindness, humility, meekness and patience"* (Col 3:12).

> "So I say to you: 'Ask and you shall receive;
> seek and you shall find;
> knock and it shall be opened to you.
> For whoever asks, receives;
> whoever seeks, finds;
> whoever knocks is admitted' " (Lk 11:9-10; Mt 7:7-8).

Last, as the Council also states:

> "Worthy too of high regard and zealous promotion
> are those associations whose rules have been examined
> by competent Church authority,
> and which foster priestly holiness
> in the exercise of the ministry
> through an apt and properly approved rule of life
> and through brotherly assistance.
> Thus these associations aim to be of service
> to the whole priestly order" (PO 8c).

In a climate of solidarity at the national and international levels, priestly associations should pursue not so much the formation of an *esprit de corps* as the promotion of the spiritual life and an intellectual updating of its members through their participation and sharing in the same priestly ideals, as Pope John XXIII already stated in his encyclical *Sacerdotii nostri primordia* of August 1, 1959. In it he expressed his satisfaction with all those diocesan priests who were seeking, in associations approved by the Church, the strength and assistance they needed to set out with greater ease and agility on the way of perfection.[50]

The phenomenon of associating is not new in the Church. And Vatican II has acknowledged the right of association not as a concession of authority but as a fundamental right of all the faithful, cleric and lay. Even for priests this right of association touches upon the area of their own autonomy and personal responsibility without constituting a useless duplication of an already existing bond.[51]

These associations, movements and groups are many, a gift of God for our time. They display a great variety of forms and charisms but have in common the search for unity of life and priestly holiness in the fulfillment of one's ministry, in a bond of fraternal charity with one's brothers, and for the benefit of the entire People of God.

Just to cite some: The Priestly Association of Prado of Anthony Chevrier (1826-1879), the groups of the "Apostolic Union" of the clergy of V. M. Lebeurier (1832-1918), the "Missionary Union" of the clergy of Paul Manna (1872-1952), the "Gospel and Mission Team," the "Priestly Fraternity Jesus-Caritas." Other priests, instead, share common bonds because of their involvement in Church movements such as the "Focolarini" of Chiara Lubich, one or another of the secular institutes such as that of "Jesus-Priest" of James Alberione, or are enrolled at various levels in the prelature of "Opus Dei" of J. Escriva de Balaguer.[52]

Priestly associations, both public and private, like spontaneous initiatives as well, for the most part sustained and encouraged and having their own statutes or not, when they are at the service of the communion of the whole presbyterate and offer a precious aid to the permanent formation of their adherents, are an authentic wealth for the Church of Christ and a gift of the Spirit who at all times suggests multiple expressions and divers shadings of priestly love.

There are some limits to keep in mind, however, as we have already indicated. These experiences, left to official institutions, run the risk of remaining fixed within general guidelines without grasping a person's most vital needs. Left instead to individual or to small group initiative, they gain in spontaneity and coherence, but with time run the risk of causing member burnout with a concomitant drop in achievement.[53]

Apart from these considerations suggested by a healthy realism, we should not forget that much remains to be done still for greater communion among priests in ministry and in life. The support of the Church, the help of the bishop, the contribution of individuals, the exchange of diverse experiences, prudence, and especially more courage and generosity will aid in finding the most successful formula and the best way to realize authentic fraternity which may give witness to the resurrection of the Lord Jesus (*cf.* Ac 4:33).

e) Fraternity and the Criteria of Vocations

At this point it seems right to us to say a few words about a subject which should assume new importance after all we have said; namely, the relationship between fraternity and the criteria of vocations.

If we regard it as true that the call to the priesthood is by nature a call to fraternity, it must also be said that this call is not improvised or produced by spontaneous generation but, like every other precious good, must be cultivated and cared for. We have seen, in fact, how the call to service in the Kingdom and the proclamation of the "good news" implies from the beginning the invitation to enter into the little company of Jesus (the *apostolica vivendi forma*); how there is no antagonism between love of God and love of a human person; that the very choice of celibacy does not exempt from fraternal love; in fact, it binds one to it even more as it enriches and purifies it,[54] thus becoming also an indispensable premise of the spirituality of the clergy.

Also ascertained, it seems, is the fact that an apostolic fraternity, deeply living communication among persons, does not become such to enclose itself in self-complacency nor does it do so for functional efficiency. It does so to be a significant presence and anticipation of the Kingdom while it cultivates in itself a passion for the communion of man with God.

In the light of these premises, is there not the possibility of looking at the concept of the priesthood in a way that is still too functional, and with a vision that is too utilitarian, which puts the idea of vocation on a par with supply and demand economics: the scarcity of vocations and the shortage of ministers, the needs of the harvest and the objective attitudes of the candidates, leaving in the background personal needs, the intention of giving oneself entirely and exclusively and the original pattern of living in communion?[55]

... APPLICATIONS OF PRIESTLY FRATERNITY

The causes of the decline in and crisis of vocations can be many. Much has been said and written about them,[56] even to suggesting the dispensation from the obligation of celibacy. (Let us not underestimate the fact that even among the Protestants and the Orthodox, where this "obstacle" does not exist, there has been an analogous drop in vocations.) Nor must we forget either that the priestly choice is a choice of a ministry ordered to help others in a process of perfection which is fulfilled only if the process of one's own personal identification and maturation is completed — a process, as we have seen, that calls for an encounter with the other. It is that "play," namely, between human love and divine love, which constitutes the central aspect of the experience and the message of Christ, where the service of the Kingdom and reciprocal love meet one another and blend, beginning with the experience of fraternity.[57]

The values of this fraternity, which are eminently evangelical values, refer to Christian maturity and treat also of an irrevocable choice. They can be interiorized only if, in an experience of fraternity, brotherly relations are lived. For the rest, even "the magisterium of the Church, deepening the experience and the teaching of Christ, has pointed to fraternal priestly communion as the necessary way for the celibate priest to protect and develop his self-giving to Christ and to the Church."[58]

This new sensibility of the magisterium which is reflected in the documents of recent years is well supported by an attentive reading of the experience of the little apostolic community which became aware of being a new reality (*cf.* Peter who speaks in the name of all: "*We have left everything and followed you . . .*" in Mt 19:27, and Jesus' answer: "*You who have followed me. . .*" *ibid.*, 19:28).

This reality is more suitable for family life than for the proclamation of the Gospel. It facilitates attention to the "*things of the Lord.*" It is offered as a sign and a pledge of the Kingdom for itself and for others,[59] carrying with it a missionary restlessness for the whole world.

In line with what Paul VI said on June 2, 1970, referring to education in community spirit — defined as "the necessary atmosphere of the believer" in which "to conceive and express religious, moral and social life in relation to the ecclesial community" — priestly formation, necessarily and *a fortiori*, must be formation to fraternity. There must be a system of integration into the group which inspires the members, accustoms them more to solidarity, to a bonding of ideals and to a fusion of human and spiritual qualities, all the while conserving the primacy of charity. The decree *Optatam totius*, of Vatican II, when speaking of the human virtues of candidates to the priesthood, refers explicitly to this new awareness of the communitarian dimension which must always grow where it is and must be created where it has not yet been given proper consideration. The qualities are:

"sincerity of spirit,
constant respect for justice,
fidelity to one's given word,
gentleness in manner,
discretion,
and charitable conversation" (OT 11a).

as also

> "the capacity to listen to others
> and to open their hearts in a spirit of charity
> to the various aspects of living together" (*ibid.*, 19a).

The very discipline of the years of formation, considered as "a support of the common life and of charity," must be imposed in such a way as gradually to instill also the habit of "collaborating with confreres and lay people." The end is obvious. In fact,

> "the whole seminary program,
> permeated with a cultivation of reverence and silence
> and with a concern for mutual help,
> should be structured as a kind of introduction to the life
> the seminarian will lead as a priest" (OT 11b-c).

Fraternity, with the values it brings with it, must become the unifying motive at the base of priestly life, not only a moment or stage of formation but the dominant note and the atmosphere it breathes. It may not remain at the surface or emotional level but is to penetrate deep within the person in his makeup and expressions. It is not to end with the admittedly important period of formation but must be the design and plan of a whole life if we hope that it be translated into concrete gestures and operative choices of true communion at a later point in priestly life.[60]

This is set down in clear terms in the *Ratio Fundamentalis*, n. 47:[61]

> "By means of seminary community life,
> let the candidates be prepared in such a way that,
> when they shall have received sacred orders,
> they will insert themselves into the larger community
> of the diocesan presbyterate 'with sacramental fraternity...
> with the bond of prayer and unconditioned collaboration...
> for the upbuilding of the Body of Christ,
> which requires many functions and new attitudes,
> especially in these times.'"

Since the fraternity that awaits them is a sacramental one, seminarians — beyond "familiar confidence with their superiors and brotherly friendship with their fellow students" from the minor seminary on (*Ratio Fundamentalis*, n. 13b), since they are "destined to model themselves on Christ the priest through sacred ordination — should become used also to living intimately united to him, like friends all their lives" (OT 8). They should make the Eucharist the center and fulcrum of their life in the seminary because from this sacrament "any education attempting to form the spirit of community must take its cues" (PO 6e).

Hence the importance of the seminary's being an authentic school of communion and a model of Christian community where one is seriously trained and pledges himself to communion; where an experience of community is lived that in its totality educates to fraternity.[62]

Specifying better, we can say that seminaries, in order to be "hotbeds of true community and priestly friendship"[63] and to foster after ordination the continuity of personal experiences of years of formation, must in the

... APPLICATIONS OF PRIESTLY FRATERNITY

highest degree attend to the formation of candidates to the priesthood so that they may reach a specifically priestly maturity which, in its particular manifestation of adult affectivity (read celibacy), sees in fraternity itself the stimulus towards a more intimate consecration to Christ and a freer gift of self to the faithful.[64]

It will be educators' special task to pay heed to the human affective equilibrium of seminarians, above all by presenting themselves as image and model; that is, as "a community of adults, joined for mutual edification and the service of mission," bearing witness to "the possibility that even adults, different and free, can realize a profound communion and friendship," conscious of thus exercising "the most efficacious moment of their educational efforts."[65] And later, at least at the time of first assignment, with tact and a sense of responsibility for the newly ordained, let there be chosen — within the limits of possibility — those ministerial settings which may offer greater guarantee of actual fraternity.

In the light of these reflections, re-enforced by a progressive historical maturation and, as has been seen, by an always clearer tendency on the part of the magisterium, the criteria of priestly vocations should be differently organized and even revised in part, both as regards the description of a choice on the part of the individual and the conditions of admission on the part of Church authority.

Once the concept of a vocation as a call coming from God (absolutely not to be confused with response or human correspondence) is well clarified, it will be necessary to face up to the problem of the discernment of a priestly vocation. It will not be enough that a man have a sincere faith, a "taste" for prayer, a "humble" concept of himself, that he know how to obey and to conquer temptations (especially against chastity), or indeed that he be brought to priestly life by circumstances (a natural inclination, the enthusiasm of superiors, the positive results of psychological tests and the like). Nor will it be enough that he have a canonical vocation (the call of the bishop) or be the one "signified" or designated by the ecclesial community.[66]

Some of these are indicative, or even necessary elements (canonical calling, for example), but they are not sufficient. The priesthood, involving a global witnessing in a completely special kind of lifestyle, supposes an action of the Spirit towards a total and exclusive plan of life and love (at the same time human and supernatural) to be realized by a deep and personal communion of life with Christ and in the priestly fraternity he established around him. To be introduced into this "order," to be incorporated into this priestly corps, re-actualizing the Lord's lifestyle with his disciples, "it will be necessary that the intuition of being able to fulfill one's own life in this manner carry with it also the awareness of being able to realize, in this state of life, this special type of authentically human love presupposed here, which is the love of Christ himself" with "the clear perception of being able to give oneself exclusively and irreversibly in this endeavor."[67]

These fundamental criteria, decisive and determinant for admission to the priesthood, are the main points to address to oneself for verification and authentication of the "call." We can even advance here an hypothesis of our own which is not meant to be anything other than suggestive. Just as the type of new life (with Christ and among themselves) was for the apostles the authentic expression of their vocation and the proof of the sincerity of their faith and love, so must it be for him who will have to show by his words and life the love lived by the Lord in the apostolic community. This fundamental criterion thus becomes a determining criterion, the one which unifies all the other cited criteria. In this sense it is also a unique criterion of discernment, understood as the capacity for "apostolic" friendship, of the choice of the apostolic lifestyle with all that it implies and all that flows from it and is necessary for admission to the priesthood as faith is for baptism.[68]

Making his way towards the priesthood with this outlook, a man who is "called" to it knows how to steer himself towards the full realization of God's design for him in perfect resonance with the priesthood of Christ.

Priestly Fraternity Is

— the sign that man is "the image of God"
— a visible proof of the love of the Father
— the reflection of Christ's charity in the world

— the gift of the Spirit who continues the action of the apostles
— the pledge of maternal fruitfulness in the Church
— a fully realized vocation
— a sharing of Christ's sentiments
— an example of communion for the whole Church
— the guarantee of pastoral charity
— the efficacious sign of evangelization
— the witness of the authenticity of the faith
— the promotion of priestly ideals
— the source of the joy of togetherness as brothers
— the seed of new vocations
— the source of enthusiasm and perseverance along the priestly way
— the forge of pastoral efforts
— the continuous thrust toward generosity in the giving of self
— the visible fulfillment of the Kingdom of Christ
— the prophetic presence of the People of God
— the anticipation of future realities.

FOOTNOTES

1. Cf. G. Cenacchi, "The Priest and the Other Priests," in *Il prete . . . , cit.*, pp. 581ff.
2. For the rest, it is a common conviction today that sexual dynamism — in so far as it refers to the desire for acceptance, reciprocal affirmation, etc. — has an important, but not an indispensable, element in the genital aspect; cf., for example, G.B. Gabrielli, "Virginity and celibacy: biopsychological aspects," in *Diz. enc. di teol. morale*, Rome 1973, pp. 1143-47; D. Goergen, *The Sexual Celibate*, New York 1974 (cf. in particular pp. 59-64 where he takes up Maslow's thinking, which can be summarized in this way: "Man is above all an animal who seeks intimacy, and one can have intimacy without genital sexuality," p. 63). D. Marzotto, "On the Nature of Priestly Celibacy," *cit.* p. 611, note 59).
3. Most useful in this regard is the letter of M. Nedoncelle, *La reciprocite des consciences. Essai sur la nature de la personne*, Paris 1942, pp. 105ff; *id.*, *Vers une philosophie de l'amour et de la personne*, Paris 1957, pp. 341ff.

... APPLICATIONS OF PRIESTLY FRATERNITY

4. Even through the presence in his life of "three types of relationships: 1) of the Twelve with Christ (experience model); 2) of the priest with Christ (priestly vocation); 3) of the priest with other priests and the bishop (concrete sacerdotal condition)" D. Marzotto, *op. cit.*, p. 28.
5. "If authentic life is love, solidarity and communion, apostolic fraternity demonstrates that authentic life is possible. If, on the other hand, the world seems to us to be threatened by non-communication and meaninglessness, apostolic fraternity presents itself as an alternative and the bearer of meaning" (F. Fernandez Alia, "Fraternities at the Service of the Upbuilding of the Church," in *De dos en dos, cit.*, p. 246).
6. Cf. also J. Rovira, "The Theological-Moral Dimension in a Life of Celibacy for the Kingdom," in *Il celibato per il Regno*, Milan 1977, pp. 296ff.
7. "Living together refines the spirit through the concrete and realistic encounter with limits and defects, virtue and goodness; the community is the agency freeing one from individual burdens and egotism, too often rationalized by the haughtiness and pride of the one who feels alone and set apart. One then can aquire the kind of dominion over the self which makes members vigilant, prompt, and persevering and which does not allow the seeking after any surrogate of dubious origin or equivocal intention" (G. Cenacchi, "The Priestly Fraternity," in *I sacerdoti, cit.*, p. 662).
8. A. Manaranche, *Come gli apostoli, cit.*, p. 133.
9. It is not our purpose here to go into detail about the problem of the retribution of the clergy. There are various studies on this topic, starting with the proposals suggested by the decree itself (PO 17), which go from an equal retribution which may assure "the means to lead an honest and dignified life" to the new qualification of "ecclesiastical office" to the establishment of a "common house," etc. For a top-level study, it suffices to examine G. Bonicelli, "The Economic Life of the Clergy," in *I sacerdoti, cit.*, pp. 1035-1078.
10. Cf. A. Favale - G. Gozzelino, *op. cit.*, p. 216. "The life of the priest is, therefore, characterized by a bipolar movement: towards God and towards men. The priest must not forget God when he entertains men; neither must he lose sight of the needs of men when he turns himself to God. True love of God and true love of neighbor are not dispersive but convergent because they are the reflection of one love" (*ibid.* p. 206).
11. Cf., for example, the latest volumes of B.I.S., Rome, the Teresianum, 1966 —, under the heading *Vita spiritualis — De Statibus vitae sacerdotalis*; J. Esquerda Bifet, *Teologia de la Espiritualidad Sacerdotal*, pp. 349-353; M. Caprioli, *Sacerdozio e Santita, cit.*
12. "This vision, stressing the ecclesial aspect, orients toward a conception of holiness which is much richer and more authentic, because founded on giving and love, and conceived as a part of the '*munus*' of priests; that is, of their task to contribute to the growth and upbuilding of the whole Body which is the Church" (P. Molinari, "The Priest's Call to Holiness," in *I sacerdoti, cit.*, p. 804).
13. This is "testimony to the scrupulous care with which they safeguard priestly chastity" (AAS, 42 [1950], p. 693).
14. Cf. G. De Rosa, *Preti per oggi*, Rome 1972, pp. 225 and 246.
15. "This double fidelity, to communion and to the truth, is sadly a source of tension; for that reason we simply cannot reach authentic ecclesial communion without conversion on the part of all. Confronting this openly and candidly, the same way the apostolic fraternities did when faced with dissembling and compromise, is the only road to true communion" (F. Fernandez Alia, "Fraternities . . . ," in *De dos en dos, cit.*, p. 243).

16. "Let us remember: To go along is easy (even if it is not always healthful); likeness is comfortable (even if it does not always stimulate growth); fraternity, on the other hand — with all the brothers the Lord gives us, favoring objective rapports over those suggested by subjective affinities — is demanding and tiring, often arid and always inconvenient for our ego. But only fraternity truly builds up a person and makes our ministry more productive" (G. Marcandelli, *op.cit.*, p. 78).
17. C. M. Martini, *La Parola nella citta, cit.*, pp. 48ff.
18. St. Strano, *Celibato e solitudine del prete, cit.*, p. 130. Cf. also the document of *CEI, Comunion e comunita*, n. 26, in *p. cit.*, col. 632: "But he (Christ) is also 'present with his virtue in the sacraments so that when one baptizes it is Christ himself who baptizes' (SC 7). He is present above all in the Eucharist by which, 'participating really in the Body of the Lord, we are elevated to communion with him and among ourselves: *Because there is only one bread, we are one body . . .*' (LG 7)."
19. "Concelebration, 'in which the unity of the priesthood is appropriately manifested' (SC 57), is not a rite solely to simplify celebration by a large number of priests, nor much less the adornment of a program for feasts. It has, to be precise, the quality of a sacramental sign (and, therefore, of some efficacy of grace), insofar as the concelebrants show that the one Priest, Christ, prolongs priestly ministry in each particular Church by means of one sign. This supposes an effective and affective concelebration with which the bishop celebrates the Eucharist with full authority, represented at least by one or by all" (J. Esquerda Bifet, *Teologia de la Espiritualidad Sacerdotal, cit.*, p. 136).
20. Cf. P. Molinari, "The Call of Priests to Perfection," in *I Sacerdoti, cit.*, pp. 793-883.
21. F. Fernandez Alia, "Fraternities. . . ," in *op. cit.*, p. 345.
22. M. Legido, "The Fraternity. . . ," in *op. cit.*, pp. 132-134.
23. F. Fernandez Alia, *op. cit.*, p. 246.
24. M. Marini, *Celibato e fraternita sacerdotale*, in *op. cit.*, p. 912.
25. "It is not easy in fact to accept not doing things by oneself, to have to discuss decisions before taking them, to accept contradiction and, indeed — as often happens — to have to make an effort or to use methods that are contrary to one's own personal point of view but decided on by the presbyterium. Priestly fraternity in a local church is not the simple result of an organizational effort, of the best directives, of a renewed institution. All these are surely helpful and even necessary, but they are certainly not enough" (G. Visconti, *L'unita tra i sacerdoti, cit.*, p. 513).
26. In this regard permit me to report something personal. A few months before my consecration to God in priestly life, a brother of mine to whom I had expressed a bit of uncertainty regarding this definitive step, answered me: "What are you afraid of? Look, a person getting married can start wondering if, even though he may be faithful, the other party will be. You don't have these problems. You have the certainty that the other party will always be faithful because God cannot be other than true to himself." It need not be said how much good these simple words did, and still do, for me.
27. "In this case the friendly thrust which is proper to fraternity, not being able to mature in friendship properly so called, will reflow into the value of fraternity to make it more consistent and deep in its essential nature. The difficulty in communicating then translates as the consolidation of the value of fraternal communion, which thus is safeguarded in its authenticity from the negative interfering of artificial or superficial communications" (G. Cristaldi, *Fraternita e amicizia sacerdotale, cit.*, p. 680).
28. *Ibid.*

... APPLICATIONS OF PRIESTLY FRATERNITY

29. "A life of fraternal, harmonious and active community, rich in human and supernatural warmth, spreads among its members a sense of relaxation, of balance, and of satisfaction through which they themselves are like vaccinated people, not seeking affective compensations outside it; and it makes more difficult the raising of complaints about the renunciation made because of the choice of celibacy" (D. Marzotto, "On the Nature...," cit., p. 621, note 87, where he mentions nos. 72-73 of *Sacerdotalis Coelibatus*).
30. These compensations can veer towards association with persons whom Jesus has explicitly invited us to leave (brothers and sisters, father and mother, etc.) or, worse, towards the deflection of one's affectivity to material things (money, buying and selling, buildings, TV, sports magazines, clubs, etc.) and animals (dogs, cats, birds, etc.). Cf. J. Murphy O'Connor, *Celibacy and Community, cit.*, p. 61.
31. "Sometimes this phenomenon even occurs: intolerance, arguments, aggressiveness, mutual excommunication — defects which once characterized our relations with others, those outside the Church — today are transferred within, among different Christian churches, among different groups or movements of Christian inspiration, between priests and their bishop..." (G. Marcandalli, *op. cit.*, p. 84).
32. "Not without cause does St. Paul, in listing charity's attributes, give the first place to patience. The patience of charity (*e agape macrothumei*) is the assumption, out of goodness, of one another's burden, of the burden of structures, the burden of situations, etc. (cf. Ep 4:2; Col 3:12ff; 1 Tm 5:14). Thus the burden, even if not suppressed, becomes rescued and freed from its oppressive thrust and made the occasion for development and the surprises of love" (G. Cristaldi, *op. cit.*, p. 683).
33. Fr. Fernandez Alia, "Fraternities...," in *op.cit.*, p. 244.
34. "Communion is the gift of the "Spirit which is to be sought continually in prayer, even because our sin entraps and constantly compromises this good. And the Spirit has seasons and times which it is not ours to know or accelerate.

    The Spirit's operations can be neither predetermined nor controlled. One must accept the long periods of expectation and tension and the hours of grace in which communion reflourishes.

    One must know how to accept the days on which communion (or fraternity) is the joy of all, and the days on which it is the burden, the cross, the tribulation of all" (G. Marcandalli, *op. cit.*, p. 80).
35. "A world from which pardon has been eliminated would be a world of only cold and unrespecting justice . . . Merciful love is highly indispensable among those who are closer" (John Paul II, *Dives in misericordia*, n. 14).
36. Perhaps notwithstanding everything, and without having left anything untried, one of our confreres, oppressed by sadness or profound crisis, can reach the point of abandoning his own vocation. Even in such a sad case as this, mindful of the unlimited love of Christ and of his heartfelt prayer (cf. Jn 9:3; 17:12), we must not cut off dialog or erect barriers between us and those "who have a right to count on charity without limits from those who are and must be their truest friends" (*Sacerdotalis Coelibatus*, n. 81; cf. 85).
37. R. Guardini, *Philosophical Writings*, ed. S. G. Sommavilla, Fabbri, Milan 1964, p. 89 (cited by G. Cristaldi, *op. cit.*, p. 683, note 10).
38. "Cultivate your sense of humor. Laugh about things, laugh over the absurdity of life, laugh at yourselves and your absurdities. In God's great universe, we are nothing more than infinitesimal and ridiculous creatures. You must be serious, but avoid being solemn because if you are solemn about everything, you will regard yourselves even with solemnity" (M. Ramsey, *Il prete cristiano oggi*, Rome 1973, cited in *L'amico del clero*, 10 [1973], p. 566).

39. For pleasant reading on this topic, see H. Cormier, *The Humor of Jesus*, Alba House, New York 1977, pp. xii-155.
40. "What is involved, for example, is 'the psychological, spiritual and economic isolation' of 'him who is most exposed by particular places, delicate situations and ministries, and difficulties arising from restricted material means which can drive one to weighty projects undertaken with zeal but not always considered with the necessary prudence or required competence. It is true there are laws which require us to be cautious, but in fact, in these cases, the priest, in good faith, finds himself entangled in situations which could have been avoided if known or discussed together from the beginning" (G. Cenacchi, "Priestly Fraternity," in *I sacerdoti, cit.*, p. 660).
41. *Ibid.*, p. 655.
42. "These can help him avoid authoritarian, paternalistic, possessive, monopolizing tendencies, typical of one who is used to living alone and who does not have the habit of dialog, co-responsibility, and normal collaboration, which are all constant elements of everyday life" (D. Marzotto, "Crisis of Vocations. . . ," in *L'Osservatore Romano*, November 7-8, 1983, p. 7).
43. "Individual updating is the best thing; the experience of personal prayer is indispensable. But it is necessary that they be done in common, that they become the 'gift of charity.' Only by giving them do we truly enrich ourselves. Otherwise, in not creating communion, they can isolate us, humanly impoverish us, and make us rush to judgment and condemnation" (G. Visconti, *art. cit.*, p. 513).
44. The *Ratio fundamentalis* is even more explicit: "Priestly formation by its nature, is such that it must be continued and always perfected throughout the entire course of one's lifetime. In this regard 'teamwork' should be preferred among priests; this approach, today especially, can offer many advantages to pastoral teaching" (*Ratio fundamentalis institutionis sacerdotalis*, n. 100: AAS 62 [1970], pp. 321-384; also *Ench. Vat.*, vol. III, p. 1215).
45. Cf. *Ench. Vat.*, Vol IV, n. 1229 (in AAS [1971], pp. 898-942).
46. "Just as the Council which hopes 'that some kind of life in common be encouraged among them . . . which can naturally assume different forms in keeping with the different personal and pastoral needs' (PO 8c), so too the Synod of Bishops (*The Ministerial Priesthood*) goes so far as to affirm that this objective can be pursued even 'by renewing pastoral structures or seeking new ones' (Part II, II, 2), if necessary, so much does it believe that the advantages offered are superior to the sacrifices required." See also A. Massoleni, "Common Life of the Presbyterate of the Parish Community," in *Presenza pastorale*, 3 (1970), pp. 145-169.
47. *CEI, Comunione e comunita*, October 1, 1981, Ch. IV, n. 35 in *Lettere pastorali, cit.*, p. 633. It is true that an authentic community requires a continual conversion and both are accomplished together. But it is also true that "interpersonal communion, to be authentic, must respect the threshold of intimacy at which communication stops and which cannot be violated by anyone. Man acknowledges in the other man an incommunicable nucleus . . . There exist a reserve and a modesty which must be respected and which have nothing at all to do with the 'gospel frankness' invoked by one or the other as a screen for a kind of interior emptiness given to intemperate chatter. This is not an instance of wanting to isolate oneself, nor of wanting a community-dormitory set up but of a true center of fraternal life. It should not be forgotten that without respect for the solitude each one needs, and in which is impressed the seal of their relationship with God, the community risks getting lost in long-winded speeches about satisfied superficialities . . . It ought to be the duty of all the members to preserve the necessary

attention to a communion in depth and at the same time to the solitude we have been talking about. Both the evangelical quality of the community and the upbuilding of persons, it seems, would thus be assured" (A. Mercatali, "Comunita di vita," in *Nuovo Dizionario di Spiritualita*, Rome 1982, p. 231).

This long citation does not seem superfluous to us both because at times we forget to respect intimacy and the need for solitude of the other and because at other times community life is given an out-of-place mystical quality or, better, the myth of community is created. Only God is absolute and unequivocal. All human realities, community life included, are ambiguous and relative. Now, community is good and positive if in this reality Christ is made present; that is, there is reflected in the atmosphere that is breathed and in the deeds that are done the genuine spirit of the "community of Christ with his Apostles." Otherwise, it ends up being negative and harmful, as when the community of Joseph's brothers is called to mind (cf. Genesis, chapters 37-49), in which instead of the good goal of "friendship," there was pursued "in complicity" the exclusion of a brother to the point of selling him to passing strangers ("a conspiracy in evil on the part of many").

Community life is abused when, instead of a *"consilium equitatis"* there is celebrated a *"consilium iniquitatis"* where in complicity decisions are taken together against a member which individually no one would have dared to take.

48. Cf. "Community Life Among the Secular Clergy," in *D. Sp.*, II-1, Cols. 1156-1184, finishing with the *Dizionario degli Istituti di Perfezione*, compiled by G. Pelliccia and G. Rocca, Rome 1974- . It treats various religious institutes, persons, and themes.
49. "It is surprising how, from this viewpoint, the priest often considers common life as a heavy burden, a form of poverty; and, on the other hand, the claim is made that solitude is the great trauma of the choice of celibacy, a solitude that should be lightened by at least the presence of a zealous female co-worker. The deduction from this would be that the mentality of the celibate priest tends towards a subtle kind of individualism. On the one hand, in fact, he does not manage to see his other confreres as a value, even if binding and strict. On the other, however, he feels the need for a human presence near him, but in a subordinate position. It must, therefore, still be asked why the priest's life is systematically organized in conditions of solitude while this fact continues to be deplored as something negative; and why forms of common life are not organized which would at least avoid those difficulties which are not inevitable" (D. Marzotto, "The Celibate and the New Testament," *cit.*, p. 370, note 154).
50. Cf. AAS, 51 (1959), p. 551. These associations were repeatedly supported even before then by Pius X in *Haerent animo*, in AAS (1908), pp. 375-376, Pius XII in *Menti Nostrae*, in AAS (1950) pp. 682 and 698, and Paul VI in *Sacerdotalis Coelibatus*, in AAS (1967), p. 689. One must, in any event, avoid the danger of disrupting the unity of the secular clergy by distancing them from their bishops and forming closed circles which make themselves unsympathetic to those who do not join them while they favor in all things their own members and let themselves be guided by affinities of the natural order more than by the supernatural ends declared in the statutes (cf. Capmany, *Espiritualidad de sacerdote diocesano, cit.*, p. 342; cf. also *The Ministerial Priesthood*, II, II, 2).
51. Cf. Del Portillo, "Priestly Associations," in *Il prete, cit.*, pp. 595-613; M. Delabroye, "Secular Institutes of Priests in the Light of Vatican II," in *Vocation*, 236 (1966), pp. 710-721.

52. For priestly figures consult, for example, the *D. Sp.*, under the corresponding entries: for movements, one can look at *Movimenti ecclesiali contemporanei*, ed. A. Favale, Rome 1980.
53. Cf. J. Esquierda Bifet, *El sacerdocio hoy, cit.*, p. 600. We do not feel that we can uncritically recommend participating in all priestly associations without distinction. Our prudence is based on the fact that some of these seem almost exclusively bent on fostering in associated and common form a deplored kind of "functionalism" or job-related "professionalism" that does not do honor to a group of mature individuals whose center is a Person, Jesus Christ.
54. Cf. M. Marini, *Amore umano e amore divino. La relazione interpersonale e l'incontro con Dio in Maurice Nedoncelle*, Brescia 1977 2, p. 149; A. Vanhoye, *La personne humaine et ses relations dans le N.T.*, *Studia Miss.*, 19 (1970), pp. 315-334.
55. Cf. A. Manaranche, *op. cit.*, pp. 84-86.
56. Cf. E. Colagiovanni, *Crisi vere e false nel ruolo del prete oggi: studio sociologico a livello mondiale*, Rome 1973, p. 275; A. D'Urso, *Le vocazioni sacerdotali in Italia: studio teologico-pastorale con documentazione statistica* (1946-74), Bologna, 1975, p. 317; R. Laurentin, "The Crisis of Vocations: Is It a Crisis of the Young?" in *Concilium*, 6 (1975), pp. 172-190; G. Martelet, *Deux mille ans d'Eglise en question-crise de la foi, crise du pretre*, Paris 1984, p. 298; *Strutture psicologiche e vocatione: motivazioni di entrata e di abbandono*, various authors, Turin, 1977.
57. In this experience of fraternity, "virginity renders possible and realizes what conjugal love seeks without exhausting it — a gift of the whole being which leads to a union without reserve . . . Human love often gives less than was expected. After having dazzled, it deludes. But virginal love always gives more than one expects. God never deludes. He is always more beautiful at the end than at the beginning and if he reserves surprises it is to make us marvel at the extent of his generosity which surpasses each time the limit one might wish to assign it. Not only is there not the least flaw in God, in his power, and in his love, but even his fullness communicates to the heart that empties itself for him an inexhaustible richness" (J. Galot, "The Heart of Mary," *Vita e pensiero*, Milan 1968, pp. 40 and 43, quoted by S. Strano, *op. cit.*, pp. 137-138).
58. "By priestly celibacy is understood a complex situation, determined by a profound love of God, by the renunciation of every matrimonial experience, by the assumption of bonds of fraternity and friendship which find their realization in particular in a common life, and finally by a generous effort on behalf of the community of the faithful. . . .

    "Going from a tendentiously essentialist vision to a vision which is more connotative historically, the reflection of the magisterium has clearly introduced even into the condition of the celibate state the theme of a profound, human, and joint relationship, and not simply as a condescension to human weakness but as an element of value for the development of this vocation" (D. Marzotto, "On the Nature . . . ," *cit.*, p. 622, where a note mentions *Sacerdotalis Coelibatus*, 79-81 and 91-95; "The Ministerial Priesthood," II, I, 3-4).
59. Cf. D. Marzotto, *The Celibate, cit.*, p. 368.
60. Cf. G. Visconti, *Unity, cit*, pp. 514-515.
61. Cf. *Ratio fundamentalis institutionis sacerdotalis*, January 6, 1970: AAS, 62 (1970), pp. 321-384 in *Ench. Vat.*, Vol. III, n. 1875. Earlier, in n. 22, it was said: "Because the education and the formation imparted in the seminary tend to be such that the candidates, one day made participants in the one and identical priesthood and ministry of Christ, may live in hierarchical communion with their bishop and their other brothers in the priesthood, forming one diocesan priesthood, it is very useful that

... APPLICATIONS OF PRIESTLY FRATERNITY

among the alumni and the bishop and the diocesan clergy strong bonds be forged starting from seminary years, based on mutual charity, frequent dialog, and cooperation of every kind.''
62. Cf. also the document of *CEI*, ''Seminaries and Priestly Vocations,'' of October 11, 1979, in *Lettere pastorali* 1978-79, Cols. 503-536 (n. 77). It seems evident that for educating to fraternity the individual efforts of seminarians or educators are not enough and that neither should the route of formation to priestly fraternity be limited to the community experience of a particular group, but ''it is the whole community of the seminary in the complex thread of its articulations and relations among persons that exercises a profound and decisive action in formation to priestly fraternity.'' Cf. G. Visconti, *art. cit.*, pp. 516-517.
63. John Paul II to the Conference of German Bishops, Fulda, November 17, 1980, in *L'Osservatore Romano*, insert with Italian translation, p. xxiv.
64. Cf. Nos. 30 and 31 of ''Educative Orientations for Formation to Celibacy,'' of April 11, 1974 in *Ench. Vat.*, Vol. V, Nos. 259-262.
65. Cf. *CEI*, ''Preparation for Priestly Ministry: Orientations and Norms,'' August 15, 1972, 271-272.
66. Cf. M. Marini, ''On the Discernment of a Priestly Vocation,'' in *Rivista di Vita Spirituale*, 30 (1976), pp. 52-54.
67. *Ibid.*, pp. 54-56.
68. Cf. *ibid.*, p. 59. ''A program of priestly life which does not interiorize sacramental fraternity as a basic value is not authentic; even existentially, it does not fulfill the definition of a priest. The priest will feel himself at a disadvantage; he will not properly express that joyful pastoral charity which interiorly unifies his life and ministry'' (G. Visconti, *art. cit.*, p. 514). ''Whoever cannot or will not live in profound friendship the life of priestly communion, which is the primary source of pastoral charity, should not be admitted to the priesthood because he must represent the love of Christ the shepherd for people'' (M. Marini, ''On the Discernment . . . ,'' *cit.*, p. 59).

IV.

Conclusion

To become a priest is to enter into a brotherly, intimate, and sacramental communion which strictly binds ministers together because they are vitally united to Christ.

Priestly fraternity is not a luxury or a prize, but a vocation, a pledge, and above all a "gift," a gift of the Spirit to be sought constantly in prayer which puts us in the condition of living it after the example of Christ. It is not a natural fact but supposes human qualities and the moral virtues of understanding, patience, pardon, generosity, dialog . . . It is a program which far surpasses human capabilities. It is the fruit of a notable attempt at asceticism. But in the faith which raises our understanding and helps us see everything and everyone with the eyes of God; in the hope that gives us the certainty of the presence of "God who *is* Communion" who helps us to hang on in time of difficulty and in the charity which unites us to him who is a Trinitarian "community of life," who purifies us and makes us saints, it will no longer be impossible to fulfill his will that *"unum sint."*

It is necessary to believe strongly in fraternity. It is necessary to believe in and want it even if such is difficult. We must be attentive to and ready for the initiatives suggested by the Holy Spirit who, beyond our weaknesses and incomprehensions, uninterruptedly guides us to a fuller communion with one another.

The priest is not alone on this simultaneously arduous and exhilarating journey. Mary is at his side, the first ring of the long chain of communion which starts with her Son and ends by embracing the whole of humanity. Through her the priesthood of Christ has begun to be efficacious, practically speaking, through the work of the Holy Spirit. Grace itself is communicated in a special manner to those who transfuse it then into their brothers.[1]

With and in Mary, "Mother of the Church,"[2] the priest will be able better to understand his priesthood, from fidelity to vocation to the grace of the sacrament, living all their requirements — not excluding communion in fraternity — with fullness and promptness.

> "A marvelous example of such promptness
> can always be found in the Virgin Mary,
> who under the guidance of the Holy Spirit,
> consecrated herself fully to the mystery of human redemption
> (cf. DV 25). She is the Mother of the supreme and eternal Priest,
> the Queen of the Apostles, and the help of priests in their ministry:
> they must therefore venerate and love her
> with filial devotion and cult" (PO 18b).

She who brought the Savior of the world into this world and assisted the "nascent Church" in its first steps, sharing with it fraternity in prayer (Ac 1:14), will not allow her maternal protection to be lacking to any priest, for all have been confided to her care by Christ himself (*cf.* Jn 19:26-27). She cared for the virgin disciple, John, the apostle of charity and model of every priest who, after Mary, was raised to an exalted and intimate participation in the very sacrifice of Christ on the cross.[3]

After the example of "those priests who, in the course of the centuries, in a service which was often humble and hidden, have left a splendid example of sanctity" (LG 41c) and heeding these privileged witnesses to the multifaceted richness of the priesthood (we are speaking here of priests such as St. John of the Cross, St. Thomas of Villanova, St. John Marie Vianney, St. Gregory Barbarigo, St. Joseph Cafasso, St. John Eudes, Cardinal Mercier, Dom Columba Marmion, Garrigou-Lagrange, and so on), priests, "acknowledging what they do and imitating what they administer" (LG 41e), will live with greater plenitude their communion with God and with their brothers of which Christ has given us the most splendid example. Our Lord even made it a precept (Mt 22:39), perfected it (*cf.* Jn 14:34; Mt 25:40), proposed it as his commandment (Jn 15:20), and made it the object of the pressing recommendation of his departing prayer at the Last Supper.[4]

> "O Father, most holy, protect them with your name
> which you have given me
> [that they may be one, even as we are one] . . .
> Consecrate them by means of truth —
> 'Your word is truth.'
> . . . I consecrate myself for their sakes now,
> that they may be consecrated in truth . . .
> As you, Father, are in me, and I in you;
> I pray that they may be [one] in us,
> that the world may believe that you sent me . . .
> I living in them, you living in me —
> that their unity may be complete.
> So shall the world know that you sent me,
> and that you loved them as you loved me . . .
> To them I have revealed your name,
> and I will continue to reveal it
> so that your love for me may live in them,
> and I may live in them" (Jn 17:11, 17, 19, 22, 23, 26).

In expectation of sitting at his table and dining with him in that full and definitive communion in heaven, let us build and consolidate on earth our apostolic fraternities, "leaven" of communion in the whole Church.

> "Inserted in the heart of history and the human condition,
> they announce new relationships among men.
> In agreement with the march of men,
> they live the freedom of Christ
> while they work for the liberation of man.
> In the midst of suffering humanity,
> they make the gospel of peace and love resound.
> And in the very People of God,
> they are a conscience which remembers,
> summons,
> and enlivens the march of the same People
> among and with other people
> towards the fullness of the Kingdom."[5]

CONCLUSION

FOOTNOTES

1. Cf. G. D'Avack, *Spiritualita sacerdotale*, II, Rome, 1971, pp. 306ff. Cf. also J. Esquerda Bifet, *Teologia de a espiritualidad sacerdotal, cit.*, pp. 236ff. (Chap. XI: "Mary, Church, and Priesthood, Priestly Marian Spirituality"). In regard to the relations between Mary and the priesthood and the Marian spirituality of the priest, we can suggest further, from a very rich bibliography: G. D'Avack, *Il sacerdozio e Maria*, Milan, 1968, p. 100; J. Esquerda Bifet, "Priestly Marian Spirituality," in *Burgense* 11 (1970), pp. 275-309; L. M. Herran, *Sacerdozio e maternidad espiritual de Maria*, in *Teologia del sacerdocio* (various authors), pp. 527-542, etc.
2. "Mary, who is justly invoked as Mother of the Church, is not only an elect part of the Church but is also its model, through faith, love and her profound union with Christ, and hence through the singular richness of grace with which she lived the grace of communion."

    "While the People of God invoke her and, with the affection of filial piety, venerate her as Mother Most Holy (LG 53), they notice in her a model of the most intense communion with God and the brethren, and consequently entrust themselves to her intercession in their effort to live ecclesial communion" (*CEI, Comunione e comunita*, n. 33, in *Lettere Pastorali, cit.*, col. 634).
3. Cf. G. D'Avack, *Spiritualita sacerdotale, cit.*, pp. 311-312.
4. Cf. S. Strano, *op. cit.*, p. 140.
5. F. Fernandez Alia, "Fraternities . . . ," in *op. cit.*, p. 247.

Instructional Models for Course Design & Development

Instructional Models for Course Design & Development

Reginald F. Melton
Institute of Educational Technology
The Open University
Great Britain

**Educational Technology Publications
Englewood Cliffs, New Jersey 07632**

Library of Congress Cataloging in Publication Data

Melton, Reginald F., 1934-
  Instructional models for course design and development.

  Includes bibliographical references and indexes.
  1. Curriculum planning. I. Title.
LB1570.M388   375'.001   81-5538
ISBN 0-87778-178-8   AACR2

Copyright © 1982 Educational Technology Publications, Inc., Englewood Cliffs, New Jersey 07632.

All rights reserved. No part of this book may be reproduced or transmitted, in any form or by any means, electronic or mechanical, including photocopying, recording, or by any information storage and retrieval system, without permission in writing from the Publisher.

Printed in the United States of America.

Library of Congress Catalog Card Number: 81-5538.

International Standard Book Number: 0-87778-178-8.

First Printing: January, 1982.

Preface

This book is concerned with describing how particular models may be used advantageously in the design and development of materials comprising courses of instruction. The models referred to are all concerned with identifying ways in which instruction may be presented to students, and as such place emphasis on the way student learning is affected by the approaches described. The models have all been designed with the needs of individualized instruction in mind, and are intended to respond to the different needs and abilities of students. However, usage is not restricted to individualized instruction.

The book is divided into four distinct parts as indicated below:

PART I provides an *introduction* to the concept of models of the type referred to, discussing why such models are needed and how they might be used.

PART II is concerned with discussing the relative advantages of different ways of presenting instruction to students. More specifically, it describes a number of alternative *models for course design*, placing these in perspective relative to one another by noting to what extent each might be described as building on well-recognized principles of learning. The models are intended to provide broad, flexible guidelines within which curriculum development might take place, and do not attempt to prescribe every facet of presentation. It is therefore possible, and in fact very desirable, for instructional developers to adopt instructional strategies within the broad constraints of any given model to meet their individual needs. Ways of achieving this are discussed in Part III.

PART III is concerned with describing a process, or a set of procedures, to be followed in order to produce course materials conforming to the requirements of any of the models described in PART II. As such, this part of the book is concerned with the development of course materials or, more specifically, with the *instructional materials development process*. To those familiar with conventional objective approaches to curriculum development, the process described may appear to be somewhat unconventional in that there is no attempt to identify detailed objectives in the earliest stages of the process. This is because the development process is seen here as an innovative one in which ideas are clarified as development proceeds. There is thus a need—particularly where development is being undertaken by groups of individuals working together in teams—for the development process to be sufficiently flexible for individuals to develop their thinking over a period of time. The process described is designed to permit such flexibility by adopting a policy of 'progressive differentiation': that is, a policy which moves gradually forward, obtaining initial agreement on broad issues and then successively on more specific ones. Thus, broad course aims are debated, and agreed on, very early in the process described, but agreement on detailed objectives is not required until much later in the process. Similarly, broad strategies, such as decisions concerning the type of course model to be adopted, are determined relatively early (once broad course aims have been clarified), but agreement on more specific unit strategies is not required until much later in the process. In order to carry out the procedures described in PART III, those involved in the development process will need to possess, or acquire, a number of basic skills that are only briefly discussed in this part of the book. These skills are elaborated on in PART IV of the book, rather than in PART III, in order to avoid disrupting the continuity of the theme being presented.

PART IV describes the additional *basic skills that are required* in order to carry out the procedures described in PART III. These include procedures for developing domain-referenced objectives and domain-referenced tests, which are characteristic features of all the models described. Much has been learned about domain-referencing in recent years, and the procedures described build on the knowledge that has been acquired from recent research.

Preface

It is worth noting here that just as this preface is intended to provide a simple overview of (and broad insights into) the contents of this book, so the introductions found at the beginning of each part of the book and at the beginning of each chapter are intended to provide successively more detailed overviews of (and insights into) the contents of each part and chapter, respectively.

RFM
May, 1981

Table of Contents

		Preface	v
		Part I. Introduction	3
Chapter	1.	*The Need for Models*	5
	1.	Why Are Models Needed?	5
	2.	How Can Models Be Used?	7
	3.	Do Appropriate Models Exist?	8
		References	12
		Acknowledgment	13
		Part II. Models for Course Design	15
Chapter	2.	*A Unit Model*	17
	1.	Section Characteristics	18
		1.1. The Advance Organizer	20
		1.2. Content Structure	21
		1.3. Domain-Referenced Objectives	21
		1.4. Domain-Referenced Tests	23
	2.	Unit Characteristics	24
		2.1. The Advance Organizer	24
		2.2. The Summary	28
		2.3. The Final Test	28
	3.	In Conclusion	29
		References	29
		Acknowledgment	30
Chapter	3.	*Some Alternative Course Models*	31
	1.	The Simple Linear Model (L)	32
		1.1. Characteristics of the Simple Linear Model (L)	32
		1.2. Characteristics Common to Both the Simple Linear Model (L) and the Keller Plan	34

		1.3. Strengths and Weaknesses of the Simple Linear Model (L)	36
	2.	The Refined Linear Model (L)	37
	3.	The Branched Model (L)	39
	4.	Variable Route Models (L)	41
	5.	The Theoretical Advantages of Unlimited Time	42
		References	46
		Acknowledgment	46
Chapter 4.		*Models in Perspective*	47
	1.	Structure and Organization	48
	2.	Feedback and Remedial Learning	49
	3.	Self-Pacing	50
	4.	Student Choice	51
	5.	In Perspective	53
		References	56
		Part III. The Instructional Materials Development Process	59
Chapter 5.		*Phase 1: Identification of Course Aims*	63
	1.	The Basic Elements of the Prescribed Approach	63
		1.1. Derivation of Course Aims from Perceived Needs	63
		1.2. Identification of Relationships Among the Aims	65
		A Simple Hierarchical Approach	65
		An Iterative Hierarchical Approach	67
	2.	Factors to Be Taken into Consideration	68
		2.1. Different Types of Aims (and Needs)	68
		Cognitive Aims	70
		Affective Aims	72
		2.2. Different Needs of Different Students	73
	3.	Procedures to Be Followed During Phase 1	74
		3.1. Exchanging Information and Ideas	75
		3.2. Obtaining Provisional Agreement on Course Aims	76

		3.3. Expressing Course Aims in Terms of Unit Aims	77
		References	79
Chapter	6.	*Phase 2: Outlining the Means of Achieving Specified Aims*	81
	1.	Identification of Course Units and Relationships Among Them	82
		1.1. Students of Average Ability	82
		A Hierarchical Approach	83
		A Progressive Differentiation Approach ...	85
		Alternative Approaches	85
		1.2. Students of Different Ability	89
	2.	Preparation of Unit Outlines	90
		2.1. Unit Aims and Assumptions Made	90
		2.2. Sequencing of Instruction	91
		2.3. Methods of Instruction	91
		A Discovery Approach	91
		Case Studies	92
		2.4. Media of Instruction	93
	3.	Frame of Reference	96
		References	97
Chapter	7.	*Phase 3: Progressive Development and Evaluation of Trial Materials*	99
	1.	Preparing the First Full-Draft Presentations ...	101
	2.	Course Team Evaluation	103
	3.	Student Testing	105
		3.1. Individual Try-out	106
		3.2. Group Try-out	107
		Analysis of Student Achievement	108
		Analysis of Student Perception of Difficulties	110
		Analysis of the Perceptions of Teachers and Administrators	111
		3.3. Field Testing	112
		References	113

		Part IV. Basic Skills Required for Course Development	115
Chapter	8.	*The Development of Domain-Descriptions*	117
	1.	The Nature of Domain-Referenced Objectives	117
		1.1. The Background	118
		1.2. Basic Characteristics of Behavioral Objectives	119
		1.3. Characteristics of Domain-Referenced Objectives	121
	2.	Developing Domain-Descriptions	123
	3.	Different Item Types	129
		References	129
Chapter	9.	*Analyzing and Developing Unit Tests*	133
	1.	Student Testing Strategy	135
	2.	Analysis of Normal Score Distributions	138
		2.1. Item Statistics	139
		2.2. Cell Statistics	140
		2.3. Test Statistics	142
	3.	Analysis of Skewed Score Distributions	143
	4.	Equivalence of Alternative Forms of Any Given Test	145
		References	146
Chapter	10.	*Monitoring Student Perceptions and Attitudes*	147
	1.	The Role of Questionnaires Within the Evaluation Process	147
	2.	Different Types of Questionnaires	149
		2.1. A Basic, Bipolar Format	150
		2.2. Different Types of Bipolar Format	152
		2.3. A Unipolar Format	154
		2.4. In Perspective	157
	3.	Interpreting Data from Questionnaires	157
		References	158
Chapter	11.	*The Interpretation of Unit Test Scores*	161
	1.	Identifying the True Performance Level Desired	161

	2.	Estimating the Student's Competency	163
		References	164

In Conclusion 167
1. The Need for Models 167
2. Course Models 168
3. The Instructional Materials Development Process 170

Subject Index 173

Author Index 181

Instructional Models for Course Design & Development

Part I

Introduction

PART I provides an introduction to the book as a whole by looking at why there is a need for models which identify ways in which instruction might be presented to students. Unlike other parts of the book, PART I is limited to a single chapter.

Chapter 1

The Need for Models

This chapter begins by looking at why instructional models are needed, and how they might be advantageous in the design and development of instructional materials and courses. The chapter then goes on to discuss existing models, and takes a close look at one model that has been widely used for two decades. Note is taken of ways in which this model could be improved in light of the existing literature, and the related discussion provides the background from which the models presented in PART II of this book emerge.

1. Why Are Models Needed?

As an educational technologist at The Open University in Britain, I have been very much concerned over the past few years with helping course teams and individuals design and develop instructional materials. As such, much of my work has been with authors who, as subject specialists, are concerned primarily with the development of course content. It has been my task to provide them with whatever knowledge of educational technology is required to ensure that the curriculum materials developed are *presented* in a way that is most likely to facilitate student learning. During the course of my work, I have become increasingly concerned with the way specific aspects of educational technology tend to be discussed in isolation from one another, not only in my own institution, but in general, for I believe that this gives rise to fundamental weaknesses in instructional materials and in the courses in which such materials are presented.

In the following paragraphs, I illustrate the problem by

reference to specific aspects of instructional design and development in The Open University. I then go on to indicate the much more general nature of the problem, and I introduce the concept of models as a means of overcoming it.

In common with most British universities, the majority of subject specialists joining The Open University have a very limited knowledge of educational technology. Despite this, they are rapidly drawn into course teams and involved in the work of instructional design and development. As busy course team members, expected to produce materials according to a prescribed schedule, they prefer to obtain advice and help in educational technology as and when the need arises, rather than spending a substantial proportion of their time on some prerequisite course in instructional design and development. Thus, during the early phases of such development, when the course contents are being discussed, course team members are likely to welcome discussion of those aspects of educational technology that relate to the structuring of material for presentation to students. However, they may prefer to defer discussion of those aspects of educational technology which relate to assessment to later phases of course development, when they feel more inclined to consider the development of assessment material. Should they treat these aspects in isolation from one another, serious problems may arise. For example, in the discussion of assessment procedures, the course team might decide to follow a criterion-referenced approach, demanding student mastery of specified objectives before students progress from one topic to another. However, recognizing that students with different abilities are likely to progress at different rates, they might decide to identify a core content to be mastered by all students and a variety of optional contents to be mastered by more able students according to their needs and abilities. Clearly, the choice of such an approach could have a profound effect on the way in which the material might best be structured, and the variety of relationships between assessment procedures and structures needs to be carefully considered. Similar consideration has to be given to the interrelationships among most facets of educational technology.

The Need for Models

The immediate reaction might be to suggest that all those interested in becoming involved in instructional design and development should first take comprehensive courses in educational technology. However, this in itself is not a complete solution, for many such courses emphasize specific aspects of educational technology, and give too little attention to relationships among them. Thus, it is too easy to discuss the advantages and limitations of such adjunct aids as advance organizers, behavioral objectives, and inserted questions in isolation from one another, and to determine whether or not to use one or all in the development of instructional materials without giving careful consideration to the relationships among them. Similarly, it is not difficult to discuss methods of assessment separately, considering, for example, the relevance of criterion-referenced or norm-referenced testing to one's own particular situation. However, when instructional materials are produced, the strategies adopted must be integrated together within the materials produced. In fact, in making decisions concerning what type of aids and strategies should be used, the designer-developer determines the form in which materials are to be presented to students, and as such, one might talk about the design format, or model, adopted. It is my contention that much more attention should be given to the development of alternative models and the way in which they can be used in instructional design and development.

2. How Can Models Be Used?

Assuming that models are available, it is of interest to consider how they might be advantageous in the situations already discussed.

In the type of situation where individuals, or groups of individuals in course teams, wish to acquire relevant knowledge of educational technology as and when the need arises, it is clear that they should nevertheless review the main characteristics of the model they plan to adopt before they become fully involved in producing related instructional materials. For this to be possible, the model must be initially described in non-technical terms, which enable the reviewers to perceive for themselves not only the advantages of the particular model, but also the relationships among its main characteristics. As long as a model is initially reviewed, it should be possible to acquire the more detailed knowledge of specific aspects of educational technology, as and when these appear relevant during the development of materials. The main advantage of this approach is that the immediate relevance of each aspect of educational technology is clearly perceived, while important relationships among these aspects are not ignored.

Prior to becoming involved in developing instructional materials, there is in fact much to be gained from reviewing several different models. Assuming that such models are available, and can be initially described in laymen's terms, it should be possible to compare the advantages and limitations of each, and the implications involved (in terms of time and effort required) in producing instructional materials according to the different models. Such an approach should permit individuals to decide for themselves in a matter of hours which model is most relevant to their own particular needs, thus increasing the motivation of authors to produce materials as well as possible according to the chosen model.

Where individuals are able to follow fairly comprehensive courses in educational technology, prior to becoming involved in instructional design and development, models have an equally important role to play. Reviewed early in a course, they can place much of the detailed learning to follow in perspective, and can ensure that the relevance of specific aspects of educational technology are kept clearly in mind. Above all, they can ensure that such aspects are not treated in isolation, and that relationships among them are given appropriate consideration.

3. Do Appropriate Models Exist?

Reviewing different instructional materials, it appears all too often that the mode of presentation does not reflect any clearly defined model; that is, it does not reflect a design format which has been carefully developed in light of the existing literature. Where an underlying model is clearly apparent, this is most

The Need for Models

commonly a model based on the use of behavioral objectives,* with the mode of presentation being basically the same as that used by Mager (1962) in his classic *Preparing Instructional Objectives*; that is, with a statement of behavioral objectives presented prior to instruction to indicate to students what they are expected to achieve, with subsequent instruction designed to help students achieve the stated objectives, and with an objectives-referenced test following the instruction to determine whether students have actually achieved the specified objectives. This simple model is still widely used, not only in this form but also as a part of more complex models. For example, in courses designed to conform to the requirements of the Personalized System of Instruction (Sherman, 1974)—or the Keller Plan (Keller, 1968) as it was originally described—each unit of instruction might typically conform to the basic requirements of the simple model just described, although one would expect to find refinements, such as alternative forms of each objectives-referenced test, to permit students to be retested following any remedial studies that might be deemed necessary.

Needless to say, much has been learned about behavioral objectives and modes of presentation of instruction since Mager first popularized the concept of behavioral objectives in the 1960s, and it is of interest to note a few of the ways in which the simple model used by Mager (as a mode of presentation of instruction) might be improved in light of the existing literature.

The first point to note is that one of the latest reviews concerning the effect of behavioral objectives on student learning (Melton, 1978) suggests that behavioral objectives are best located at frequent intervals immediately following—rather than preceding—related instruction. The review suggests that if behavioral objectives are placed immediately prior to related instruction, they are likely to orient students towards relevant learning (that is, learning relevant to the stated objectives), but away from incidental learning, and any enhancement of relevant learning is

---

*Readers unfamiliar with behavioral objectives may wish to introduce themselves to the concept by referring to Chapter 8.

likely to be offset to some extent by a depression of incidental learning. In contrast, the review indicates that if behavioral objectives are placed immediately after related instruction, they are likely to reinforce relevant learning without depressing incidental learning when first encountered. In situations where not every possible objective can be stated, and where depression of incidental learning is viewed as undesirable, this suggests that the most logical location for behavioral objectives is immediately following related instruction. This has the additional advantage that statements of objectives may be clarified by the use of terms that have been introduced and defined in the preceding instruction, whereas similar statements placed prior to the related instruction would often be meaningless.

Although there are advantages in using behavioral objectives in the way described above, there are still some disadvantages. Thus, once statements of objectives have been met and studied for the first time, they are still likely to orient students away from incidental learning and towards relevant learning during subsequent review of the related materials, and this might be seen as leading towards an undesirable narrowing of horizons, even if this is delayed until after the first reading or presentation of instruction. The problem arises from the fact that, in order to be specific, behavioral objectives tend to be narrow. Thus, a single test item might be described as providing a measure of whether or not students have achieved a related objective. One way of broadening statements of objectives without loss of precision is to relate each objective to a domain of test items rather than to single items. The concept of domain-referencing is not new, having been pioneered by Glaser (1963) and Popham and Husek (1969), and it has already contributed to a more sophisticated approach to criterion-referenced testing, which is reflected in related reviews by Meskauskas (1976) and Hambleton, Swaminathan, Algina, and Coulson (1978).

The foregoing arguments suggest that the simple model for the presentation of instruction which was used by Mager might be improved by using domain-referenced objectives placed at frequent intervals immediately following related instruction. Howev-

The Need for Models

er, if this is done, one must also ask how students might best be introduced to the related instruction. After all, one of Mager's (1962) reasons for placing objectives prior to instruction was to provide students with some indication of where they were going. In fact, the advance organizer (Ausubel, 1968) is seen as providing an appropriate mechanism for this purpose. Basically, it might be described as a special form of introduction designed to place subsequent detailed learning in perspective. It also provides a cognitive framework under which new concepts can be subsumed, and it follows that it must be written at a higher level of generality and abstraction than the detailed learning which follows. This is in marked contrast to behavioral objectives, which in order to be specific are written at the same level as the learning tasks themselves, and it is this difference which can often lead to statements of behavioral objectives having very limited meaning until after related instruction has been studied. Clearly, advance organizers and behavioral objectives have different characteristics, and the advance organizer is in fact seen here as providing a more appropriate mechanism than behavioral objectives for the introduction of instruction. Having said this it is worth noting that an advance organizer may still include statements which indicate what students are expected to achieve. However, such statements would be expressed in much more general terms than those normally found in statements of behavioral objectives.

The models described in PART II of this book were developed with factors such as the above in mind. It is not suggested that the models described are the only ones possible, or even the best, but simply that they are models which have been carefully developed in light of the existing literature for use in the design and development of courses. Care is taken in fact to place the models in perspective by noting the extent to which they might be described as building on well-recognized principles of learning. It is noted that most of the models reflect a limited number of principles. This is not seen as a cause for concern in itself, for once a particular model has been adopted, attention may be given to the development of instructional strategies within the constraints of the model, and such strategies may be chosen to reflect further principles of learning or to reinforce those already reflected within the adopted model. In other words, the adopted model simply provides a broad frame of reference within which course development proceeds, and this is emphasized in PART III of this book, which pays attention to the development of strategies within the constraints of adopted models.

References

Ausubel, D.P. *The Psychology of Meaningful Verbal Learning.* New York: Grune and Stratton, 1968.

Glaser, R. Instructional technology and the measurement of learning outcomes. *American Psychologist,* 1963, *18,* 519-521.

Hambleton, R.K., Swaminathan, H., Algina, J., and Coulson, D.B. Criterion-referenced testing and measurements: A review of technical issues and developments. *Review of Educational Research,* 1978, *48,* 1-47.

Keller, F.S. Good-bye, teacher. *Journal of Applied Behavior Analysis,* 1968, *1,* 78-89.

Mager, R.F. *Preparing Instructional Objectives.* Palo Alto, California: Fearon, 1962.

Melton, R.F. Resolution of conflicting claims concerning the effect of behavioral objectives on student learning. *Review of Educational Research,* 1978, *48,* 291-302.

Meskauskas, J.A. Evaluation models for criterion-referenced testing: Views regarding mastery and standard-setting. *Review of Educational Research,* 1976, *46,* 133-158.

Popham, W.J., and Husek, T.R. Implications of criterion-referenced measurement. *Journal of Educational Measurement,* 1969, *6,* 1-9.

Sherman, J.G. (Editor) *PSI, Personalized System of Instruction.* Menlo Park, California: W.A. Benjamin, Inc., 1974.

Acknowledgment

This chapter is reproduced with some modifications from PART I of the following paper:

Melton, R.F. The use of models in the design and development of curriculum materials. *British Journal of Educational Technology*, 1980, *11*, 5-24.

Part II

Models for Course Design

PART II is concerned primarily with describing a number of models which identify ways in which instruction may be presented to students. The models discussed include a basic *unit model* and a number of *alternative course models.* Underlying each to varying extents is an individualized approach to student learning that is intended to respond to the different needs and abilities of different students. As the names imply, the unit model prescribes a mode of presentation for a discrete unit of instruction, such as a self-study package or an audio-visual learning unit, while the course models prescribe modes of presentation for entire courses. The course models are similar to one another in that each consists of a number of units, each of which must conform to the requirements of the unit model. However, they differ from one another in that the units in the different models are integrated together in different ways to form total courses of instruction.

Although the models are designed to meet the needs of an individualized approach to learning, they may be applied much more widely to different forms of instruction. Thus, the unit model may be applied to a chapter in a text, a lesson or a lecture, or even a group of two or three lessons, as long as these form a coherent unit of instruction. Similarly, although articles, books, case studies, experiments, projects, and audio-visual materials are likely to provide course developers with the most flexible, and most appropriate, media for the presentation of courses conforming to the requirements of the various course models, nevertheless more conventional lectures can still be included within the design of such courses. Underlying all the models is an objective approach to student learning that may be applied to any course of instruction where it is possible in advance to design tests to measure related student learning.

Within this context, *Chapter 2* provides an overview of the main characteristics of the *unit model*, while *Chapter 3* provides an overview of the different *course models*. In each case, the theoretical basis on which each model is founded is discussed in terms of the existing literature. *Chapter 4* is designed to place the *models in perspective*. It does this by reviewing a variety of principles that have emerged from a careful study of theories of learning, and by identifying the extent to which the models described build upon these principles. From this it should be clear that the relative emphasis placed on different principles is likely to determine the type of model developed. It would be illogical, therefore, to suggest that the models described in this book are the only ones that can be conceived, for this is clearly not the case. All that is contended is that there is a need for such models, particularly ones that are well founded in the literature relevant to instructional design.

Chapter 2

A Unit Model

This chapter is concerned with describing a model for the presentation of a unit of instruction. Typically, a unit is seen as presenting a fairly discrete topic of instruction. Normally, it is broken down into subtopics, with each presented within a separate section of the unit. Thus, a unit of instruction on the human body might be concerned with such subtopics as the blood system, the nervous system, the bones, the muscles, and so on, depending on the way the author wishes to develop student understanding of the human body. This is, of course, a loose description of a unit, and one might ask whether there is any real difference between a unit and a section of instruction. In terms of the unit model, there is in fact a clear distinction between the two based on the way in which assessment is used to involve both the student and the teacher in the learning process. Thus, a unit is the amount of instruction that may be presented before the *teacher* is required to use formal tests to check student progress, whereas a section is the amount of instruction that may be presented before the *student* is required to check his or her own progress. Thus, each section is brought to a close with self-assessment questions, which are designed to help the student determine whether he or she has mastered the related content and to indicate what remedial studies may be required. In contrast, each unit concludes with a formal test designed to help the teacher determine whether the student has achieved sufficient mastery of the unit to permit him or her to move on to study further related units.

Needless to say, units may vary considerably in the amount of content they contain and in the time required by the average student to master that content. Thus, a unit might be designed to be studied in as little as 30 to 40 minutes or in as much as ten to 12 hours. Although the total study time may be several hours, this can be broken down into a series of short study sessions, and from this point of view, time does not create a major problem. However, if a unit is rather long, there is always the risk that student misconceptions may become firmly entrenched before they are discovered by the teacher using formal tests, and well-established misconceptions are often difficult to erase. Conversely, there is the risk that if a course is broken down into a large number of smaller units, the amount of formal testing involved might be too demanding for both student and teacher. Clearly, the number of units and their related length is a matter to be determined in light of the circumstances concerned.

Although units may vary considerably in the amount of content they contain, they do have a number of major characteristics in common. These are described in the following pages, first with regard to those characteristics which are repeated in each section of a unit, and then with regard to the characteristics of the unit as a whole, that is, with regard to *section characteristics* (*Section 1*) and then *unit characteristics* (*Section 2*), respectively.

1. Section Characteristics

Before looking at each section characteristic individually, it is useful to review them briefly and to note how they relate to one another. This is done with the help of Figure 1, which illustrates diagrammatically the main characteristics of each section. It will be noted that an advance organizer is used to introduce the detailed learning within each section. Among other things, the advance organizer should identify new concepts to be met and should indicate the relationships among them. The model requires that the content of instruction be structured in a manner which clearly reflects these relationships. At the end of each section, there is a statement of objectives to be achieved. These are described as domain-referenced objectives, since each is related to, and defined by, a domain of test items. Self-assessment questions placed alongside each objective to help students determine

Figure 1

Characteristics of a Section of Instruction Within the Unit Model

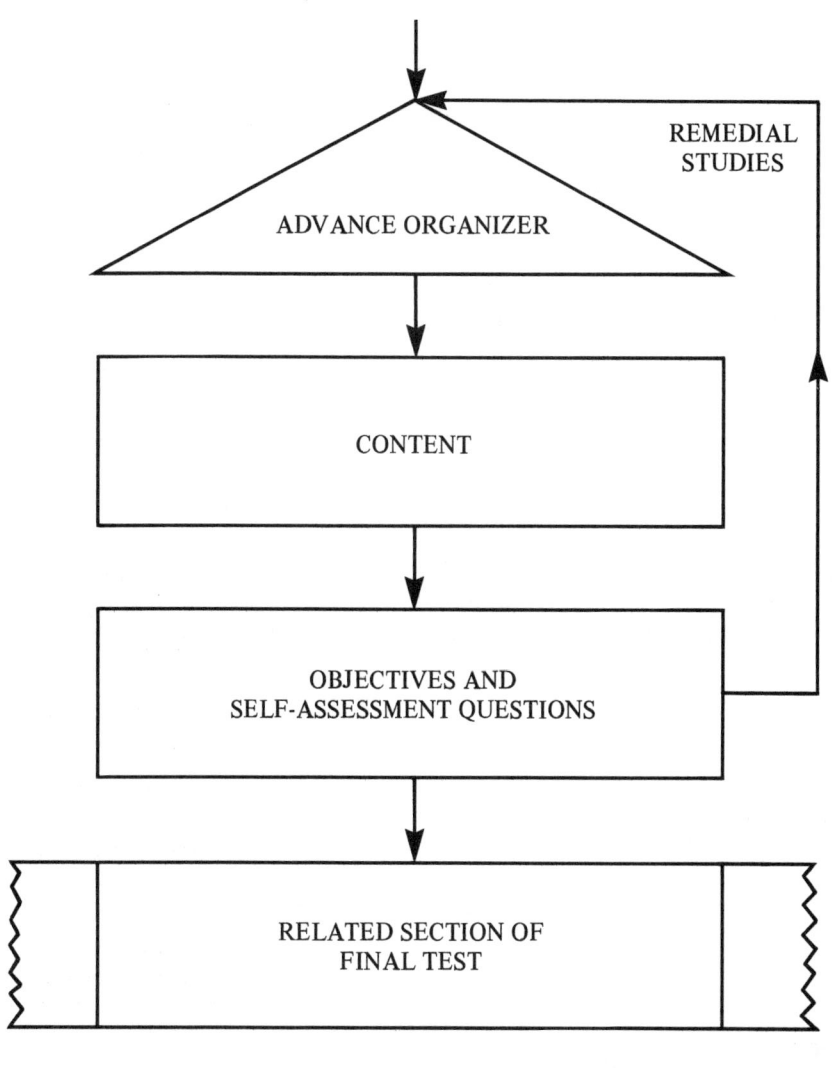

whether they have achieved the stated objective are, in fact, drawn from the related domain of items as a representative sample of the domain. Where the self-assessment questions indicate that students have not mastered a given objective, or part of an objective, remedial studies are advocated before students move on to further sections. Final test items are drawn from the same domains, and students are advised that upon completion of their study of the unit as a whole they will be required to demonstrate (to the teacher) their mastery of the stated objectives by responding to a final test in which the questions will be equivalent, but not identical, to those provided for self-assessment purposes.

These, then, are the main characteristics of each section, and each is now reviewed separately in greater detail.

1.1. The Advance Organizer

Most readers have experienced at one time or another the type of instruction which discusses concept after concept in detail without any advance explanation of where all of this is taking the student. However, students need to know where they are going. They need to know in advance what topics are to be discussed, and why. They need to be able to relate what is to be learned to what they already know. In fact, students need a logical frame of reference to which subsequent detailed learning can be related. With this in mind, it is suggested that detailed instruction should always be preceded by an advance organizer (Ausubel, 1968). This is a special form of introduction providing students with an overview of the more detailed learning to follow. It must be written in terms that are meaningful to the student, and must take into account his or her existing knowledge. Similarities and differences between concepts to be acquired and old, familiar concepts may be identified, as well as similarities and differences between the new concepts themselves.

However, the advance organizer is more than a simple introduction. Ausubel argues that the prime factor influencing student learning of new material is the student's existing cognitive structure—that is, the organization, the clarity, and the stability of his or her existing knowledge. If the student's cognitive structure is disorganized, ambiguous, or unstable, Ausubel believes that this will inhibit his or her learning of new material. The advance organizer, by taking into account the student's existing knowledge, is designed to become a part of his or her cognitive structure. As such, it is intended to provide a clear, well-organized framework under which new concepts can be subsumed. Not surprisingly, it may be noted that it is written at a level of generality and abstraction that is higher than that of the detailed learning which follows.

1.2. Content Structure

Since the advance organizer is intended to provide a clear framework under which new concepts can be subsumed, it is logical to present the new concepts within each section in a way which relates most clearly to the framework of the advance organizer. Thus, if the advance organizer indicates that a group of concepts are closely related, it might be decided that these might be best discussed under a single subheading. Similarly, if the advance organizer indicates that a given concept derives from certain other concepts, this should be reflected in the way the concepts are treated within the section. In other words, the structure of the content should reflect the relationships indicated in the advance organizer.

1.3. Domain-Referenced Objectives

Each section is followed by a statement of objectives.* These are behavioral objectives in so far as they indicate what students should be able to do before proceeding further. However, each objective is related to a domain of test items, rather than a single

---

*Throughout this book, the terms 'aims' and 'objectives' are used to refer to what students are expected to achieve. The only difference between the terms is that 'objectives' stated in curriculum materials must be expressed in terms which are sufficiently explicit to indicate how achievement of the 'objective' might be measured. In contrast, 'aims' are usually expressed in more general terms. The term 'behavioral objective' is reserved to refer to objectives with the characteristics defined by Mager (1962).

item, and they are more aptly described, therefore, as domain-referenced objectives.

In stating objectives after the related instruction has been presented, it is recognized that students may internalize the content in a variety of different ways. Thus, one student may attempt to recall all the specific details presented. Another might concentrate more on understanding the broader relationships involved, and yet another might spend most of his or her time analyzing the strengths and weaknesses of the arguments presented. In contrast, the designer-developer or teacher may have intended that the student be able to use his or her newly acquired knowledge to solve particular types of problems, and it is important, therefore, that he or she state his or her objectives clearly, particularly if he or she intends that student progress be assessed in terms of these objectives, or if he or she intends to develop subsequent instruction on the assumption that students will have already mastered the stated objectives.

Since the objectives indicate what is expected of the student, one might ask why they are presented *after* the related instruction rather than *before* it. There are two good reasons for this. First, since objectives are precise statements of what students should be able to do, they tend to be written in terms which are often meaningless to students until after the students have studied the related content in detail. Placed prior to instruction, such objectives may not only be meaningless when first encountered, but also may reduce student interest in the learning to follow. It is accepted that prior to instruction students need guidance concerning the detailed learning to follow. However, it has already been indicated that the advance organizer is seen as most appropriate for this purpose. Since statements of objectives are written at the same level of generality and abstraction as the learning tasks themselves, they cannot function as advance organizers, and are considered to be an inappropriate means of introducing subsequent learning.

Second, in using behavioral objectives, it is commonly claimed that they result in the enhancement of student learning. The literature (Melton, 1978) indicates that this is an oversimplification of the situation. Thus, where objectives are placed immediately prior to instruction, it appears that during the first study of the related material they are likely to orient students towards instruction that is relevant to the stated objectives but away from that which is incidental. Therefore, although relevant learning may be enhanced, this may be offset by a depression of incidental learning. This is likely to be seen as an undesirable state of affairs where instruction has been specifically designed to meet the needs of a particular target group. In contrast, placed immediately after related instruction, it appears that objectives are likely to reinforce relevant learning without depressing incidental learning. Relevant learning may thus be enhanced without incidental learning being depressed, and an undesirable narrowing of horizons may be avoided during the first study of the material. Where the materials are re-studied with the stated objectives in mind, there is likely to be a subsequent orientation away from the incidental and towards the relevant. In other words, a narrowing of horizons may still occur, but this process will have been delayed.

1.4. Domain-Referenced Tests

One of the main reasons for relating each objective to a domain of test items rather than a single item (as is conventionally the case with the behavioral objective approach of the 1960s) is to avoid an over-narrowing of the approach during any re-study of the instructional materials. How this is achieved depends very much on the way in which self-assessment questions and final test questions are related to one another and the stated objectives.

A representative sample of items is in fact drawn from each domain, and placed under each objective, under the label of self-assessment questions, to help students diagnose their weaknesses and to provide guidance concerning remedial studies that may be required. Where instructional material has been particularly well-developed, it may be sufficient for students to re-study the instruction concerned with the stated objectives clearly in mind. However, weaker students may require additional instruction to reinforce their understanding of the concepts presented.

Students are advised that upon completion of their study of all sections within the unit, their mastery of all the objectives in the unit will be measured by means of a *final test* in which the questions will be similar, but not identical, to the self-assessment questions. The final test questions are in fact drawn from the same domains as the self-assessment questions (as illustrated in Figure 2) with the intention that the two types of questions will produce equivalent tests (Angoff, 1971) of the stated objectives. Students should thus have little difficulty in recognizing the importance of the stated objectives and the relevance of the related self-assessment questions. At the same time, they should recognize that what is required is not simply mastery of a limited number of self-assessment questions, but of broader domains, and that the self-assessment and final test questions simply provide equivalent samples of items from those domains.

2. Unit Characteristics

It has already been indicated that within the unit model a unit typically consists of a number of sections of instruction, each with the characteristics just described. In addition, the unit is characterized by the use of an advance organizer to introduce the total learning within the unit and by the use of a summary to review or summarize the total learning. The unit concludes with the final test, to which we have already referred. The unit characteristics are illustrated in diagrammatic form in Figure 3 for a unit consisting of three sections. The number of sections may vary considerably, but this variation does not alter the basic nature of the unit characteristics which are described below.

2.1. The Advance Organizer

It follows logically that just as each section requires an advance organizer, so the unit as a whole requires its own advance organizer. The latter might be seen as a means of introducing the subtopics represented by each of the section headings, while the advance organizers for the individual sections might be seen as a means of introducing more detailed concepts within each section. There is thus a hierarchical progression in which the advance organizer for the unit is written at a higher level of abstraction and

A Unit Model

Figure 2

Domain of Test Items Related to a Given Objective, Indicating Selection of Equivalent Items for Self-Assessment Questions and Final Test

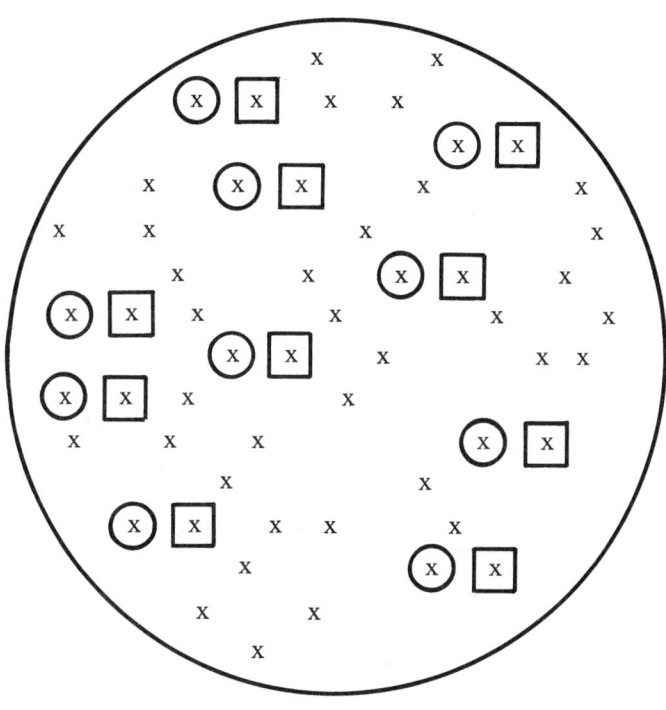

x = Test Items

(x) = Self-Assessment Questions

[x] = Final Test Items

Figure 3

Characteristics of the Unit Model for the Presentation of a Unit of Instruction (Containing, in This Case, Three Sub-Sections)

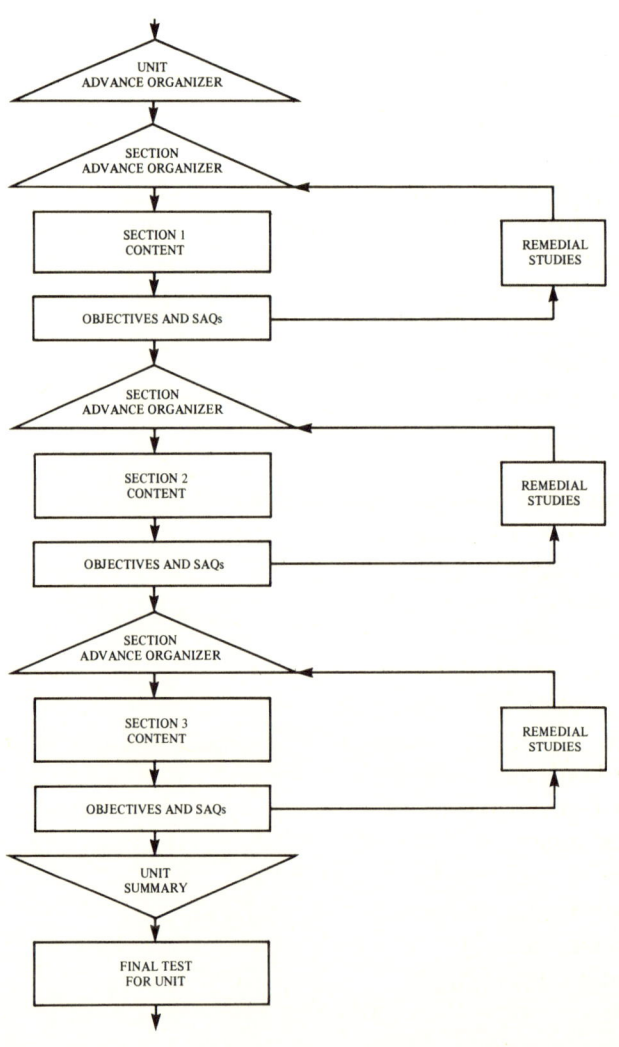

A Unit Model

generality than the advance organizers for the individual sections. In the same way that the structure of the content within a given section should reflect the relationships indicated in the advance organizer for that section, so the structure of the unit content as a whole should reflect the relationships indicated in the advance organizer for the unit.

At this point it is worth noting that this book provides a useful illustration in itself of the way in which advance organizers may be used to aid instruction. Advance organizers are used to introduce the book as a whole, each part of the book, and each chapter. It may be noted that the advance organizer for the book as a whole, namely the preface, is written in the most general terms, and is simply intended to place the major parts of the book in perspective. The advance organizers for each part describe the related contents in somewhat greater detail, and are intended to place the chapters within each part in perspective. In the same way, the advance organizers for each chapter are intended to place related sections of each chapter in perspective, and as such focus on more specific aspects than the advance organizers for the major parts of the book. There is thus a process of "progressive differentiation" as one moves forward from the advance organizer for the book, to those used respectively for the parts and for the chapters within the parts. Advance organizers may also be used for even smaller elements of instruction, and it is a matter of judgment whether this is likely to serve a useful purpose. Thus, within this book advance organizers are used to introduce the more complex sections within each chapter, particularly those sections which are divided into a number of related sub-sections.

The book also provides a useful illustration in itself of the way in which the structure of instructional content might be related to advance organizers, and readers have only to look at any of the advance organizers used within the book to see examples of the type of relationship referred to. However, at this point in time, the preface is likely to provide readers with the most convenient illustration of the point.

2.2. The Summary

The advance organizer for the unit as a whole is followed by a number of sections of instruction, each with the section characteristics already described. Instruction within the unit is brought to a close by means of a summary. In a sense, the summary complements the advance organizer in that the one looks backward over the unit while the other looks forward. Both provide a means of emphasizing relationships among concepts, but here the similarity ends.

Typically, the summary is prepared by highlighting and repeating the most important aspects of instruction, and where this is done the summary (in contrast to the advance organizer) might generally be described as being written at the same level of generality and abstraction as the related instruction. Nevertheless, having said this, it is possible to envisage summaries being written at different levels of generality. Thus, a summary looking back over a short unit of instruction may well be fairly detailed and specific, whereas a summary looking back over a block of units may well be written in much more general terms. In looking back at related instruction, a summary may, of course, make full use of terms and concepts that have been developed within the unit, whereas similar usage in advance organizers is normally impossible.

The summary is in fact an ideal place for reinforcing concepts and relationships that have already been met in the preceding instruction. However, it should be emphasized that it is not a place for new learning.

2.3. The Final Test

The unit concludes with the final test, already mentioned in discussing section characteristics. Little needs to be added, other than to re-state that whereas the self-assessment questions are designed to help *students* diagnose and eliminate weaknesses, the final test is designed to help *staff* determine the degree to which students should be advised to undertake further, remedial studies before proceeding to further units of study.

3. In Conclusion

Readers wishing to review an example of instructional material produced according to the requirements of the unit model may be interested to note that such a unit was produced under the author's direction (Melton *et al.,* 1979) and is available in the form of an audio-visual learning package.

It has already been noted that such units may be combined in different ways to produce different types of courses, and it is worth adding that just as each unit requires its own advance organizer and summary, the same is true for each block of units within a course and for the course as a whole. As such, advance organizers and summaries, respectively, provide a means of continuously looking forward and backward at the learning within a course of instruction. (Extending the logic in the opposite direction, some readers may suggest that each *section* within a unit should have a summary as well as an advance organizer. This is certainly a debatable point. However, summaries were not included as an essential characteristic of each section in the unit model, since the *objectives* and *self-assessment questions* were designed to encourage students to review and summarize the contents of each section for themselves.)

The unit model is a model in its own right in that it prescribes a mode of presentation for a discrete topic of instruction. However, it is also a building block which may be used in different ways to produce courses with different types of characteristics. Chapter 3 looks at different ways of relating units to one another, and as such describes different course models.

References

Angoff, W.H. Scales, norms, and equivalent scores. In Thorndike, R.L. (Editor), *Educational Measurement.* Washington, DC: American Council on Education, 1971, pp. 508-600.

Ausubel, D.P. *The Psychology of Meaningful Verbal Learning.* New York: Grune and Stratton, 1968.

Mager, R.F. *Preparing Instructional Objectives.* Palo Alto, California: Fearon, 1962.

Melton, R.F. Resolution of conflicting claims concerning the effect of behavioral objectives on student learning. *Review of Educational Research,* 1978, *48,* 291-302.

Melton, R.F. (Director), Oxtoby, P.J. (Associate Director) *et al. The Basic Principles of Multicoloured Map Making.* Enschede, The Netherlands: The International Institute for Aerial Survey and Earth Sciences, 1979.

Acknowledgment

This chapter is reproduced with some modifications from PART II of the following paper:

Melton, R.F. The use of models in the design and development of curriculum materials. *British Journal of Educational Technology,* 1980, *11,* 5-24.

Chapter 3

Some Alternative Course Models

This chapter is concerned with discussing the advantages and limitations of a number of different course models, namely, *the simple linear model (Section 1), the refined linear model (Section 2), the branched model (Section 3)*, and examples of *variable route models (Section 4)*. All the models are similar in that each consists of a number of units, each of which must conform to the requirements of the unit model (see Chapter 2). However, they differ from one another in that the units are integrated together in different ways. As the names imply, the units in the two linear models are linked together in a way which leads to a linear approach to learning, whereas those in the branched model are linked together in a way which leads to a branched approach to learning. The variable route models differ from the other three in that they offer *all* students a choice of different routes through the units.

Each mode of linkage produces two alternative versions of the same model: an *'L' version* and a *'U' version* according to whether the time available for completion of the related course is *limited* or *unlimited*. In practice, most courses are limited by economic and administrative considerations to a specific period of time, such as a term or a year. With this in mind, initial discussion of the course models (Sections 1 to 4) is centered around the *'L' version* of the models. However, the idea of unlimited time being available for completion of any course does have strong appeal, and the final section of this chapter *(Section 5)* is concerned, therefore, with reviewing the *theoretical advantages* to be gained if *no time limits* are imposed. Section 5 is thus concerned with discussing the advantages of the *'U' versions* of the models introduced in Sections 1 to 4. (It is worth noting that since the two versions of any given model discussed have precisely the same structure, there is no need to distinguish between 'L' and 'U' versions of the models in Figures 4 to 8, which illustrate their different structures.)

Finally, it may be noted that although the simple linear model is unsatisfactory in that it offers students very little choice in what they may, or may not, study, it is discussed in some depth in this chapter. This is because the other models evolved from a consideration of the strengths and weaknesses of the simple linear model, and the same considerations provide a logical introduction to the discussion of the other models.

1. The Simple Linear Model (L)

The discussion of the simple linear model (L) begins here (*Section 1.1*) with a review of *its characteristics*. These are then compared (*Section 1.2*) with those of the Keller Plan (Keller, 1968), about which much is already known, and note is made of *characteristics common to both*. Since there is much in common between the two, it is possible to infer (*Section 1.3*) some of the *strengths and weaknesses of the simple linear model (L)* from what is known about the Keller Plan.

1.1. Characteristics of the Simple Linear Model (L)

The simple linear model (L) described here (see Figure 4) consists of a series of units which are related sequentially to one another, and students are advised to master the objectives specified for each unit before proceeding to the next. The final test for each unit provides an indication of student mastery of the objectives. Students who fail to achieve a specified level of performance are redirected to relevant remedial learning, and advised to take an equivalent form (Angoff, 1971) of the final test when they feel confident that they have mastered the stated objectives. Once they have achieved the specified level of performance, they are advised to proceed to the next unit of instruction. The approach is of particular relevance where the

Figure 4

Simple Linear Model

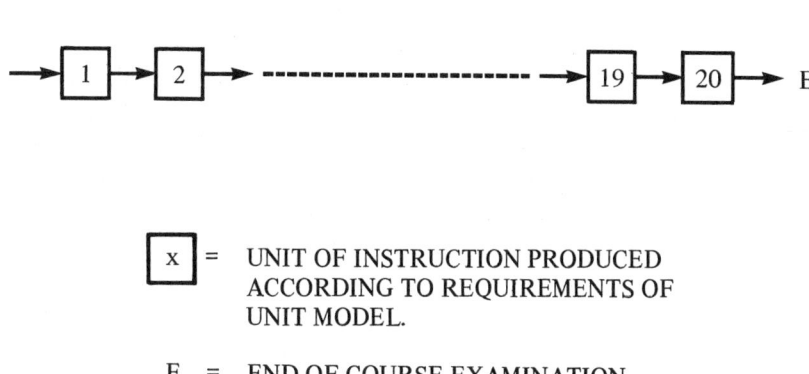

| x | = UNIT OF INSTRUCTION PRODUCED ACCORDING TO REQUIREMENTS OF UNIT MODEL.

E = END OF COURSE EXAMINATION.

acquisition of knowledge and skills presented in later units of a course depends on the acquisition of knowledge and skills presented in earlier units.

Since students with different abilities tend to progress through the units at different rates, students will tend to master different numbers of units in a given period of time. Ideally, one might suggest that the time available to complete a mastery-based course of this type should be completely open. However, it has already been noted that in practice administrative requirements tend to impose a time limit, such as a term or a year, for the completion of a course. Unfortunately, this creates an innate problem which is not readily resolved. Thus, if the number and difficulty of units are limited, then it is possible that the majority of students concerned will be able to master all the units presented in the time available. However, in such circumstances, more able students will tend to finish the course with time to spare, and will probably find the course undemanding and insufficient for their particular needs. In contrast, if the number and difficulty of units are increased to meet the needs of more able students, then a substantial proportion of students is likely to be unable to master all the units concerned. In practice, an intermediate position is generally adopted. Thus, the number and difficulty of units are typically such that a substantial proportion of students is normally able to master all the units. However, since a significant proportion of students will still tend to fail to master all the units, it is important to record what each student ultimately achieves in the form of a profile. At the minimum, a profile needs to indicate the content of each unit studied, and whether or not the student concerned achieved the desired level of mastery. More informatively, it might also indicate the student's score on each unit test, an estimate of the probable error in each unit score, and the score accepted as demonstrating mastery of the unit.

It should be noted that the profile described records the student's knowledge at the time of completing each unit test. Not all this knowledge will necessarily be retained, and it is useful to use equivalent testing techniques (Angoff, 1971) to subsequently determine to what extent the student has retained the knowledge initially acquired. This may be achieved by producing an end-of-course examination consisting of test items equivalent to those included in the unit tests. Student performances on the final course examination should be kept separate from those recorded for each unit (final test) during the course, since they provide quite different measures of student retention of knowledge: the one being short-term retention and the other long-term retention.

1.2. Characteristics Common to Both the
Simple Linear Model (L) and the Keller Plan

The Keller Plan is similar to the simple linear model (L) in so far as its major characteristics are concerned. As with the simple linear model (L), it consists of a linear sequence of units of instruction which students are expected to master before proceeding to subsequent units. Emphasis is placed on unit tests, which are designed to determine whether or not students have mastered the objectives for the related unit. Four or more versions of each test are normally produced, and students undertaking remedial learning respond to different versions of the test whenever they are retested on a given unit. The Keller Plan, in fact, makes use of undergraduates—described as proctors—to administer tests and provide related guidance. The proctors may simply be students in the same course who have already mastered the units concerned (Sherman, 1974a), but they play nevertheless a key role in the successful implementation of a Keller Plan approach. The tests used by the proctors are designed by the course instructor, and tend to favor the use of objective test items, since these can usually be processed more quickly and reliably than subjective, essay-type test items. However, the latter are not excluded from the test, and proctors may be asked to make subjective judgments concerning levels of performance in addition to similar judgments concerning what remedial learning is required. The simple linear model (L) does not describe in detail how tests should be administered and how guidance should be determined, but it is clear that the system used in the Keller Plan could be adopted, if desired.

The main difference between the Keller Plan and the simple linear model (L) resides in the way units of instruction are constructed. The simple linear model (L) requires units to conform to the requirements of the unit model. Thus, each unit makes use of advance organizers, domain-referenced objectives, diagnostic self-assessment questions, related final tests, and other interrelated characteristics. The Keller Plan adopts a more simplistic approach. The instructor, who functions as the designer-developer, selects instructional material for each unit from existing materials, such as articles, books, and laboratory exercises. He or she then prepares a study guide, which typically includes both a statement of behavioral objectives to be mastered and a set of questions to guide students in their studies, and may include a self-test for students to measure their own progress. The proctor is relied upon to provide students with guidance concerning remedial studies. Although the approach adopted in constructing each unit of instruction in the Keller Plan is less rigorous than that adopted for each unit in the simple linear model (L), it is clear that the two approaches are similar in that both place prime emphasis on self-pacing and student mastery.

1.3. Strengths and Weaknesses of the Simple Linear Model (L)

A large number of studies have been centered around the Keller Plan, and some 41 of these have been compiled by Sherman (1974b) to provide some useful insights into the strengths and weaknesses of the Keller Plan approach.

A large number of the studies make comparisons between the Keller Plan approach and more conventional lectures, and, although the studies concern students at different stages in the academic hierarchy and courses in different disciplines, they nevertheless indicate in study after study that the Keller Plan approach tends to enhance student learning and tends to be preferred by students. Thus, in studies by Hoberock *et al.* (1972), McMichael and Corey (1969), and Sheppard and MacDermot (1970), 'end-of-course' examinations were used to make comparisons between students following a Keller Plan approach and those following a more conventional lecture approach. In each study, the Keller Plan groups performed better on the examination, and also recorded their preference for the Keller Plan approach. These advantages of the Keller Plan are largely attributed to the unit mastery requirement and the freedom to proceed at one's own particular rate, both of which are also major characteristics of the simple linear model (L). One might logically argue, therefore, that the simple linear model (L) should possess the same advantages.

Unfortunately, the characteristics of unit mastery and self-pacing also lead to one of the major weaknesses of both the Keller Plan and the simple linear model (L). Thus, it has already been noted that students with different abilities tend to proceed through units at different rates, and that if a course is limited to a fixed period of time, students with different abilities tend to master different numbers of units in the time available. A typical approach adopted with the Keller Plan (Sherman, 1974a) is to award student grades, which are related to the number of units mastered. Although this might appear to be a logical approach, it tends to hide a basic comprehension problem which might best be illustrated by means of a simple example.

Consider the case of a course which has been designed to provide students with a basic foundation in science, and imagine that the course consists of a sequence of units covering aspects of earth science, biology, chemistry, and physics, in that order. Students failing to study the last few units may acquire no knowledge of physics whatsoever, and in such circumstances, one could hardly claim that the students concerned had acquired the comprehensive foundation in science that the course was intended to provide. One solution is to suggest that there should be no time limits on courses based on the Keller Plan or the simple linear model (L). An alternative solution is to develop more flexible models which can meet the needs of both more able and less able students at one and the same time; and the models described in the subsequent sections were designed with this in mind.

One further point of common concern should be noted concerning the Keller Plan, and hence the simple linear model (L); that is the fact that students following such an approach show an increased tendency to drop out of courses in the early stages. However, there are those who see this as an advantage, arguing that if students do not have either the prerequisite knowledge, the ability, the time, or the interest to successfully master the content of the course presented, it is far better that they recognize this earlier, rather than later, in the course concerned. It might be argued that continuous testing and the demand for unit mastery make it easier for students to recognize at an early stage whether or not they are likely to master the contents of the course presented.

2. The Refined Linear Model (L)

The refined linear model (L) described here provides one of the simplest solutions to the lack of flexibility that is seen as a particular weakness in the simple linear model (L). The refined linear model (L) (see Figure 5) consists of a linear sequence of

Figure 5

Refined Linear Model

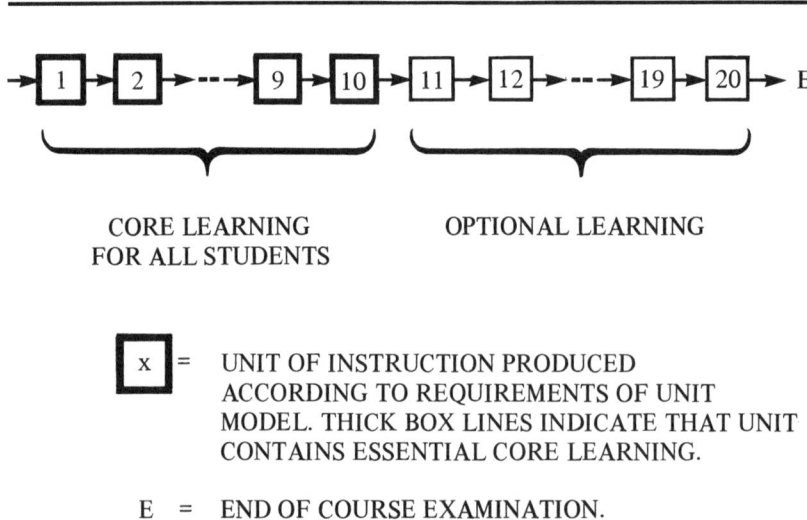

core units followed by a related sequence of optional units, with each unit produced to conform to the requirements of the unit model. As with the simple linear model (L), students are required to master the content of each unit before proceeding to the next. The major difference between this model and the simple linear model (L) is that the refined linear model (L) takes particular note of the number of units that all students are expected to master and those that only a limited number will master. Thus, if the course is designed to provide all students with a basic foundation in science, that foundation must be contained completely within the core units; the optional units providing something above and beyond that minimum foundation. This situation might be contrasted with a more conventional course in science, in which students tend to master varying percentages of the objectives in each unit. Clearly, in the latter situation, it is difficult to identify a common core of knowledge which students may be assumed to possess upon completion of the course.

As with the simple linear model (L), student performance should be recorded in the form of profiles; the only difference in the case of the refined linear model (L) being that the profile should distinguish clearly between those units identified as essential core learning and those identified as optional learning. If desired, grades may be related to the number of units mastered, and, in this case, the lowest acceptable performance for a course grade (say grade D) would be mastery of all the core units. However, the main point is that the student's performance should be profiled, thus making it clear what has, or has not, been achieved.

3. The Branched Model (L)

One of the weaknesses in all the linear models so far described is the fact that it is extremely difficult to build group activities into related courses. This is because at any given point in time the degree of mastery achieved varies considerably from student to student. This was recognized from the beginning by the Keller Plan, which limited group activities to optional lectures and demonstrations (Keller, 1968). These were typically presented only after a certain percentage of students had mastered a specified number of units, and, as such, they were designed simply to motivate students rather than to provide essential learning. In fact, according to Hoberock *et al.* (1972), lectures (as used) do not have a significant role to play in the Keller Plan, and could be eliminated from the approach without serious consequences. The branched model (L) described here was designed, therefore, not only to offer greater flexibility to students of varying ability, but also to offer the opportunity for more meaningful group activities.

As with the refined linear model (L), the branched model (L) consists of both core and optional units (see Figure 6), each produced according to the requirements of the unit model. However, whereas with the refined linear model (L), optional units cannot be studied until after all the core units have been mastered, this is not the case with the branched model (L). A schedule is

Figure 6

Branched Model

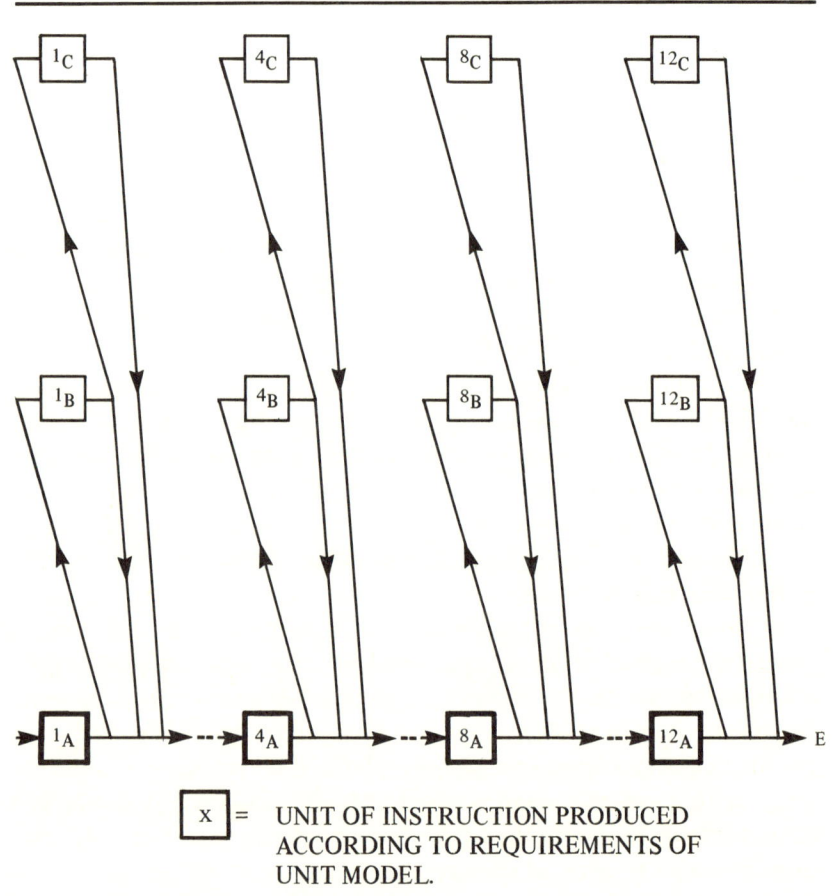

☐ x = UNIT OF INSTRUCTION PRODUCED ACCORDING TO REQUIREMENTS OF UNIT MODEL.

A = SUFFIX A INDICATES ESSENTIAL LEARNING.

B, C = OPTIONAL LEARNING.

E = END OF COURSE EXAMINATION.

Some Alternative Course Models

prepared to advise students as to approximately when they should have completed each of the core units. The time allowance is sufficiently generous to permit most of the less able students to master the content of each of the core units. More able students with time on hand upon completion of a particular core unit are encouraged to turn to some of the optional units available up to this particular point in the course. As with the refined linear model (L), the award of a course pass is dependent on students mastering all the core units. Again, it is important that profiles indicate not only the units mastered by students, but also whether or not these units contain core learning considered essential to the mastery of the basic course aims. As with the refined linear model (L), grades may be related to the number of units mastered, a grade of any type being dependent on mastery of all the core units.

The advantage of the branched model (L) over the refined linear model (L) is that group activities can be readily built into the course. Thus, it is possible to arrange lectures and demonstrations to introduce all students to each new core topic, and to arrange related follow-up discussions.

4. Variable Route Models (L)

In discussing the various models so far, emphasis has been placed on mastery learning and the need for students of different abilities to be able to proceed at their own individual rates. However, there has been very little discussion of the need to cater to different student needs and interests. Admittedly, the optional units in the refined linear model (L) and the branched model (L) do provide an element of choice, but the choice that exists is open primarily to the average and above-average student rather than to the less able student. In fact, with courses produced according to any of the course models so far discussed, the greatest potential for choice lies not within the course, but in whether or not students choose to study the course concerned. It is relevant, therefore, to consider to what extent a greater degree of choice might be built into course models. Variable route models (L) are discussed here with this in mind.

The first variable route model (L) to be considered (see Figure 7) is a simple variation of the refined linear model (L); the main difference being that the variable route model (L) offers students alternative routes through the optional units. In the case illustrated, there are three alternative routes (A, B, and C), but the number involved is arbitrary. With such a model, the number of core learning units to be mastered by all students should be limited as much as possible to permit even weaker students a choice of alternative routes. Needless to say, weaker students may be expected to proceed much more slowly through the units. Therefore, just as with the refined linear model (L), there is a need to profile student learning and to identify the number of units which must be mastered in following any given route if a minimum grade for a course credit is to be awarded.

With such a model, each core unit must serve the needs of each of the alternative routes, and it is likely that any given core unit will contain learning that is seen to be irrelevant to the needs of any one route. In other words, the amount of core learning considered to be irrelevant to the needs of any single route will increase as the number of alternative routes increases. This could be offset by creating alternative routes through the core learning as indicated in Figure 8. Thus, some units (such as unit 2) might be broken down into separate components for the alternative routes on the grounds that the original unit contained too much that was irrelevant to the needs of any single route. On the other hand, some units (such as units 1 and 3) might be retained in their original form, despite such irrelevance, on the grounds that the content of the unit as an integrated whole is of interest and importance in its own right. Optional units from the alternative routes might be reviewed in a similar manner, with some units being integrated on the grounds that they serve the needs of two or more routes, and that any irrelevance introduced is acceptable in view of the interest and importance of the unit itself as an integrated whole.

5. The Theoretical Advantages of Unlimited Time

All the models discussed in this chapter are considered to be

Figure 7

Variable Route Model with a Predominant Core of Common Learning for All Students

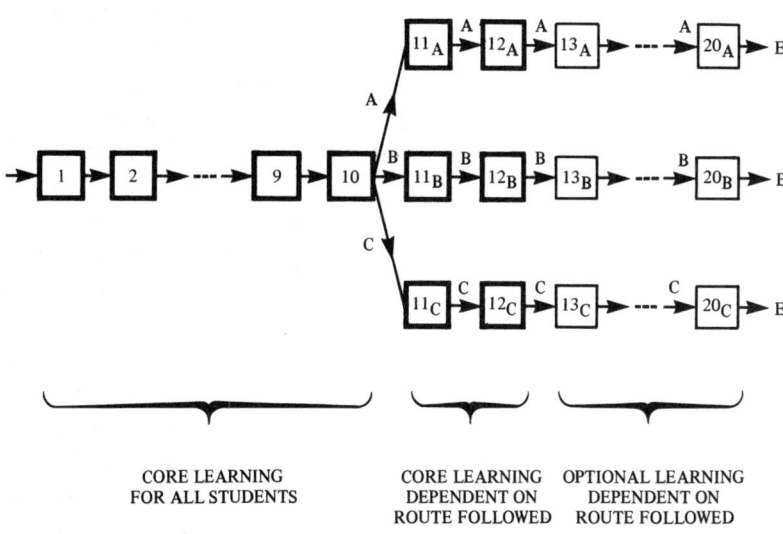

x_A	= UNIT OF INSTRUCTION PRODUCED ACCORDING TO REQUIREMENTS OF UNIT MODEL. THE INTEGER, x, INDICATES SEQUENTIAL NUMBER OF UNITS, WHILE THE SUFFIX (A, B, C) INDICATES THE ROUTE FOR WHICH UNIT IS DESIGNED. THICK BOX LINES INDICATE THAT UNIT CONTAINS ESSENTIAL CORE LEARNING.
E	= END OF COURSE EXAMINATION.

44 Instructional Models for Course Design and Development

Figure 8

Variable Route Model with Alternative Routes Through Core Learning

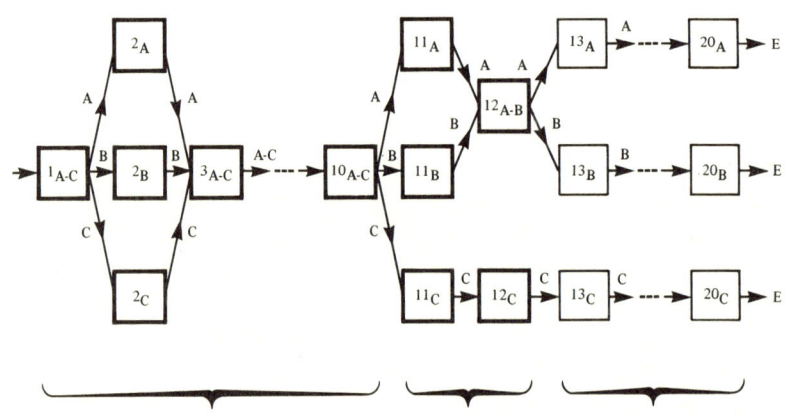

CORE LEARNING FOR ALL STUDENTS

CORE LEARNING DEPENDENT ON ROUTE FOLLOWED

OPTIONAL LEARNING DEPENDENT ON ROUTE FOLLOWED

 = UNIT OF INSTRUCTION PRODUCED ACCORDING TO REQUIREMENTS OF UNIT MODEL. THE INTEGER, x, INDICATES SEQUENTIAL NUMBER OF UNIT, WHILE THE SUFFIX (A, B, C) INDICATES THE ROUTE FOR WHICH UNIT IS DESIGNED. THICK BOX LINES INDICATE THAT UNIT CONTAINS ESSENTIAL CORE LEARNING.

E = END OF COURSE EXAMINATION.

Some Alternative Course Models 45

particularly appropriate for the presentation of instruction where it is desirable to pay particular attention to what might be loosely described as the structure of learning; that is, to pay attention to the way in which concepts are related to one another, to the way in which instruction might best be sequenced, to the knowledge which students actually acquire, and to the coherence of that knowledge and hence its meaningfulness. All the models pay attention to the need for students to progress at their own rates, while the variable route models pay attention to offering *all* students freedom of choice within a given course, as well as the freedom of choice between courses which may exist with any of the models. Models offering students greater choice within a given course could have been included in those discussed, but were not, since increasing flexibility of choice tends to be accompanied by undesirable side effects. Thus, on the one hand, increased flexibility of choice may be achieved by increasing the complexity of the design of related models, but this tends to lead to models which are too complex to implement in practice. On the other hand, increased flexibility of choice may be achieved with relatively simple models, by paying less attention to, or by ignoring, the importance of structure. Although this might be possible for certain topics in particular disciplines, it is generally undesirable, and this point will be elaborated on in Chapter 4, which follows.

Given the above constraints and the models so far described, it is of interest to contemplate the extent to which freedom of choice might be gained by removal of time constraints from related courses. As already pointed out, time constraints tend to be imposed by economic and administrative considerations, but if these could be removed, certain advantages might be gained. Thus, in the case of *unlimited time (U) versions* of the refined linear model, the branched model, and the variable route models, all students, regardless of ability, might be free to study a selection of optional units, whereas in the *limited time (L) versions* of these models such choice is very limited, or nonexistent, for weaker students. However, with unlimited time available for the study of any given course, one must then ask to what extent such time is gained at the expense of the variety of courses that might otherwise have been studied.

References

Angoff, W.H. Scales, norms, and equivalent scores. In Thorndike, R.L. (Editor), *Educational Measurement.* Washington, DC: American Council on Education, 1971, 508-600.

Hoberock, L.L., Koen, B.V., Roth, C.H., and Wagner, G.R. Theory of PSI evaluated for engineering education. *IEEE Transaction on Engineering,* 1972, E-15.

Keller, F.S. Good-bye, teacher.... *Journal of Applied Behavior Analysis,* 1968, *1*, 78-89.

McMichael, J.S., and Corey, J.R. Contingency management in an introductory psychology course produces better learning. *Journal of Applied Behavior Analysis,* 1969, *2*, 79-83.

Sheppard, W.C., and MacDermot, H.G. Design and evaluation of a programmed course in introductory psychology. *Journal of Applied Behavior Analysis,* 1970, *3*, 5-11.

Sherman, J.G. Logistics. In Keller, F.S., and Sherman, J.G. (Editors), *PSI, The Keller Plan Handbook.* Menlo Park, California: W.A. Benjamin, Inc., 1974a, 25-49.

Sherman, J.G. (Editor) PSI: Personalized System of Instruction. Menlo Park, California: W.A. Benjamin, Inc., 1974b.

Acknowledgment

Sections 1 to 3 (inclusive) of this chapter are reproduced with some modifications from PART III of the following paper:

Melton, R.F. The use of models in the design and development of curriculum materials. *British Journal of Educational Technology,* 1980, *11*, 5-24.

Chapter 4

Models in Perspective

This chapter is intended to place the models discussed in Chapters 2 and 3 in perspective. It does this by considering to what extent the different models might be described as building on recognized theories of learning, and by noting to what extent strategies based on such theories may still be adopted within the constraints imposed by the different models.

The first point to note is the existence of several different theories of learning. This is not surprising in itself, for it reflects the fact that the learning process may be viewed from several different perspectives. This is healthy, for different perspectives tend to highlight different principles, and suggests that note should be taken of principles which emerge from all the recognized theories of learning and not simply those from a single theory. Where principles emerging from different theories reinforce one another, they may be accepted with increased confidence. However, where they conflict with one another, they need to be reviewed with extreme care.

The work of Hilgard and Bower (1975) is particularly helpful in identifying the extent to which the models discussed in Chapters 2 and 3 might be described as building on recognized theories of learning, for, after carefully reviewing some 13 theories of learning (ranging from early reinforcement theories to physiological and neurological theories), Hilgard and Bower identify 21 principles which they believe would be acceptable, by and large, to almost all the schools of thought concerned. This chapter is concerned with identifying the extent to which the different models might be perceived to build on these principles. It does this by reviewing the extent to which the major characteristics of *structure and organization* (*Section 1*), *feedback and remedial learning* (*Section 2*), and *self-pacing* (*Section 3*) are founded on particular principles. The degree to which *student choice* is built into the different models is also reviewed in similar terms (*Section 4*), not because this is seen as a major characteristic of the models, but because it highlights an apparent conflict between two principles which needed to be taken into account in designing all the models. The extent to which the models might be described as being founded on the principles identified by Hilgard and Bower is placed *in perspective* in *Section 5*. There, note is taken not only of the principles which underlie the models, but also of the remainder which do not contribute to the design of the models in any significant manner. It is suggested that in developing strategies of instruction within the constraints of the models, every attempt should be made to build further on these principles. Examples of how this may be achieved are identified in Section 5 and discussed in greater detail later, in PART III of this book.

1. Structure and Organization

> "The organization of knowledge should be an essential concern of the teacher or educational planner." Hilgard and Bower (1975)

> "Learning with understanding is more permanent and more transferable than rote learning or learning by formula." Hilgard and Bower (1975)

Both the unit model and related course models are firmly built on these two principles. Thus, the use of advance organizers and summaries—not only for each unit, but also for each block of units and the course as a whole—is a reflection of the stress placed on the structure and sequence of learning in all the models. The advance organizer is also seen as providing a logical frame of reference which encourages students to pay attention to relationships, rather than isolated specifics, and, as such, encourages learning with understanding. Summaries have a similar role to play in that they are able to highlight important relationships as well as

Models in Perspective

fundamental concepts. In all the models, emphasis is placed on the logical sequencing of instruction, and this will become more evident in reviewing the procedures (described in PART III of this book) for developing instructional materials according to any of the models. In particular, the refined linear model (L), the branched model (L), and the variable route models (L) are all designed to ensure, as far as possible, that all students are able to acquire a coherent body of knowledge, and this is reflected in the distinction between essential core learning and optional learning adopted in these models.

2. Feedback and Remedial Learning

> "Cognitive feedback confirms correct knowledge and corrects faulty learning..... This is, of course, the equivalent of reinforcement in stimulus-response theory." Hilgard and Bower (1975)

The way in which objectives and self-assessment questions are used to provide guidance concerning remedial learning is seen as fulfilling the important role of feedback in the unit model, and hence in the related course models. Remedial materials may be designed to fulfill a number of different functions. On the one hand, they might simply explain the misunderstood concepts in greater detail. On the other hand, they might look at the concepts from different points of view, or identify prerequisite knowledge which students may not have acquired. In contrast, it is quite possible that the only remedial learning required is dependent on a repetition of the original instruction. As Hilgard and Bower indicate, repetition is still an important factor in learning. After all, one does not learn to play a musical instrument or to speak a foreign language without some degree of repetition.

The way in which objectives and self-assessment questions are used is, of course, not only intended to provide feedback and to identify appropriate remedial learning. It is also intended to lead to success in mastering the specified objectives as measured by the final tests. The work of Liebert and Allen (1967) is of interest in this respect, for it suggests that if students are exposed to a sufficiently consistent reward system (e.g., indicators of success), they will tend to develop an internalized expectancy concerning the standard of performance required. In other words, they will tend to set standards for themselves related to those required by the system.

3. Self-Pacing

> "The learners' abilities are important, and provisions have to be made for the slower and more rapid learners, and for those with specialized abilities." Hilgard and Bower (1975)

> "Anxiety level of the individual learner may determine whether certain kinds of encouragement to learn will have beneficial or detrimental effects." Hilgard and Bower (1975)

It is recognized that students with different abilities tend to progress at different rates through the same instructional material, particularly where mastery of specified objectives is required. This is taken into account by all the course models, which are designed to permit students to proceed at their own preferred rates. In this respect, the refined linear model (L), the branched model (L), and the variable route models (L) are seen as more appropriate than the simple linear model (L), for they are designed to ensure that slower learners have every opportunity of acquiring a coherent body of knowledge.

Permitting students to progress at their own individual rates has the added advantage that weaker students are more likely to perceive stated objectives as achievable. This is important, for as Stotland (1969) points out, the extent to which an individual is motivated to achieve a particular goal* is in part dependent on the

---

*The term 'goal' is used in a general sense by Stotland to refer to that which is to be achieved. The terms 'aims' and 'objectives' as used in this book are more limited in that they refer to what students are expected to achieve. However, the terms are often used interchangeably in the literature.

extent to which he or she perceives the goal to be achievable. If a goal or objective is seen to be less and less achievable, and increasingly unachievable, one might anticipate an increasing level of anxiety, with the student ultimately relinquishing the goal in order to escape from anxiety. Studies by McCandless and Castaneda (1956) are of interest in this respect in that, in 28 out of 30 correlations which they reviewed, they noted a fall-off in academic performance with increasing anxiety. This is not always the case, as is clear from a study by Lynn (1957), and it would seem that below a certain level, increasing anxiety can lead to arousal and increased academic performance, but beyond that level, increasing anxiety leads to *reduced* academic performance.

4. Student Choice

> "Goal setting by the learner is important as motivation for learning, and his successes and failures are determiners of how he sets future goals." Hilgard and Bower (1975)

The extent to which students may 'set' their own objectives, or goals, within the constraints of the different models has already been discussed, in so far as it has been noted that students may proceed through instruction at their own particular rates and may identify for themselves the objectives that they wish to achieve, and which they perceive to be achievable. However, in other respects, the models presented in this book offer students a very limited choice in the selection of objectives. There is, of course, a degree to which average and above-average students may select different objectives from optional units within the refined linear model (L) and the branching model (L), but only the variable route models (L) and the unlimited time (U) versions of all these models offer all students a degree of choice, and even this may be seen to be limited. The reason for this is that the degree to which students may be offered freedom of choice is limited by the extent to which structure is seen to be desirable. Although choice between courses, and selection of objectives within courses, is desirable, it is also important that students be given guidance in selecting aims and objectives and in determining how these might best be achieved, if frustration and failure are to be avoided. This apparent conflict between freedom of choice and the need for structure is resolved within the constraints of the models by suggesting that what is of prime importance is not that students should be completely free to select their own objectives, but that with whatever strategy is adopted, students should be strongly motivated to achieve the objectives identified. This is aimed at within the constraints of the models by placing emphasis (in PART III) on the need to develop strategies to motivate students towards specified aims and objectives, and the concepts of self-pacing and student choice built into the models are only partly relied on for realizing such motivation.

An example of how student motivation can be achieved might illustrate the point more clearly. A teacher of French might arrange regular exchange visits to France for students, and then encourage follow-up contacts in the hope that some students will want to communicate in French and, therefore, will be motivated to learn the language. Whether or not the teacher is successful will depend very much on the extent to which he or she is able to ensure that the stimuli to which students are exposed are able to provide adequate motivation. This may be placed in perspective by considering the case of a child who goes to France for two or three months every year, because his or her parents have a holiday cottage in the French Alps. Exposed for long periods to a French environment, the child may find himself or herself strongly motivated to learn to speak French in order to communicate with those around him or her. It might be suggested that the child has selected for himself or herself the aim of learning to communicate in French, but this may not be the full story. It is quite possible that his or her parents decided to take him or her to France (rather than leave him or her at home with his or her grandparents, for example) in order to motivate him or her (among other things) to learn French. The only difference between this situation and that of the teacher would be, therefore, in the degree to which the teacher could manipulate the environment surrounding the student in order to affect his or her motivation. The point being

Models in Perspective

made is that if due attention is paid to motivating students towards certain aims and objectives, students may well accept, and be strongly motivated towards achieving them, without necessarily being the prime movers in selecting them in the first instance.

5. In Perspective

> "Drive conditions are important in learning, ... [and] it may be taken for granted that motivational conditions are important."
> Hilgard and Bower (1975)

> "The learner should be active, rather than a passive listener or viewer." Hilgard and Bower (1975)

The discussion of student choice in Section 4 is of particular interest in that it highlights the fact that, although the need for student motivation is accepted as a basic principle, this is only partly reflected in the design of the various models. In fact, it is suggested that particular attention must be paid subsequently to the need for the development of strategies, within the constraints of the models, which focus attention on the motivation of students towards specified goals.

The same point may be made with regard to the need for students to be active rather than passive learners. To a certain extent, the use of objectives and self-assessment questions to diagnose weaknesses and to guide remedial learning might be seen as a mechanism for actively involving students in the learning process. However, this does not mean that the degree of involvement achieved through this design characteristic in the models is sufficient in itself. In fact, in discussing (in Chapter 6) the development of strategies within the constraints of the models, attention is focused on how the adoption of a discovery approach to learning might be used to stimulate a higher degree of involvement.

It should now be clear that the models developed reflect a limited number of principles, and that there is undoubtedly room for further development of alternative models. Ultimately, in reviewing the acceptability of any particular model, it would seem important not only to ask to what extent the model is based on the principles identified by Hilgard and Bower, but also to ask to what extent strategies may be adopted within the constraints of the model to reflect these principles.

Finally, to place the models more clearly in perspective, the 21 principles derived by Hilgard and Bower are reproduced below under three subheadings according to whether they have been derived from stimulus-response (S-R) theory, cognitive theory, or from motivation, personality, and social psychology theories. Those wishing to look more carefully at the theories from which these principles were derived may wish to refer to Hilgard and Bower's (1975) book, *Theories of Learning*, or to the equally thorough book, *Learning: Systems, Models, and Theories,* edited by Sahakian (1976).

Principles Emphasized Within S-R Theory

- The learner should be an *active*, rather than a passive listener or viewer. The S-R theory emphasizes the significance of the learner's *responses*, and "learning by doing" is still an acceptable slogan.
- *Frequency of repetition* is still important in acquiring skill, and in bringing enough overlearning to guarantee retention. One does not learn to type, or to play the piano, or to speak a foreign language, without some repetitive practice.
- *Reinforcement* is important; that is, repetition should be under arrangements in which desirable or correct responses are rewarded. While there are some lingering questions over details, it is generally found that positive reinforcements (rewards, successes) are to be preferred to negative reinforcements (punishments, failures).
- *Generalization and discrimination* suggest the importance of practice in varied contexts, so that learning will become (or remain) appropriate to a wider (or more restricted) range of stimuli.
- *Novelty* in behavior can be enhanced through imitation of models, through cueing, through "shaping," and is not inconsistent with a liberalized S-R approach to learning.
- *Drive conditions* are important in learning, but not all personal-social motives conform to the drive-reduction principles based on food-deprivation experiments. Issues concerning drives exist within S-R theory; at a practical level, it may be taken for granted that motivational conditions are important.
- *Conflicts and frustrations* arise inevitably in the process of learning difficult discriminations and in social situations in which irrelevant motives

Models in Perspective

may be aroused. Hence, these have to be recognized and provision made for their resolution or accommodation.

Principles Emphasized Within Cognitive Theory

- The *perceptual features* according to which the problem is displayed to the learner are important conditions of learning (figure-ground relations, directional signs, "what-leads-to-what," organic interrelatedness). Hence, a learning problem should be so structured and presented that the essential features are open to the inspection of the learner.
- The *organization of knowledge* should be an essential concern of the teacher or educational planner. Thus, the direction from simple to complex is *not* from arbitrary, meaningless parts to meaningful wholes, but is from *simplified wholes* to *more complex wholes*. The part-whole problem is, therefore, an organizational problem and cannot be dealt with apart from a theory of how complexity is patterned. Also, studies of cognitive growth inform us that the appropriate organization of knowledge may depend on the developmental level of the learner.
- *Learning with understanding* is more permanent and more transferable than rote learning or learning by formula. Expressed in this form, the statement belongs in cognitive theory, but S-R theories make a related emphasis on the importance of meaningfulness in learning and retention.
- *Cognitive feedback* confirms correct knowledge and corrects faulty learning. The notion is that the learner tries something provisionally and then accepts or rejects what he [or she] does on the basis of its consequences. This is, of course, the cognitive equivalent of reinforcement in S-R theory, but cognitive theory tends to place more emphasis on a kind of hypothesis-testing through feedback.
- *Goal-setting* by the learner is important as motivation for learning, and his [or her] successes and failures are determiners of how he [or she] sets future goals.
- *Divergent thinking*, which leads to inventive solutions of problems or to the creation of novel and valued products, is to be nurtured along with *convergent thinking*, which leads to logically correct answers. Such divergent thinking requires appropriate support (feedback) for the person's tentative efforts at originality so that he [or she] may perceive himself [or herself] as potentially creative.

Principles from Motivation, Personality, and Social Psychology

- The learner's *abilities* are important, and provisions have to be made for the slower and the more rapid learners, and for those with specialized abilities.
- *Postnatal development* may be as important as hereditary and congenital determiners of ability and interest. Hence, the learner must be understood in

terms both of inherent maturational factors and of special influences that have shaped his [or her] development.
- Learning is *culturally relative*, and both the wider culture and the sub-culture to which the learner belongs may affect his [or her] learning.
- *Anxiety level* of the individual learner may determine whether certain kinds of encouragements to learn will have beneficial or detrimental effects. The generalization appears justified that with some kinds of tasks, high-anxiety learners perform better if *not* reminded of how well (or poorly) they are doing, while low-anxiety learners do better if they *are* interrupted with comments on their progress.
- The same objective situation may tap *appropriate motives* for one learner and not for another, as, for example, in the contrast between those motivated by affiliation and those motivated by achievement.
- The *organization of motives and values* within the individual is relevant. Some long-range goals affect short-range activities. Thus, college students of equal ability may do better in courses perceived as relevant to their majors than in those perceived as irrelevant.
- *Self-esteem* and its related manifestations (self-confidence, level of aspiration, self-awareness) cannot be overlooked.
- The *group atmosphere* of learning (competition versus cooperation, authoritarianism versus democracy, individual isolation versus group identification) will affect satisfaction in learning as well as the products of learning.

Reprinted from Hilgard, E.R., and Bower, G.H. *Theories of Learning*, Fourth Edition, © 1975, pp. 608-609. Reprinted by permission of Prentice-Hall, Inc., Englewood Cliffs, New Jersey.

References

Hilgard, E.R., and Bower, G.H. *Theories of Learning.* Englewood Cliffs, New Jersey: Prentice-Hall, Inc., 1975.

Liebert, R.M., and Allen, M.K. Effects of role structure and reward magnitude on the acquisition and adoption of self-reward criteria. *Psychological Reports*, 1967, 21, 445-452.

Lynn, R. Temperamental characteristics related to disparity of attainment in reading and arithmetic. *British Journal of Educational Psychology*, 1957, 27, 62-67.

McCandless, B.R., and Castaneda, A. Anxiety in children, school achievement, and intelligence. *Child Development*, 1956, 27, 379-382.

Sahakian, W.S. (Editor) *Learning: Systems, Models, and Theories.* Chicago: Rand McNally College Publishing Co., 1976.

Stotland, E. *The Psychology of Hope.* San Francisco: Jossey-Bass, Inc., 1969.

Part III

The Instructional Materials Development Process

PART III is concerned with describing a process to be followed in order to produce instructional materials conforming to the requirements of the course models (and the unit model on which they depend). In describing the procedures to be followed within the process, it is assumed that the development of the materials will normally be undertaken by a group of individuals acting as a course team. Comments thus are addressed to such a team. However, it is worth noting that individuals, responsible alone for the development of instructional materials, may follow very much the same procedures. The only difference is that whereas course team members are advised to discuss specific issues with one another, the individual is advised to discuss such issues with colleagues and other experts in the field.

For convenience, the process is divided into three consecutive phases. *Phase 1 (Chapter 5)* is concerned primarily with the course team's *identification of course aims** based on an analysis of

---

*It is worth recalling at this point that the terms 'aims' and 'objectives' are used in a similar sense throughout this book to identify what students are expected to achieve upon completion of their studies. The only difference between the terms is that an 'objective,' when stated in instructional materials, must be expressed in terms which are sufficiently explicit to indicate how achievement of the 'objective' might be measured. In contrast, 'aims' are usually expressed in more general terms. Thus, the transition from discussion of 'aims' to discussion of 'objectives' usually represents a progression from consideration of general issues to consideration of more specific issues.

perceived needs and the ability of the course team to meet these needs. *Phase 2* (*Chapter 6*) is concerned mainly with *outlining the means of achieving specified aims.* *Phase 3* (*Chapter 7*) is concerned with the *progressive development and evaluation of trial materials.*

The development process outlined above is one which progresses gradually from the general to the specific. Thus, in the early stages, emphasis is placed on obtaining general agreement on broad course aims, which are intended to provide a broad frame of reference for subsequent development. Consideration is then given to more specific aims and objectives and the means by which they are to be achieved, with the first fully detailed presentations emerging during Phase 3. The intent is to avoid unnecessary re-drafting of materials in later phases of the process with all that this might entail in terms of inefficiency and conflict. An example might usefully illustrate the point. Let's imagine a course team developing instructional materials without paying serious attention to Phases 1 and 2, and moving rapidly into the development of full-draft presentations of units of instruction as required in Phase 3. In such a situation, a unit might be developed by an individual author to achieve certain aims which other course team members may feel are unimportant or irrelevant. In such circumstances, the author is likely to be required to modify his or her aims and the related instructional materials. At such a late phase in the development process, this is likely to require considerable re-drafting of materials, and few authors are likely to welcome such criticism and demands, particularly if earlier, more timely discussion could have avoided the situation. In fact, faced with criticism from colleagues, and a demand for substantial re-drafting of materials, course team members are likely to feel considerable pressure and anxiety, and may withdraw from the team. The effect on the individual may be highly traumatic, while the effect on the course team is likely to be very disruptive. Such undesirable effects have been reported in some detail by Lawrence and Young (1979), and should be avoided as far as it is possible to do so.

Running parallel to, and serving as an integral part of, the development process is a continuous process of evaluation which is designed to help develop and progressively improve the instructional materials as they emerge, rather than to make judgments on the final product. The process is thus concerned with 'formative' rather than 'summative' evaluation, to use Scriven's (1967) widely accepted terminology. Reflecting the nature of the development process, the formative evaluation is designed to focus initially on broad issues, but as development proceeds, it focuses progressively on more specific issues. The logic of such a relationship might be illustrated by a simple example. Let's imagine that the course team is interested in determining to what extent students perceive the broad course aims as relevant to their needs. This needs to be determined early in the development process when broad aims are still being discussed (Phase 1), for this is a time when related student opinions can be taken into account. If student perception of the aims is not determined until later in the process, when instructional materials are emerging in considerable detail (Phase 3), any proposed modification is likely to be ignored, since this may require massive re-drafting of related instruction.

Although the process described moves gradually from a consideration of the general to the specific, with the products of each phase providing guidance for development in the next phase, this does not prevent the process from being an innovative one. Thus, although Phases 1 and 2 are very much concerned with developing a broad frame of reference to provide individual course team members with guidance during Phase 3, the development of this frame of reference is in itself very much an innovative process, even if it normally reflects the thinking of the team as a whole rather than that of any one individual. Individual innovation is also encouraged within the broad frame of reference developed. Throughout the process, it is recognized that as development proceeds, thinking tends to be clarified, and initially held ideas are likely to be modified in what is essentially an iterative process. However, it is also recognized that broad frames of reference must be developed if iteration is not to lead to conflict and inefficiency.

Chapter 5

Phase 1: Identification of Course Aims

This chapter is concerned with discussing how the course team might go about the identification of course aims in terms of perceived student needs. It does this in three stages. First (*Section 1*), it describes *the basic elements of the prescribed approach* which might be used by the course team in group interactions, or by individual members of the course team, to help identify course aims and the relationships among them. It then identifies (*Section 2*) a number of *factors to be taken into consideration* in applying the approach. Finally (*Section 3*), it describes a set of *procedures to be followed during Phase 1*. The latter indicates how the course team as a whole, and individuals within it, might make use of the basic approach described in Section 1.

1. The Basic Elements of the Prescribed Approach

The basic approach is described here in two distinct stages: the first (*Section 1.1*) is concerned with the *derivation of course aims from perceived needs* and the second (*Section 1.2*) with *identification of relationships among the aims.*

1.1. Derivation of Course Aims from Perceived Needs

The approach recommended here is based very much on Tyler's (1949) thinking concerning the way in which course aims might be derived. Tyler, in fact, suggested that those concerned with determining the aims of teaching institutions (schools, in particular) need to take note of the needs of students and society, the opinions of subject-matter specialists, and the educational and social philosophies of the teaching institution, as well as taking note of what is known about the learning process itself. It is suggested here that a course team needs to act in a similar manner, undertaking a broad analysis of perceived student needs and determining to what extent these might be met through the development of related instructional materials. In undertaking such a process, the course team might usefully address itself to the questions which follow.

- What are the needs (perceived by students, society, master performers, and subject-matter specialists) to which the course team wishes to address itself?
- What are the characteristics of the target group which the course team wishes to help?
- What assumptions are made concerning the knowledge, abilities, interests, and motivations of the target group?
- To what extent do existing courses meet, or fail to meet, the needs identified?
- To what extent is the course team likely to be able to meet the perceived needs through the adoption of instructional materials already in existence?
- To what extent is it logical, and feasible, for the course team to attempt to meet perceived needs through the development of new instructional materials?
- Does the course team have sufficient resources (including manpower, expertise, and finances) to develop appropriate instructional materials?

It is important that discussion of the above questions be as informed as possible, and a number of strategies may be adopted to ensure this. Thus, interviews and questionnaires may be used to help determine the extent to which students, society, subject-matter specialists, or master performers perceive the importance of particular needs, and to help identify the characteristics of the target group requiring help. They may also be used to determine the degree to which members of the groups referred to agree with the aims of alternative scenarios under consideration. National and international reports may be reviewed to identify what work has already been done in developing related instructional materials, for, apart from not

Identification of Course Aims

wanting to 'reinvent the wheel,' the study of existing materials provides the course team with a sound knowledge of instructional materials on which to base subsequent development work.

1.2. Identification of Relationships Among the Aims

As possible course aims begin to emerge, it is suggested that attention be paid to the identification of relationships among them. What is required is not identification of all possible relationships, but a clear indication of the relationships on which subsequent materials are to be built. Hierarchical relationships are of particular value in this respect, for they may be used (during Phase 2) to help determine an appropriate sequence for related instruction. However, in more immediate terms, they may also be used (during Phase 1) to help identify aims that might otherwise have been ignored, as well as to identify assumptions made with regard to the target group.

Two methods of identifying relationships are described here. The first is *a simple hierarchical approach* recommended by Krathwohl and Payne (1971), which pays attention to broad general aims in the first instance and then derives more specific aims from these. The second is *an iterative hierarchical approach*, which proceeds not only from a consideration of more general to specific aims, but also from more specific to general aims, and is the approach most likely to be adopted in practice. Both approaches lead to the identification of relationships among aims in terms of hierarchical flow diagrams.

A Simple Hierarchical Approach. The approach recommended by Krathwohl and Payne (1971) suggests that attention should be focused in the first instance on obtaining agreement on the broadest possible aims, and that once this has been done, one should proceed to obtaining agreement on more specific sub-aims on which each of the broader aims depends. In this way, aims may be identified, and agreed upon, with increasing precision to the point where they can provide meaningful guidance to those involved in the development process. A simple example of how this can occur might usefully illustrate the point.

Let us consider the case of a university department of education which is concerned with the inability of graduate students to critically review articles in certain educational journals, particularly as the department sees progress towards higher degrees as very much dependent on this ability. The department decides to rectify the problem by developing a course to meet the perceived need. The department creates for this purpose a small course team from among its members, and after limited debate is able to agree that the primary aim of the course should be that all graduate students completing the course should be able to:

- critically review articles in certain educational research journals (which the team lists).

This being a very general aim, it is somewhat ambiguous, and the course team goes on to discuss in more specific terms what is meant by it. From this emerges two sub-aims which it is decided students must achieve if they are to achieve the broader general aim to the satisfaction of all concerned. The two sub-aims require that students should be able to:

- use statistical tests commonly used by researchers in the journals identified; and
- demonstrate a knowledge of experimental methods commonly used by researchers in the journals identified.

The course team continues in the same manner, breaking down the aims even further, as indicated in the hierarchical flow diagram in Figure 9, to identify the specific statistical tests and the experimental methods that need to be mastered if the above two aims are to be realized.

The process of breaking down general aims into more specific aims continues in this manner until the aims being identified may be assumed to be already achieved by students in the target group. The flow diagram in Figure 9 may thus help to clarify the assumptions being made with regard to the target group.

Needless to say, other educators starting from the same overall aims as the department course team might derive different sub-aims. However, the derivation of aims in this way opens up the aims and the logic behind their derivation for inspection and debate by the course team, and provides a useful frame of

Figure 9

*The Use of a Hierarchical Flow Diagram
to Identify the Logic Behind Specific Aims
Derived (or Selected) for a Course*

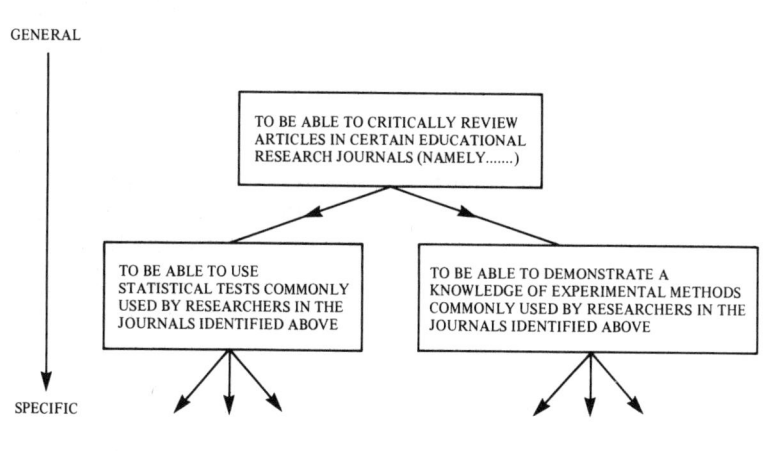

reference for the development of subsequent instructional material.

An Iterative Hierarchical Approach. In practice, the analysis of perceived needs (described in Section 1.1) is likely to lead to the identification of a number of aims which vary considerably in specificity. In such a situation, two complementary approaches may be adopted for the clarification of relationships among the aims and for identification of further related aims.

The first approach is similar to that already described in that the starting point is one or two of the broadest aims, and consideration is given to the identification of more specific aims on which each of these depends. This may lead to the identification of a number of new, more specific aims, but some of the prerequisite aims may have been already identified in discussing perceived student needs.

In the second approach, the course team has to consider to what extent some of the more specific aims might be logically grouped, and (when this is possible) if each set of specific aims grouped can be described under a more general aim. This may lead to the identification of new, more general aims, or may simply identify the relationship between a group of specific aims and a more general aim that has already been identified.

Combining the two approaches results in an iterative approach with thinking concerning general aims leading to clarification of more specific aims, while thinking concerning specific aims leads to clarification of more general aims. As with the simple hierarchical approach, the end-product is one or more hierarchical flow diagrams, which identify the way in which aims will be subsequently realized. The hierarchical flow diagram indicated in Figure 10 was derived from such an iterative process, and represents very early thinking concerning possible aims for a science foundation course for mature students.

2. Factors to Be Taken into Consideration

It is too easy for a course team to follow the approach described earlier (*Section 1*) without paying sufficient attention to the wide variety of aims (and needs) that might be taken into consideration and without differentiating between the needs of different types of students. This section is concerned, therefore, with highlighting the *different types of aims (and needs)* that need to be considered (*Section 2.1*) and with emphasizing the importance of recognizing the *different needs of different students* (*Section 2.2*).

2.1. Different Types of Aims (and Needs)

In considering possible course aims, it is logical to focus attention in the first instance on different types of *cognitive aims*, that is, on the knowledge, intellectual abilities, and skills that students will be expected to achieve. However, this is not sufficient in itself, for one must also pay attention to the motivation of students towards achieving such aims. Consideration must also be given, therefore, to *affective aims*, that is, to student

Identification of Course Aims

Figure 10

A Hierarchical Flow Diagram Used as a Provisional Frame of Reference for Planning a New Foundation Course in Science for Mature Students

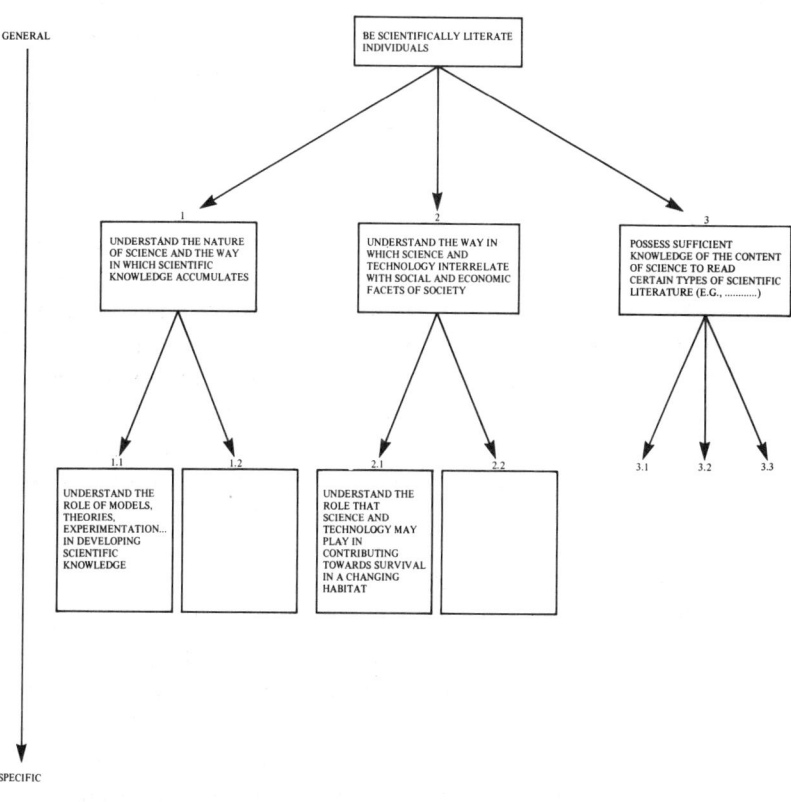

interests, attitudes, and values, particularly to the degree that they determine the students' motivation to achieve specified cognitive aims.

Cognitive Aims. Although instructional designers and developers often express high ideals about what they hope students will achieve through following certain courses, very often they end up providing students with factual information which the students are simply expected to recall. It is important, therefore, for the course team to ask what it *really* wants students to achieve. Initially, this may be expressed in terms of knowledge or skills which students are expected to acquire, but ultimately it should be expressed in terms of what the students should be able to *do*.

In making the above suggestion, it is recognized that there is a difference between students possessing a certain element of knowledge and demonstrating behavior which, it is assumed, is based on that knowledge. This is an important point made clear by Pask and Scott (1973), and it should not be forgotten. However, the advantage of expressing aims in terms of what students should be able to do is that if the aims have been expressed clearly enough (in objective terms), it is possible to *measure* whether or not the aims have been achieved. At the same time, it provides some insight into whether or not the desired knowledge has been acquired.

With the above factors in mind, it is suggested that the course teams consider the following questions during the process of identifying course aims and the relationships among them.

- To what extent will students be expected (upon completion of the course) to demonstrate their *knowledge* of the information provided? For example, to what extent will they be expected to recall specific facts, ways and means of dealing with things, principles, theories, and so on? Is such recall sufficient in itself, or is some higher level of intellectual ability to be demonstrated?
- One might expect students at least to be able to demonstrate a minimum level of *understanding* of information provided, for example, by expressing this in their own terms. However, is this sufficient in itself?

Identification of Course Aims

- Will students be expected to *apply* what they have learned (for example, rules, methods, principles, or theories) to various types of data or information that may be provided?
- Will they be expected to *analyze* information provided; for example, distinguishing between factual and hypothetical statements?
- To what extent will they be expected to *synthesize*; for example, putting ideas together in new ways in the form of reports or plans?
- Will students be expected to identify weaknesses in data, arguments, proofs, principles, or theories? In other words, will they be expected to *evaluate* what is put in front of them?

The above questions are based on the 'Cognitive Domain' of Bloom's (1956) *Taxonomy of Educational Objectives*, which was developed to provide a standardized system for classifying cognitive objectives (that is, educational objectives concerned with the acquisition of knowledge, intellectual abilities, and skills). This is not the only system of classification that has been developed, but it is the one that has been most widely adopted in practice.

If a course team is inadvertently paying too much attention to the simple recall of information and too little to other aspects, such as the understanding and application of knowledge, this will soon become clear if the aims identified are reviewed with Bloom's taxonomy in mind. It may be that the aims ultimately identified might be related usefully to different parts of the taxonomy, but they should not be forced into an unnatural format simply to conform to specific categories within the taxonomy. What is required ultimately is a meaningful statement of aims rather than a contrived one which can be neatly categorized. In other words, the taxonomy should be used to help stimulate thinking rather than to restrict it. With this in mind, the course team may wish to review its aims with other classification systems, and in this context they may find Gagné's (1970) system of classification of interest—particularly if the team is concerned with primary education.

In the same context, the course team might review its aims

taking note of the extent to which stated aims pay attention to relationships which make information predictable or redundant. Bruner (1957) argues that careful attention should be paid not only to propositions that permit the maximum reconstruction of material unknown to the constructor, but also to axioms and theories that maximize the ability of the student to go beyond the information given. Some students are able to see relationships being spelled out in detail. Such students adopt what Marton (1975) describes as a 'deep approach' to the processing of information; making connections among points for themselves, perceiving relationships between new and old ideas, reflecting on the soundness of arguments presented, and drawing conclusions for themselves. However, many students, if not most, tend to adopt what Marton describes as a 'surface approach,' doing little more than trying to recall information provided. For such students, it is important that relationships of interest be made explicit.

Affective Aims. It is logical in the first instance for the course team to concentrate its attention—as already indicated—on determining the knowledge, intellectual abilities, and skills that it would like students to achieve. However, having done this, it must pay careful attention to the need to motivate students towards achievement of the cognitive aims identified. Thus, prior to cognitive instruction commencing within the course as a whole, or within individual units within the course, one might aim to ensure that students are already motivated towards achieving certain broad cognitive aims, while once cognitive instruction is underway, one might aim to ensure that such motivation is maintained. Instruction must be developed with this need clearly in mind.

If students are to be motivated towards achieving the cognitive aims identified, they must see these as both relevant and important. This point is reinforced by Rogers (1975) and Stotland (1969). Thus, Rogers suggests that significant learning takes place when the subject matter is perceived by the student as having relevance to his or her purposes, while Stotland reinforces this in his terms by arguing that the motivation of an individual to achieve a particular goal is, in part, dependent on the individual's

Identification of Course Aims

perception of the importance of that goal. Unfortunately, one cannot assume that students will see specified cognitive aims as relevant to their needs and important simply because the course team *believes* this to be the case, and instruction will have to be developed to ensure that students do perceive the relevance and importance of stated cognitive aims.

The extent to which students perceive stated cognitive aims to be relevant and important, and the extent to which they feel motivated towards achieving these aims, may be measured subsequently (during student testing of materials in Phase 3) with the help of related questionnaires. Affective aims may be stated, therefore, with questionnaire responses in mind. However, course teams wishing to use more standardized forms of measurement may consider relating their aims to the 'Affective Domain' of the *Taxonomy of Educational Objectives*. This was developed by Krathwohl, Bloom, and Masia (1964) to provide a means of standardizing educational objectives concerned with the development of interests, attitudes, and values.

2.2. Different Needs of Different Students

In following the basic approach described in Section 1, the course team might initially limit itself (in the interests of simplicity) to considering the needs of typical or average students in the target group. However, it must be recognized that different students have different abilities and need to be treated differently. Thus, less able students should not always be expected to achieve the same aims as more able students. If students, particularly less able ones, are to be motivated towards achieving specified cognitive aims, they must perceive these to be achievable. This point is reinforced by Stotland (1969), who suggests that an individual's motivation to achieve a particular goal is, in part, a function of the individual's perception of the probability of attaining the goal. It is suggested, therefore, that in determining course aims, and the relationships among them (using the basic approach described in Section 1), the course team should give separate consideration to the needs of students of above- and below-average ability as well as to the needs of those of average ability. Separate hierarchical flow diagrams may also be produced for these three sub-groups, while note should be made of the different assumptions that may be made with regard to each sub-group.

It is worth noting at this point that in discussing the need to treat students differently according to their different abilities, we are once again concerned with factors which affect student motivation towards the achievement of specified cognitive aims, reflecting the same type of concern that was expressed in discussing the need to develop materials oriented towards ensuring that students recognize the relevance and importance of stated cognitive aims. The way in which these factors are interrelated is summarized in the four propositions quoted below. These are taken from a well-supported theory concerning goal achievement developed by Stotland (1969).

"An organism's motivation to achieve a goal is, in part, a positive function of its perceived probability of attaining the goal and of the perceived importance of the goal."

"The higher an organism's perceived probability of attaining a goal, and the greater the importance of that goal, the greater will be the positive affect experienced by the organism."

"The lower an organism's perceived probability of attaining a goal, and the greater the importance of that goal, the more will the organism experience anxiety."

"Organisms are motivated to escape and avoid anxiety; the greater the anxiety experienced or expected, the greater the motivation (to escape)."

3. Procedures to Be Followed During Phase 1

It has already been noted that the recommended 'basic approach' for identifying course aims is based upon a careful examination of student needs, consideration of the extent to which these might be met through the development of related course materials, and study of the relationships (among specified course aims) upon which the development of subsequent instruction is to be based. Similarly, it has also been noted that in

Identification of Course Aims

applying the '*basic* approach,' a number of '*factors*' must be taken into account. These include the need to give careful consideration to a variety of different cognitive and affective aims, and the need to recognize that different students (particularly those of different ability) tend to have different needs.

The task of the course team during Phase 1 is to use the 'basic approach' to help identify course aims and the relationships among them, taking all relevant 'factors' into consideration. This section is thus concerned with describing how this might be achieved. The process described is broken down into three stages as follows.

The first stage in the process is concerned with the course team *exchanging information and ideas (Section 3.1)*. What is required at this stage is a course team discussion, which identifies major concerns and provides some indication of course team thinking concerning student needs and the extent to which these might be met through the development of instructional materials. There is no attempt to come to decisions at this stage, and course team members are encouraged to remain open-minded and flexible in their thinking.

In contrast, the second stage in the process is concerned with *obtaining provisional agreement on course aims (Section 3.2)* and on the relationships among them that will be used as a basis for the development of subsequent materials. The 'basic approach' already described is applied here, taking careful note of all relevant 'factors.' The end-product is a statement of broad course aims for each sub-group of interest together with related hierarchical flow diagrams.

The final stage in the process is concerned with *expressing course aims in terms of unit aims (Section 3.3)*, by providing some indication of the way in which individual course team members might contribute to the realization of specified course aims through the development of related units of instruction.

3.1. Exchanging Information and Ideas

Stage 1 is concerned with discussing possible course aims in terms of student needs, and the questions included in the 'basic approach' (see Section 1.1) provide a natural starting point for this. As aims emerge, each course team member is encouraged to identify aims which he or she perceives to be relevant to the needs of the course and to indicate the relationships (see Section 1.2) which he or she sees among them. What is required at this stage is a free-flowing discussion, which identifies major concerns from a number of different points of view. The intent is not to discuss each viewpoint in great detail, but to ensure a free exchange of information and ideas. More than one meeting may be required for this purpose.

3.2. Obtaining Provisional Agreement on Course Aims

Stage 2 is concerned not only with obtaining agreement on broad course aims and the extent to which these should differ for different sub-groups within the target group, but also with identifying relationships (among the aims) that are seen as providing a logical basis for the subsequent development of instructional materials. It is suggested that the course team appoint a small working group (or an individual, such as the course team chairperson) to undertake this task, bearing in mind the ideas and information which emerged from stage 1. Once the working group has completed the initial task, it should present its findings to the course team for discussion, modifying statements of aims and perceived relationships as necessary in light of the feedback received. The end-product provides a broad frame of reference for subsequent development of instructional materials.

In undertaking its task of identifying course aims and relationships, it is suggested that the working group follow the recommended 'basic approach' (Section 1), taking note of all relevant 'factors' (Section 2) in a series of related steps. Thus, in the first instance, the working group might limit itself to a consideration of cognitive aims to be achieved by students of average ability, given subsequent consideration to affective aims that need to be realized if the cognitive aims are to be achieved. The working group might then examine the assumptions being made with regard to the needs, interests, knowledge, and abilities of the average-ability student. This should help to identify cognitive and affective aims

Identification of Course Aims 77

that many less able students will need to acquire, if they are to achieve the 'core aims' already identified. Finally, the working group might give similar consideration to 'optional aims,' which more able students might be expected to achieve in addition to the 'core aims' already identified.

3.3. Expressing Course Aims in Terms of Unit Aims

Stage 3 is concerned with the extension and refinement of the broad frame of reference emerging from stage 2. Each course team member is invited to indicate—in terms of related aims—the extent to which he or she might contribute to the achievement of one or more course aims through the development of one or more related units of instruction. The process might be illustrated by means of a simple example.

Let's consider the case of a course team concerned with the development of a new foundation course in science for mature students, and let's assume that the team has completed stages 1 and 2 of the process described here. The products available at the beginning of stage 3 include a number of hierarchical flow diagrams, one of which indicates the relationships between 'core aims' to be achieved by all students regardless of ability. This flow diagram is shown in Figure 10.

Let's look now at how one course team member identifies what he or she perceives to be a relevant contribution towards achievement of one of these course aims. The aim on which he or she focuses attention (aim 2.1) indicates that students should be able to 'understand the role that science and technology may play in contributing towards survival in a changing habitat.' The course team member believes that he or she can make a significant contribution towards realization of this aim through the development of a unit of instruction concerned with 'The Role that Energy Plays in Contributing Towards Survival,' and he or she expresses his or her thinking in the form of a hierarchical flow diagram (Figure 11). From this it is clear that he or she sees his or her unit as a means of helping students to understand both 'the importance of energy to survival' (aim 2.11) and 'the dangers of energy to survival' (aim 2.12). He or she also sees achievement of these two aims as contributing to the realization of the broader

Figure 11

A Hierarchical Flow Diagram Used as a Provisional Frame of Reference for Planning a Unit of the Science Foundation Course Referred to in Figure 10

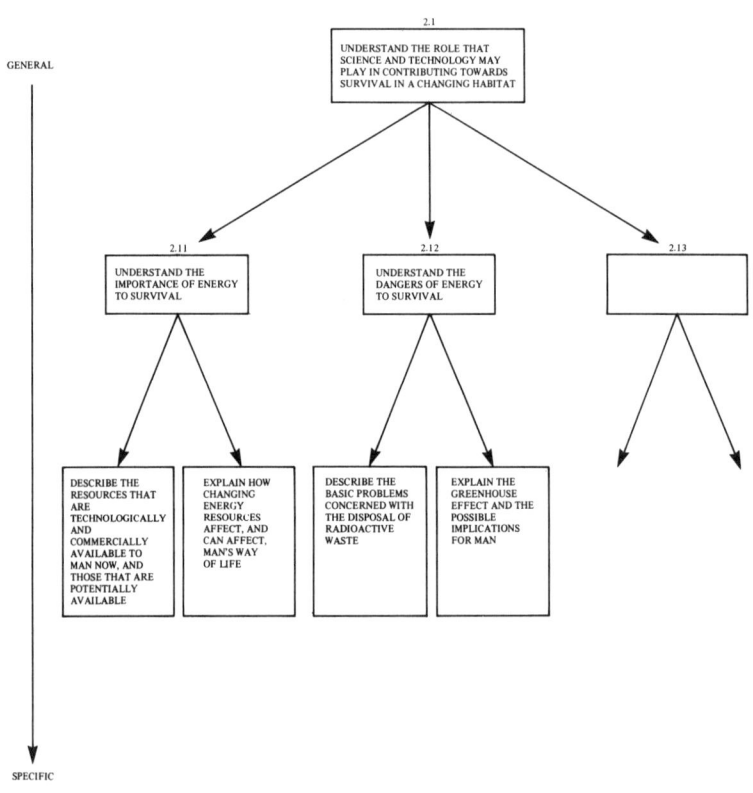

course aim already identified (aim 2.1). The blank space for aim 2.13 simply indicates that he or she recognizes that realization of the broader course aim will be only partly accomplished through the proposed unit and that other contributions will need to be considered.

With contributions such as the above from each course team member, the course team is in a position to discuss the relevance of each individual's proposed contribution and the extent to which it is likely to contribute towards achievement of course aims identified. It may be decided that an individual's contribution is recognized as both relevant and desirable but not sufficient in itself to realize a particular aim. In such circumstances, it may be decided to obtain additional contributions, even if additional authors have to be invited to join the course team for this purpose. However, it may also be decided that it is financially impossible to increase the size of the course team, and in such circumstances, it may be more realistic to modify the broad course aims to reflect what can be achieved. Clearly, the process is an iterative one, leading to both the extension and refinement of the hierarchical flow diagram. Applied to all relevant flow diagrams, it leads to the development of a basic frame of reference for use in subsequent Phase 2 activities.

References

Bloom, B.S. (Editor). *Taxonomy of Educational Objectives. Handbook I: Cognitive Domain.* New York: Longman, Inc., 1956.

Bruner, J.S. Going beyond the information given. In Bruner, J.S. et al., *Contemporary Approaches to Cognition.* Cambridge, Massachusetts: Harvard University Press, 1957.

Gagné, R.M. *The Conditions of Learning* (Second Edition). New York: Holt, Rinehart, and Winston, 1970, 237-276.

Krathwohl, D.R., Bloom, B.S., and Masia, B.B. *Taxonomy of Educational Objectives. Handbook II: Affective Domain.* New York: Longman, Inc., 1964.

Krathwohl, D.R., and Payne, D.A. Defining and assessing educational objectives. In Thorndike, R.L. (Editor), *Educational Measurement*. Washington, DC: American Council on Education, 1971, 17-45.

Lawrence, W.G., and Young, I. *The Open University. TIHR document no. 2T-271.* London: The Tavistock Institute of Human Relations, 1979.

Marton, F. What does it take to learn? In Entwistle, N., and Hounsell, D. (Editors), *How Students Learn*. Lancaster: Institute of Research and Development in Post Compulsory Education, University of Lancaster, 1975, 125-138.

Pask, G., and Scott, B.C.E. A system for exhibiting learning strategies and regulating uncertainties. *International Journal of Man-Machine Studies*, 1973, 5, 17-52.

Rogers, C. Freedom to learn. In Entwistle, N., and Hounsell, D. (Editors), *How Students Learn*. Lancaster: Institute of Research and Development in Post Compulsory Education, University of Lancaster, 1975, 149-158.

Scriven, M. The methodology of evaluation. In Tyler, R.W., Gagné, R.M., and Scriven, M. (Editors), *Perspectives of Curriculum Evaluation*. AERA Monograph on Curriculum Evaluation, No. 1. Chicago: Rand McNally, 1967, 39-83.

Stotland, E. *The Psychology of Hope*. San Francisco: Jossey-Bass, Inc., 1969.

Tyler, R.W. *Basic Principles of Curriculum and Instruction*. Chicago: University of Chicago Press, 1949.

Chapter 6

Phase 2: Outlining the Means of Achieving Specified Aims

Whereas Phase 1 was concerned with identifying broad *aims* for the course materials to be developed, Phase 2 is concerned with an initial consideration of the *means* by which these aims are to be achieved. During this phase, the course team needs to think about the *content* of the course and the *strategies* that might be adopted to facilitate learning of the course.

During this phase, each member of the course team should prepare an outline of his or her contribution to the course, indicating his or her thinking concerning the content of the unit and the strategies to be adopted within it. However, before undertaking such tasks, the responsibilities of each course team member have to be clarified, and in turn this requires clarification of the way in which the course is to be structured. *Section 1* of this chapter is concerned, therefore, with the *identification of course units and relationships among them*, while *Section 2* is concerned with the *preparation of unit outlines* by individual course team members. Once these have been prepared, they need to be discussed within the course team and modified in light of the feedback received. The end-product should be a much clearer *frame of reference* (*Section 3*) for the activities which follow in Phase 3.

In developing the outlines, the intent is not to commit authors to detailed strategies but to ensure that each member of the course team has a clear understanding of each author's aims prior to the development of related instructional material. As an author develops materials during Phase 3, his or her thinking concerning detailed aims and strategies may change, but this may be realized without affecting other course team members, if the author is working within the terms of a broad frame of reference. Outlines prepared during Phase 2 are intended to serve this purpose. They are not intended to function as 'straight jackets,' and authors are encouraged to develop their thinking during the subsequent development of materials, along with a full awareness of the implications that major modifications may have on other course team members.

1. Identification of Course Units and Relationships Among Them

The natural starting points for the activities suggested here are the hierarchical flow diagrams produced during Phase 1. These identify the course aims to be achieved, and the relationships among them, and may be used to help determine how the course may be broken down into units and to indicate how these units may be related to one another. Initial discussion is limited to the needs of *students of average ability* (*Section 1.1*), but this is then extended to include consideration of the needs of *students of different ability* (*Section 1.2*).

1.1. Students of Average Ability

In the interests of simplicity, it is suggested that during this first stage the course team limit itself to considering the needs of students of average ability only, and the starting point for the related activities is thus the flow diagrams (such as those in Figures 10 and 11), which identify course aims for the average student. Three ways of using these diagrams are discussed here. The first is *a hierarchical approach* recommended by Gagné (1970), which sees related instruction as moving upwards through the hierarchy. The second is *a progressive differentiation approach* advocated by Ausubel (1968), which sees related instruction as moving downwards through the hierarchy. At first glance, the two approaches would appear to be incompatible, but they may in fact be combined, and this is explained within the related discussion. Finally, it is recognized that the hierarchical flow diagram is not the only tool which may be used in determining the way in which instruction might be broken down into units and sequenced and that *alternative approaches* might be adopted. However, it is noted

Outlining the Means of Achieving Specified Aims

that in such situations the proposed sequence of instruction may still be usefully examined with the help of hierarchical flow diagrams.

A Hierarchical Approach. The type of hierarchical approach recommended by Gagné (1970) is best illustrated with reference to one of his own hierarchical flow diagrams (see Figure 12). According to Gagné, the way to produce such a diagram is to focus on the major objective, and to ask what prerequisite objectives must be acquired if the major objective is to be realized. The same question is then asked with regard to the newly emergent subordinate objectives, thus identifying a further set of related subordinate objectives. The analysis of prerequisite objectives is repeated as often as necessary, until one can assume that the subordinate objectives emerging have already been acquired by students in the target group. Gagné argues that such an analysis not only identifies prerequisite objectives that must be acquired in order to achieve the major objective, but it also identifies a logical order in which these might be achieved. This suggests a related sequence of instruction which permits objectives to be achieved in the order indicated. Thus, if each unit were aimed at the realization of a particular objective, the sequence of units would be related to the order in which objectives are to be realized. If a unit covers more than one objective, the sequence of instruction within each unit would similarly be related to the order in which objectives are to be achieved.

This type of hierarchical approach can be extremely helpful in determining the sequence of instruction, but it needs to be interpreted with some caution. Thus, Figure 12 identifies a logical order for achieving a major objective—namely, that of being able to subtract numbers of any size—and it opens up the logic to ready discussion. However, it need not be the only way of achieving the objective. Thus, some subject specialists might consider that the major objective stated may be achieved without any reference to the concept of borrowing. For example, the objective might be achieved by learning to determine what must be added to the smaller of two numbers in order to realize the larger number. Alternatively, it might be achieved by learning to use a calculator.

84   Instructional Models for Course Design and Development

Figure 12

*A Hierarchical Flow Diagram Showing the Breakdown
of a Major Skill into Prerequisite Skills and Indicating
the Order (I-XI) in Which the Prerequisite Skills Should
Be Achieved (From Gagné and Briggs, 1974)*

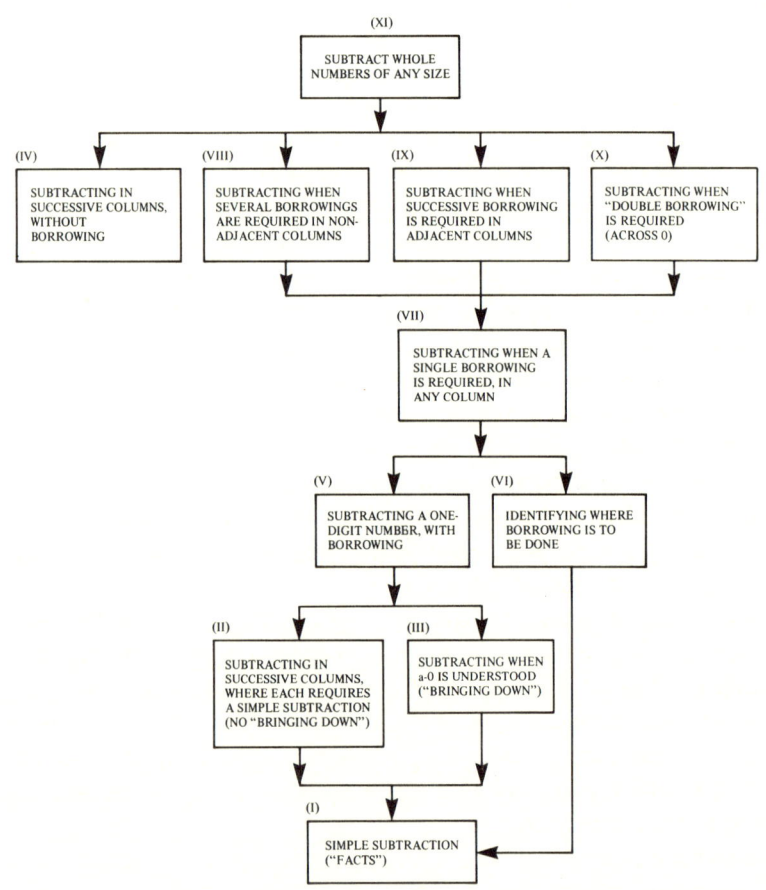

From *Principles of Instructional Design* by Robert M. Gagné and Leslie J. Briggs. Copyright © 1974 by Holt, Rinehart, and Winston, Inc. Reprinted by permission of Holt, Rinehart, and Winston.

It would seem wiser, therefore, to use hierarchical flow diagrams to identify the logic behind one's thinking than to suggest that this implies there is only one way of achieving a particular objective.

A Progressive Differentiation Approach. The concept of advance organizers for introducing students to detailed learning within a unit of instruction has already been discussed, and it is suggested that advance organizers be ultimately developed to introduce related blocks of units and the course as a whole. Such advance organizers may be units in their own right. It has already been noted that *one* of the functions of the advance organizer is to indicate to students how concepts are related to one another, and hierarchical diagrams provide course team members with a valuable way of reviewing these relationships.

The concept of advance organizers may be used not only to introduce a course, but also a program of courses, and one might envisage an advance organizer to a program which is a course in itself. Thus, at the primary level, a simple course in science might be seen as an advance organizer for related secondary level courses, and the latter as advance organizers for much more complex science courses at a tertiary level. Used in this way, advance organizers might be seen as contributing to a process which Ausubel (1968) describes as progressive differentiation; that is, a process in which attention is paid initially to the most general ideas and then to progressive differentiation between these in more and more specific detail. There is in fact a close parallel between the progressive differentiation approach and the spiral approach to the sequencing of instruction recommended by Bruner (1970).

From the above comments, it can be seen that the use of advance organizers permits the designer-developer to combine the advantages of a progressive differentiation approach with those of a hierarchical approach.

Alternative Approaches. The hierarchical flow diagram is not the only tool which may be used in determining the sequence of instruction, and there may be occasions when course teams find alternative approaches more illuminating. However, in such situations, aims still need to be clearly identified, and hierarchical flow diagrams may still be used to examine the way in which aims are to be realized through the proposed process. An example might usefully illustrate the point.

Let's consider the case where a course team is concerned with the teaching of a process, and careful examination of the skills to be acquired suggests that each may be acquired independently of the others. Let's imagine that the process consists of consecutive sub-processes A, B, and C, with sub-process A converting a product P_1 to a new form P_2, and sub-processes B and C, respectively, converting this to form P_3 and then P_4, as indicated in Figure 13. The sub-processes may be taught in any order as long as the appropriate raw materials (P_1, P_2, or P_3) are made available for the sub-process concerned (A, B, or C).

It might appear most logical, at first glance, to teach the sub-processes in the order in which they occur, for this has the advantage of each sub-process providing the materials required for the next sub-process, as well as relating instruction directly to the process as it occurs in practice. Such an instructional approach might be described as a *forward chaining approach*.

However, there will be occasions when a process is long and elaborate, and it will not be obvious in the early stages of the process why certain procedures are being followed. In such circumstances, advance organizers may be used to good effect, but this is not the only way of solving the problem. An alternative approach is to teach the sub-processes in reverse order (C, B, then A) in what Gilbert (1969) describes as a *backward chaining approach*. The advantage of this approach is reflected in the related hierarchical flow diagram (see Figure 14), which indicates the order in which objectives are to be achieved. From this it is clear that very early in the learning process the student is able to produce the ultimate end-product (P_4) from given raw materials (P_3), thus placing in perspective the need for related sub-processes to produce the raw materials provided. In this case, the hierarchical flow diagram may only clarify what may have already been obvious, but in more complex situations, it may identify anomalies which can then be rectified.

Outlining the Means of Achieving Specified Aims 87

Figure 13

Backward Chaining of Instruction

SEQUENCE OF SUB-PROCESSES A, B, AND C IN PROCESS OF INTEREST, WITH INDICATION OF PRODUCTS P_1, P_2, P_3, AND P_4 AT EACH STAGE IN PROCESS

$$P_1 \xrightarrow{A} P_2 \xrightarrow{B} P_3 \xrightarrow{C} P_4$$

SEQUENCE OF SUB-PROCESSES IN RELATED INSTRUCTION WITHOUT REPETITION OF NEWLY MASTERED SUB-PROCESSES

SEQUENCE	SUB-PROCESSES
1	$P_3 \xrightarrow{C} P_4$
2	$P_2 \xrightarrow{B} P_3$
3	$P_1 \xrightarrow{A} P_2$

SEQUENCE OF SUB-PROCESSES IN RELATED INSTRUCTION WITH REPETITION OF NEWLY MASTERED SUB-PROCESSES

SEQUENCE	SUB-PROCESSES
1	$P_3 \xrightarrow{C} P_4$
2	$P_2 \xrightarrow{B} P_3 \xrightarrow{C} P_4$
3	$P_1 \xrightarrow{A} P_2 \xrightarrow{B} P_3 \xrightarrow{C} P_4$

88   *Instructional Models for Course Design and Development*

Figure 14

Hierarchical Flow Diagram and Related Table, Indicating Order in Which Objectives Are Realized Through Backward Chaining Process Illustrated in Figure 13

UPON COMPLETION OF THE RELATED STUDIES, STUDENTS SHOULD BE ABLE TO EXPLAIN HOW:

V

THE FINAL PRODUCT (P_4) MAY BE PRODUCED FROM THE RAW MATERIALS PROVIDED (P_1)

III

THE FINAL PRODUCT (P_4) MAY BE PRODUCED FROM THE RAW MATERIALS PROVIDED (P_2)

IV

PRODUCT P_2 MAY BE PRODUCED FROM PRODUCT P_1 BY MEANS OF *SUB-PROCESS A*

I

THE FINAL PRODUCT (P_4) MAY BE PRODUCED FROM THE RAW MATERIALS PROVIDED (P_3) BY MEANS OF *SUB-PROCESS C*

II

PRODUCT P_3 MAY BE PRODUCED FROM PRODUCT P_2 BY MEANS OF *SUB-PROCESS B*

ORDER IN WHICH SUB-PROCESSES ARE TO BE STUDIED	ORDER IN WHICH OBJECTIVES ARE TO BE ACHIEVED
C	I
B	II AND III
A	IV AND V

Outlining the Means of Achieving Specified Aims

1.2. Students of Different Ability

So far the sequencing of instruction has been discussed with only the average student in mind, and there is a need to expand discussion to include all types of students. However, before becoming too involved in this, the course team should give consideration to the type of model to be adopted for the presentation of instruction. Such models, discussed in PART II of this book, indicate alternative ways in which instruction may be designed in order to cater to the different needs of different students. In this respect, it should be noted that core units are designed with the average student in mind, whereas optional and remedial units are designed, respectively, with the above- and below-average students in mind. This means that in developing instruction for a given unit, a course team author can limit his or her thinking concerning any one unit to the needs of a specific target group.

The type of model adopted will reflect the degree to which the course team wishes to treat students differently, and in turn this will depend on the resources available to the course team: the time, the expertise, and the financial resources. However, a final decision concerning the model to be adopted will depend to a certain extent on the activities which immediately follow.

It is suggested that the course team repeat the activities already outlined in Section 1.1 concerning the identification and sequencing of course units, but this time with students of varying ability in mind. The starting points on this occasion will be hierarchical flow diagrams identifying course aims for students of above- and below-average ability as well as for those of average ability. The only difference during this stage of activities will be that the course team will need to think carefully not only about how instruction might be sequenced, but also how this might be done within the constraints of the adopted model. This should help determine to what extent the model is appropriate to course team needs.

Other models could be developed, of course, as long as these are well founded on theories of learning and can be substantiated. However, if this is done, course team members would also need to ascertain for themselves whether or not the procedures described here (PART III) for the production of instructional materials also apply to their new model.

At this stage in the proceedings, the course team should have little difficulty in confirming which course team members will be responsible for the subsequent development of specific units, particularly as individual interests should have emerged clearly during the Phase 1 discussion of course aims.

2. Preparation of Unit Outlines

Each unit author should now undertake to prepare an outline of the contribution which he or she is proposing to make. This may be limited to four or five pages of manuscript notes and diagrams, but it should include clarification of thinking concerning *unit aims and assumptions made* with regard to the target group (*Section 2.1*), proposed *sequencing of instruction* (*Section 2.2*), *methods of instruction* to be adopted within the constraints of the unit model (*Section 2.3*), and *media of instruction,* which may be used in presenting the instruction (*Section 2.4*). Sub-sections 2.1 to 2.4 are concerned with describing how the individual author might go about the preparation of this outline.

2.1. Unit Aims and Assumptions Made

The unit author needs to develop and clarify his or her thinking about the aims to be realized through study of the proposed unit, and may do this by following basically the same procedures as those described for Phase 1 activities. In other words, he or she needs to think more carefully about student needs and the extent to which he or she can meet these through the development of his or her unit. In doing this, he or she needs to give careful thought not only to possible cognitive aims to be achieved, but also to affective aims, particularly those that indicate motivation of the student to achieve the cognitive aims identified. He or she should develop hierarchical flow diagrams to help clarify aims and the relationships among them, and to help identify assumptions made concerning the knowledge, abilities, interests, and motivations of students within the target group concerned. The task is

Outlining the Means of Achieving Specified Aims

somewhat simpler than that described in Phase 1, in that the author may confine his or her thinking to the requirements of a specific target group.

2.2. Sequencing of Instruction

Once appropriate hierarchical flow diagrams have been produced, the unit author may proceed to consider the content of instruction and the way in which it might be sequenced by following the same procedures as those described in Section 1 of this chapter. More specifically, he or she might use a hierarchical approach to help determine the way in which the unit can be broken down into sections and to consider how these might best be sequenced with regard to one another.

2.3. Methods of Instruction

In choosing a particular course model for the presentation of instruction, the course team has already made important decisions concerning methods of instruction to be adopted. Thus, adoption of any one of the models implies that an individualized, objective approach to student learning has already been adopted. The particular model selected determines the extent to which students may be treated individually according to their interests and abilities, and also determines the type of group activities that may be possible.

However, within the constraints of the selected model, there is room for further decision-making concerning methods of instruction that might be adopted, and it is with these that we are concerned here. A variety of methods could be discussed, but the following paragraphs are limited to a brief discussion of two methods. These are of particular interest in that they may be related to the motivation of students to achieve specified cognitive aims. The methods referred to are concerned with *a discovery approach* to learning and the use of *case studies* in instruction.

A Discovery Approach. One of the major principles arising from theories of learning is that students should be actively involved in the learning process (Hilgard and Bower, 1975). This may be achieved to a certain extent by the use of self-assessment questions with feedback and remedial cycles within the adopted model. However, involvement may be increased within the constraints of the model by adopting a discovery approach rather than a reception, or didactic, approach. This does not mean a completely open-ended form of inquiry, where the outcome is unknown to anyone, but, as Skinner (1968) describes it, a guided form of discovery in which the teacher arranges the environment in which the discovery is to take place, suggests the line of inquiry, and provides guidance to the student as necessary. The main point is that the end point should be a discovery *for the student*. The approach attempts to capitalize on the natural curiosity which Rogers (1975) believes to exist in all individuals unless it has been blunted by experience. According to Berlyne (1960), novel stimuli arouse curiosity within the individual, and a discovery approach is intended to provide such stimuli. However, if the prime purpose of the approach is to ultimately achieve certain cognitive aims, it is important to ensure that the aims be realized without too much difficulty and that students perceive the aims to be achieved as important and achievable (Stotland, 1969). If the discovery approach creates too many difficulties, it may lead to frustration and anxiety and a tendency for students to try to escape from the stated goals.

The discovery approach, as described above, is not intended to lead to an understanding of the process of discovery. If the latter is the aim of a particular course, then much more is likely to be required. *Science—A Process Approach*, sponsored by the AAAS Commission on Science Education (1965), is an example of a course that was specifically designed to help students learn something about scientific discovery. As such, it was very much concerned with teaching students basic processes that are commonly used by scientists in experimental inquiry. Its prime concern was with the acquisition of specific process skills rather than with the learning of scientific knowledge. Needless to say, both are required in scientific inquiry.

Case Studies. Real-life case studies may be used in a variety of ways to underline the relevance and importance of concepts presented in a unit. For example, they may be used in the manner of

Outlining the Means of Achieving Specified Aims 93

advance organizers to introduce students to a unit of instruction, by identifying the relevance of concepts to be met within the unit. They also may be made a part of a unit to indicate how newly acquired concepts may be applied to new situations. The prime purpose is to underline the relevance and importance of new concepts within the unit, and to help motivate students towards mastery of these.

2.4. Media of Instruction

The final step in developing a strategy of instruction for a unit is for the author to think carefully about the media to be used in the transmission of information to and from students. Thus, there is a need to consider to what extent media, such as books, slides, tape recordings, filmstrips, films, videotape recordings, television programs, computer programs, and the like, may be used for this purpose.

A number of analytical approaches have been devised by those such as Briggs (1970) and Gagné (1970) to help identify relevant media, but these tend to be oversimplistic in view of the wide variety of factors that need to be taken into account. This is a viewpoint shared by Heidt (1978), based on his analysis of theories and taxonomies that have been proposed for the selection of media. The approach adopted here is to identify the wide variety of factors that need to be taken into consideration through the series of questions which follow. These, and the related comments, are intended to stimulate each author in his or her thinking about his or her particular situation. It may be noted that a factor which appears to be of prime importance in one instance may be of limited importance in another. What is required in each instance is clear, intelligent thinking about the alternatives available, bearing in mind the questions and comments which follow.

Is achievement of any particular aim or objective dependent on the use of any one sense (sight, hearing, smell, taste, or touch) more than any other? Individual course team authors need to ask this question with regard to specific unit aims and objectives which they have identified, and to ask what implications the answer has on the choice of media. For example, if in a course on the environment a particular unit aim is that students should be able to recognize certain bird calls, it is clear that achievement of the aim depends on use of the sense of hearing. Thus, related instruction should make full use of an audio medium. A number of alternatives might be considered, ranging from that of listening to calls in the natural environment to listening to calls on tape recorders, radio, sound film, television, and so on, but at least there is some indication of the type of medium that should be used.

Does the sequencing of instruction affect the choice of media? Considering specific aims and objectives in isolation, as indicated above, normally leaves one with a wide choice of possible media. However, consideration of related aims and objectives can often narrow that choice. For example, in the case referred to above, a tape recorder might be considered appropriate for listening to bird calls, but if a series of related objectives concerning bird recognition is to be achieved with the help of 16mm sound film, it may be more convenient to use this same medium also for listening to the bird calls.

Do decisions concerning the method of instruction to be adopted affect the choice of media? The choice of media can often be influenced by the method of instruction adopted. For example, although radio and television are often used in distance teaching to reach out to large student audiences, these media are much more difficult to use where emphasis is to be placed on an individualized approach to student learning. This is because students progressing at their own individual rates are likely to have very different degrees of knowledge at any fixed point in time when a program might be presented. In such situations, tape recorders, film projectors, and videocassette recorders may often be more appropriate because of their greater flexibility.

Similarly, if emphasis is to be placed on mastery learning within the above individualized approach, then it will be necessary to ensure that feedback and remedial help be available on an individualized basis. Programmed learning materials and computer-aided instruction may be considered for the routine aspects of this work, particularly where large numbers of students are involved and teachers are in short supply.

Outlining the Means of Achieving Specified Aims

Are the media of interest readily available at an acceptable cost? Since in practice many aims can be achieved using alternative forms of media, it makes sense to ask what media are already available. For example, in setting up a distance teaching system in a developing country, it might make little sense to suggest using the medium of television (among others), if this is not already available on a sufficiently wide scale.

Similarly, if potential users of instructional materials do not already have sufficient access to film projectors, videocassette recorders, and the like, care must be taken to ensure that such equipment can be readily obtained and operated. Cost may be a major factor in determining this. However, the question of cost cannot be divorced from that of efficiency in use.

Thus, before deciding, for example, that the cheapest way of teaching students to recognize certain common species of birds is to take them on field trips into the local environment, one should ask whether the necessary learning experiences can be organized in a logical order and within a reasonable space of time, and one must ask whether or not there are more logical and more efficient means of achieving the same ends. It may be that classroom-based media are more appropriate for the detailed learning required. This is not to suggest that field trips are of little value. On the contrary, they may be of considerable value, but for a variety of different purposes. For example, they may be used to introduce students to the study of birds with the intention of identifying the relevance of the subject and to provide students with related motivation. Additionally, they might be used after detailed learning to encourage students to apply what they have learned.

Are the media considered acceptable to both student and teacher? Care must be taken not to overuse any particular medium. Media such as films, television, slides, computer display screens, and the like may result in eye strain when viewed continuously for long periods of time, while any prolonged period of passive viewing of audio-visual programs may too easily lead to boredom on the part of the student.

Care must also be taken to make sure that students and teachers are able to manipulate technical equipment without difficulty, while teachers need to know that if equipment breaks down they have the necessary technical support to have it repaired without major disruption to the teaching program.

Do the abilities of students in the target group suggest any one medium as being more appropriate than another? Bruner (1966) makes an interesting distinction between three types of learning, namely Enactive, Iconic, and Symbolic Modes. The Enactive Mode involves learning through doing, for example, learning to walk. The Iconic Mode involves learning through use of the sensory organs such as one's visual senses, while the Symbolic Mode involves abstract thinking. Bruner sees the Symbolic Mode as the most powerful of the three and the Enactive Mode as the least powerful. He illustrates this by discussing the way in which one might attempt to teach the concepts of longitude and latitude using the different modes in turn. Quite rightly, he points out that if limited to the Enactive Mode one would not get very far. However, permitted to use imagery, as in the Iconic Mode, one could use an orange as a model, by removing the peel in appropriate sections, and laying these out on a horizontal surface to represent almost all the principles of latitude and longitude, including distortion at the poles. In subsequent discussions, one could refer to these concepts in abstract terms as one might do in using the Symbolic Mode.

In considering the appropriateness of a particular mode, it is not sufficient to ask which is the most powerful. One must also ask whether students are able to make full use of the mode proposed. Thus, young children may have much more difficulty in learning with the more powerful modes, whereas more able adults may find less powerful modes sometimes inappropriate to their needs.

3. Frame of Reference

Each author's thinking concerning the development of his or her unit should be summarized in the form of an outline, as already mentioned, and submitted to the course team for discussion purposes. Inevitably, as unit aims and proposed strategies are clarified, interrelationships among units will become clearer, and outline proposals may need to be modified. This should not be a major problem in so far as the outlines available at this stage are relatively brief. Once the outlines have been modified, they will provide a sound frame of reference for the much more extensive development activities to follow in Phase 3.

References

AAAS Commission on Science Education. *Psychological Bases of 'Science–A Process Approach.'* AAAS Publication 65-8. Washington, DC: American Association for the Advancement of Science, 1965.

Ausubel, D.P. *The Psychology of Meaningful Verbal Learning.* New York: Grune and Stratton, 1968.

Berlyne, D.E. *Conflict, Arousal, and Curiosity.* New York: McGraw-Hill Book Co., 1960.

Briggs, L.J. *Handbook of Procedures for the Design of Instruction* (First Edition). (Second Edition: Educational Technology Publications, 1981.) Pittsburgh, Pennsylvania: American Institutes for Research, 1970.

Bruner, J.S. *Toward a Theory of Instruction.* New York: Norton, 1966.

Bruner, J.S. *The Process of Education.* Cambridge, Massachusetts: Harvard University Press, 1970.

Gagné, R.M. *The Conditions of Learning* (Second Edition). New York: Holt, Rinehart, and Winston, 1970.

Gagné, R.M., and Briggs, L.J. *Principles of Instructional Design.* New York: Holt, Rinehart, and Winston, 1974.

Gilbert, T.F. Mathetics: The technology of education. Reprinted in *Recall Supplement No. 1.* London: Longman, 1969.

Heidt, E.V. *Instructional Media and the Individual Learner.* London: Kagan Page, 1978.

Hilgard, E.R., and Bower, G.H. *Theories of Learning.* Englewood Cliffs, New Jersey: Prentice-Hall, Inc., 1975.

Rogers, C. Freedom to learn. In Entwistle, N., and Hounsell, D. (Editors), *How Students Learn.* Lancaster: Institute of Research and Development in Post Compulsory Education, University of Lancaster, 1975, 149-158.

Skinner, B.F. *The Technology of Teaching.* New York: Appleton-Century-Crofts, 1968.

Stotland, E. *The Psychology of Hope.* San Francisco: Jossey-Bass, Inc., 1969.

Chapter 7

Phase 3: Progressive Development and Evaluation of Trial Materials

Phase 3 is concerned with the progressive development of instructional materials through a series of full drafts, each draft being subjected to evaluation at each stage in the process, and developed and refined in light of the feedback received. The process is designed to reduce the probability, and magnitude, of errors in the final instructional materials. The intent is to reduce the probability of such errors at each successive stage in the process, following an approach which Schutz (1970) has described as one of "reducing uncertainty."

This chapter is concerned with describing the basic elements of such an approach. *Section 1* begins the process by describing how authors might set about *preparing the first full-draft presentations* of their units starting from the related outlines which emerged from the Phase 2 activities. Assessment material is not developed at this stage, while media usage may be restricted in the interests of flexibility and economy. For example, if audio-visual materials (such as films, slide-tape presentations, television programs, etc.) are ultimately to be included in a unit of instruction, the first full-draft presentation may make provisional use of simpler and less expensive media (such as scripts, diagrams, and pictures) to indicate how the media will ultimately be used. The intent at this stage is for each author to elaborate on his or her thinking and planning, by opening this up to discussion within the course team. The intent is that the author should clarify his or her thinking, but should not add further detail, such as assessment and media materials, which may discourage further modifications due to the cost and effort involved in related changes. Once the first draft materials have been developed, it is suggested that they be subjected to *course team evaluation* as described in *Section 2*. The second full-draft presentations of instruction emerging from this stage of instruction should not only take note of the feedback received, but should also be developed to include assessment materials and to make fuller use of the media. Nevertheless, the materials are still likely to be restricted in a number of senses. For example, tape recordings and videocassette recordings may be used at this stage instead of radio and television broadcasts, while the assessment material may still need further validation and development. The final stage in the process is described in *Section 3*, and is concerned with *student testing* of the materials with feedback leading to further modification and refinement. The stage of student testing is a particularly extensive one in which materials may first be tested by individual students, then by representative groups of students in controlled conditions, and finally by students in normal field conditions. Each sub-stage referred to may lead to further modifications in the materials.

As the development process proceeds, it may be noted that the evaluative data collected tend to become more objective and reliable, with the most reliable data being collected in the final stages of student testing in the field. However, as the process proceeds, the degree to which substantial changes are possible decreases, simply because materials are added to, and refined, at each successive stage, and a given change has greater implications later in the process, as compared with those done early. This is a problem highlighted by the author (Melton, 1977) in a study of course evaluation at The Open University, and it has two major implications as far as the process of development is concerned. The first point is that although information collected early in the process may be less reliable, it should be acted on when it appears likely that this will reduce the probability of substantial errors in the materials, for such action is more feasible early in the development process. The second point is that although data collected later in the process may suggest the desirability of a number of modifications, it may be necessary to recognize that at this late stage in the process certain (more substantial) changes are not feasible. Where this is the case, it is suggested that related data be stored in an appropriate information bank for use at a later point in time, when the course is likely to be remade. In The Open University, such remakes are usually planned to take place within four to six years of a course being initially presented to students.

1. Preparing the First Full-Draft Presentations

Prior to commencing work on first drafts, it is suggested that each unit author carefully review the related unit outlines which emerged from the Phase 2 activities, refining them further if it is necessary. The outlines provide basic guidance for the development of each unit, for they identify unit aims and objectives to be achieved, assumptions made concerning the target group, perceived relationships among specified aims, and early thinking concerning ways of achieving the aims.

It is suggested that each unit author logically follow a basic process of progressive differentiation (Ausubel, 1968) in developing unit materials. This might be realized through the development of provisional advance organizers, first for the unit and then for related sections within the unit. As development of the unit proceeds, the author is likely to re-draft the initial advance organizers, for development work may clarify the author's earlier thinking. Nevertheless, preparing initial advance organizers in itself is likely to help the author clarify his or her intentions, and it is a process which follows naturally from the outlines available—particularly from any hierarchical diagrams that have been developed.

In drafting an advance organizer for the unit as a whole, the author might usefully address himself or herself to questions such as the following. How is the unit to be broken down into subtopics? Do hierarchical flow diagrams provide useful guidance in identifying an appropriate breakdown into sections? How are the subtopics in the different sections related to one another? How are the subtopics related to the students' existing knowledge? How are the subtopics similar or different from one another? It is not essential to provide answers to each and every one of these questions in drawing up an advance organizer for the unit, but answers should be given if this is to provide students with useful guidance concerning the detailed learning to be presented within the unit. Provisional advance organizers may be prepared for each section of the unit, following a similar process. The only difference is that an advance organizer for a section is concerned with introducing concepts within the section rather than subtopics within the unit. This provisional work should help to identify section headings within the unit and subheadings within each section, providing a natural basis on which to build subsequent instruction. Needless to say, the structure of the content of each unit should reflect the structure perceived in the advance organizer developed.

Chapter 6 has already indicated the type of considerations to be taken into account in determining the strategies of instruction to be adopted, and these have to be borne in mind in developing this presentation and subsequent draft presentations. It has already been noted that the first draft does not need to include assessment materials, but materials should otherwise conform to the requirements of the unit model. Statements of objectives should be included to indicate as clearly as possible what students should be able to do on completion of their studies. However, there is no need to attempt to relate these to domains of test items, although some authors may wish to add a few sample test items to each objective to provide some indication of the type of performance to be achieved. It may be noted here that techniques for producing objectives in general and domain-referenced objectives in particular are discussed in detail later in the book (Chapter 8, PART IV).

As development proceeds, the author will often find himself or herself re-drafting materials in what is basically an iterative process. Ultimately, the intent is to present materials within a consistent system, and the author should aim towards a consistent relationship within each unit between the unit advance organizer, the unit subtopics (and section headings), and the unit summary; and within each section between the section advance organizer, the concepts within each section, and the objectives stated for each section. Once this has been realized to the author's satisfaction, the unit is ready for course team evaluation.

2. Course Team Evaluation

Instructional materials under development have to be evaluated from at least two different points of view, namely that of the subject specialist and that of the student learner. This is a need identified by Scriven (1967) in distinguishing between what he describes as "intrinsic evaluation" and "pay-off evaluation," the former being concerned with evaluation of the content of instruction from the expert's point of view and the latter with evaluation of its learnability from the student's point of view.

In discussing the first full-draft presentation of the units developed, it is suggested that the course team review each unit from both the expert's and the student's point of view, recognizing, of course, that at this stage the course team can only predict the degree to which students will find the materials to be learnable, and that measurement of this will ultimately have to be determined through student testing of the materials (as described in Section 3).

From *the expert's point of view*, the course team has to examine the instructional materials to determine if they are free of errors, if they are logically sequenced, and whether the strategies of instruction adopted appear to be appropriate for presenting the ideas they contain. It may be that the course team will wish to have outside experts also comment on the materials.

From *the student's point of view,* the course team has to examine the instructional materials with the following considerations in mind. *With respect to each unit,* the course team has to ask to what extent the objectives appear to be achievable, bearing in mind the target group and the materials provided. To what extent are students likely to be motivated towards mastering the content of the unit? Will students perceive the objectives to be relevant and important? Are the assumptions made concerning the knowledge, interests, and abilities of the target group acceptable? Are some members of the target group likely to need remedial materials to help them achieve the stated objectives? To what extent are relationships between advance organizers, content, and objectives consistent within the unit? Is instruction sequenced in a logical manner? Are the media and teaching strategies appropriate? Will the unit motivate students to study the subject further? How long will it take the students to master the content of the unit? Is the load too great? *With respect to the course as a whole*, the course team has to look carefully at the relationships between each unit and the course as a whole. Thus, there is a need to examine to what extent each unit presumes to build on learning from prior units and the extent to which each unit may contribute to the prerequisite needs of subsequent units. There is in fact a need to ensure continuity in general throughout the course, and this extends to continuity in matters such as the use of symbols, terms, and concepts, to mention but a few factors. Finally, it should be noted that student learning may be affected by factors that may have their origin some distance from the student-teaching interface, and the course team should review such factors as much as possible. Thus, it should ask whether the materials developed are likely to give rise to teaching or administrative problems. It may be that the cost of support services is prohibitive, that the administration required is unacceptably complex, or that the load placed on teachers is too great, and such factors should be taken into consideration.

Second draft presentations of each unit should be prepared in light of the feedback received. The new drafts should make use of media in line with the ultimate intentions, while assessment material should be developed so that each second draft unit will conform as closely as possible to the requirements of the unit model. Use will need to be made of the techniques described in Chapter 8, PART IV for generating domain-referenced objectives. As far as related assessment materials are concerned, all that can be expected is that self-assessment materials and final unit tests will appear to be equivalent to one another. The production of equivalent forms of tests depends on fairly rigorous development procedures (Chapter 9, PART IV), and these cannot be undertaken until the materials are subjected to student testing. Apart from developing new drafts for each unit, the course team chairperson should prepare advance organizers and summaries for each block of units within the course and for the course as a whole. All related materials should then be reviewed by the course team before being subjected to student testing.

3. Student Testing

This section describes three sequential stages of student testing to which instructional materials might be submitted. The stages described are effectively the same as those discussed by Thiagarajan (1976) and are well recognized in the literature. The first stage is one of *individual try-out* (*Section 3.1*), that is, one in which the instructional materials are tried out by an individual student, or by a small number of successive individuals. It is particularly useful for identifying errors and for illuminating aspects that require further investigation. The second stage is one of *group try-out* (*Section 3.2*), that is, one in which the materials are tried out by a small group of students under controlled conditions. The objectivity of findings and recommendations at this stage will depend very much on the number of students involved, but the intent is to identify common difficulties, problems, and errors, and to suggest ways in which these might be reduced or eliminated. The third stage is one of *field testing* (*Section 3.3*), that is, one in which the materials are tried out under the conditions for which they have been designed. Thus, new national instructional materials might be field tested on a large scale across the country, rather than in a limited number of pilot locations. The idea of three sequential stages of student testing of materials can be traced back well beyond Thiagarajan. In this respect, it may be noted that Markle (1967) described an almost identical process much earlier, although she used somewhat different terminology, describing the corresponding stages as being concerned with "developmental testing," "validation testing," and "field testing."

Whether or not a course team decides to proceed through each and every stage described here will depend very much on the particular circumstances involved. It is argued that some form of student testing is essential, but it is also recognized that a full three-stage program of testing would make considerable demands on a course team in terms of time, effort, and expenditures, and that this needs to be justified in the circumstances involved. Thus, an extensive testing program is more likely to be justified in circumstances where the target population is large, where the new materials are likely to be used without modification over a number of years, where the materials have a particular uniqueness and importance, and where the investment in the materials (in terms of time, effort, and expenditures) is already considerable.

Where a course team decides to reduce the number of stages involved in student testing, it may be tempted to eliminate stage 1. Thus, in reviewing a number of evaluation projects, Henderson and Nathenson (1980) indicate that it is difficult to find any example of materials that have passed through all three stages of student testing, although they identify a number of instances where materials passed through the last two stages, in some cases with successive repetition of one or both stages. Baker (1974), in fact, has described a two-stage process of testing encompassing the latter two stages only. Should such an approach be adopted, care should be taken to ensure that the group try-out stage includes an element of open-endedness about the investigation. Thus, although many questions will suggest themselves to the course team before the testing begins, it should be recognized that the group try-out may illuminate issues that previously had not been given consideration. In Parlett and Hamilton's (1976) terms, the importance of illuminative evaluation must not be ignored.

3.1. Individual Try-out

Although the individual try-out approach has often been used in the development of programmed learning materials, and there are those, such as Gilbert (1960), who claim that fewer than ten successive try-outs will lead to the development of a program which will be found acceptable to the vast majority of students, it does have severe limitations as far as most course development is concerned. The major problem is the time required for such an approach. Thus, in The Open University, a full credit course involves the average student in about 400 hours of study, and it would clearly be impractical to submit all materials to a process of successive individual try-outs. Nevertheless, there are specific components that may be tested following this approach, while there are authors who find feedback from the individual student valuable in identifying overlooked errors and aspects that need to be reviewed on a more careful basis.

3.2. Group Try-out

The group try-out stage is designed to identify problems that are likely to affect students in the target group and to suggest ways in which these problems might be eliminated or reduced. Being very much concerned with measurement and prediction, it should be carried out, as far as possible, under controlled conditions using students representative of the target group. Inevitably, there will be ways in which the group try-out situation will fall short of the ultimate field conditions, but this does not prevent the collecting of valuable information. However, it does mean that care should be taken in interpreting the information, taking careful note of the way in which predictions might need to be modified under field conditions.

A wide variety of evaluation techniques may be used in any group try-out or field testing situation, and Steadman (1976) provides a broad perspective of techniques that might be considered, ranging from the use of questionnaires, attainment tests, and controlled experiments to case studies, group discussions, and conferences. However, the intent here is not to discuss all possible techniques, but to focus on a limited number which might readily be adopted by any course team to rapidly illuminate the effect of a wide range of factors on student learning and attitudes. The approach described is based on techniques and procedures developed by the author (Melton, 1977, 1978) for use in The Open University.

Central to the approach is *the measurement of student achievement of the stated objectives*, both cognitive and affective, for the prime purpose of the instructional materials is to ultimately ensure that students are able to achieve the stated objectives as far as this is possible. All other aspects of the evaluation approach are concerned with *identifying factors which explain failure to achieve the stated objectives*, this being undertaken with a view to hypothesizing ways in which subsequent student achievement might be improved by related modifications of the instructional materials. Within this framework, the sub-sections which follow are concerned with describing how related factors affecting student achievement may be identified. Three basic approaches are adopted. The first is based on an *analysis of student achievement* itself. The second is based on an *analysis of student perception of difficulties*. The third is based on an *analysis of the perceptions of teachers and administrators* as to factors giving rise to student problems. The main point of the latter is that the cause of some student problems may have their origins well removed from the student-teaching interface, and teachers and administrators may be more able to identify the original cause.

Analysis of Student Achievement. Figure 15 indicates in algorithmic format the basic approach to the use of tests in any group try-out of instructions. It is suggested that pre-tests and post-tests be developed for each unit of instruction.

The pre-test for each unit should be designed to measure to what extent students possess the knowledge, skills, and motivations which the author has assumed in preparing the related instruction. When a substantial proportion of students fails to demonstrate possession (or mastery) of a particular requirement, the course team must give careful consideration to questions such as the following. Does the pre-test provide an acceptable measure of the prerequisite requirements? Should some of the test items be modified before accepting related data as reliable? Should any of the assumptions be modified? If so, to what extent will the instructional materials need to be modified to take the new assumptions into account? Could the test be used in the future as a means of advising students on the extent to which they possess the necessary prerequisites? If so, is it possible to identify remedial materials which might be studied by those without the necessary requirements? To what extent is the course team able to identify, provide, or develop remedial materials for such purposes?

The post-test for each unit may be the final test already developed by the unit author, and this may be used in a manner similar to the pre-test. As with the pre-test, the post-test itself has

Figure 15

*Algorithm Indicating How Pre-Tests and Post-Tests
May Be Used to Review Both the Appropriateness of
Specified Objectives and Stated Assumptions and
the Adequacy of Existing Instruction*

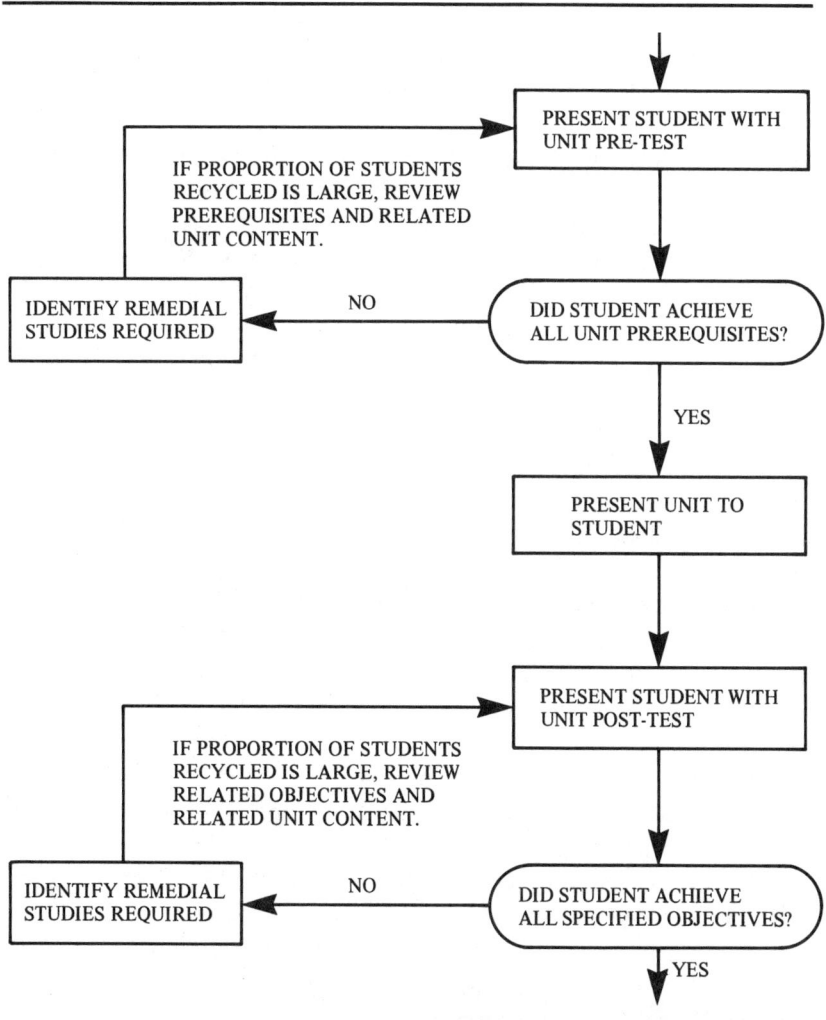

still not been validated, and if a substantial proportion of students fails to master any particular item, then the first requirement is to examine the item itself for weaknesses. This done the course team needs to review related instruction to determine whether the explanation of poor performance can be identified there. Item analysis may be used to good effect for this purpose, and it is discussed in greater detail later in the book (Chapter 9, PART IV). It may be that errors exist in the instruction. However, it is possible that all that is required is for students to re-study the related material more carefully. Nevertheless, failure to understand a particular point may suggest that the point might be clarified further in the instruction concerned. It may be decided that remedial materials might be required for some of the weaker students. This could, for example, include alternative ways of looking at a particular concept. It might also be decided that it is unreasonable to expect all students to master a particular objective, and that it should be either removed altogether or transferred elsewhere in the course as optional learning for more able students.

Although item analysis is helpful in identifying weaknesses in instruction, it does have limitations, and it is particularly helpful, therefore, to have available a review of problem areas perceived by students, teachers, and administrators to reinforce course team discussions.

Analysis of Student Perception of Difficulties. Student perception of difficulties might be illuminated by two different forms of inquiry conducted in parallel with one another. The two forms of inquiry, namely open-ended and strongly-guided, are complementary to one another.

An open-ended form of inquiry might be pursued through discussion with individual students or groups of students, with the intent of identifying strengths and weaknesses that have not been previously considered. Inevitably, the problems of one or two individuals may not turn out to be representative of those of the target group, and wherever possible, such discussions should be followed by related questionnaires to determine to what extent perceived problems are common to the group as a whole.

Progressive Development and Evaluation of Trial Materials

For the strongly-guided form of inquiry, questionnaires may be designed prior to the commencement of the group try-outs, and the following paragraphs indicate the type of questions which might be included. Needless to say, the questions would need to be expressed in terms of related instructional material and presented in a manner that lends itself readily to analysis, and techniques for doing this are discussed later in this book (Chapter 10, PART IV).

Since one of the prime concerns of any course is to enable students to achieve the objectives specified, this provides a logical starting point. Thus, students may be asked to what extent they had difficulty in mastering specified objectives. Although one might anticipate a close correlation between perceived difficulty and the degree of relative mastery observed, this need not always be the case. For example, students may have considerable difficulty with instruction leading towards mastery of a particular objective, and yet a large proportion may still achieve the desired mastery. Such data are thus complementary rather than simply repetitive. Questions concerning difficulty with objectives lead naturally to questions concerning difficulties with related concepts, principles, terms, and skills. In turn, this suggests the need to investigate the acceptability of assumptions made concerning the knowledge, skills, interests, and motivations that students would have on beginning their studies. There is a need to examine the clarity of the materials and the consistency of relationships between various elements, such as advance organizers, content, objectives, assessment, and summaries, to examine the logical development of concepts, and to review the acceptability of strategies adopted. Motivation towards specified cognitive objectives may be monitored at various points in time during the course of related studies, and note made of the extent to which students perceive particular goals to be both relevant and important to their needs as well as achievable. There may be other student perceptions which the course team will wish to explore, and these will be determined in light of the situation concerned.

Analysis of the Perceptions of Teachers and Administrators. Student learning may be affected by factors that are not obvious to the student, and an analysis of student perception of difficulties may in itself be insufficient to identify the root cause of a problem. Both open-ended and strongly-guided forms of inquiry may be pursued to complement those concerning student perception of difficulties. In this respect, it is logical to look at factors which affect administrators and teachers and thereby affect the quality of instruction. Thus, one might investigate to what extent teachers and administrators are overloaded by the project, whether supporting facilities are adequate, and whether equipment and other resources, such as space, are adequate to meet the perceived needs. One might explore attitudes of teachers and administrators towards the instructional materials developed. Their motivation towards achieving the goals of the program may be a vital factor in determining its success.

Once the various forms of analysis have been completed, the course team will want to discuss what modifications should be made to the instructional materials, and the revised drafts will need to be reviewed again before they are considered ready for the final field testing stage.

3.3. Field Testing

Whereas the group try-out may be conducted under somewhat limited conditions, field testing should be carried out under the conditions for which the instructional materials were designed. In many respects, the field testing may resemble the group try-out, with the use of similar tests and questionnaires focusing on similar issues. Inevitably, there will be some additional questions raised in light of the new conditions under which the materials are being tested, but by and large this stage should be seen more as one of refinement rather than one of substantial change.

The later stages of field testing are particularly appropriate for determining the equivalence (Angoff, 1971) of alternative forms of given unit tests, that is, for determining how scores on one form of a given test may be equated to scores on alternative forms of the same test. However, this cannot be done until after the alternative forms of tests have been finalized, since any change to a given form of test is likely to invalidate comparisons that have been made between it and alternative forms of the same test. Techniques for establishing the equivalence of alternative forms of test are in fact discussed later in the book (Chapter 9, Part IV).

In discussing the findings of field testing, the course team will need to decide to what extent modifications can still be made in the materials, bearing in mind all the implications involved. Much can be done at this stage in the way of refining materials, but substantial changes should be avoided as much as possible, unless the new materials can be recycled through the evaluation described in Phase 3. The fact that some information may not be acted upon at this point in time should not be a matter of major concern. Most instructional materials can be improved on a continuous basis, and it is logical to collect relevant data from this point onwards with a view to using them in the remaking of the course at some subsequent point in time.

References

Angoff, W.H. Scales, norms, and equivalent scores. In Thorndike, R.L. (Editor), *Educational Measurement.* Washington, DC: American Council on Education, 1971, 508-600.

Ausubel, D.P. *The Psychology of Meaningful Verbal Learning.* New York: Grune and Stratton, 1968.

Baker, E.L. Formative evaluation of instruction. In Popham, W.J. (Editor), *Evaluation in Education: Current Applications.* Berkeley, California: McCutchan, 1974, 531-585.

Gilbert, T.F. On the relevance of laboratory investigations of learning to self-instructional programming. In Lumsdaine, A.A., and Glaser, R. (Editors), *Teaching Machines and Programmed Learning: A Source Book.* Washington, DC: National Education Association, 1960, 475-485.

Henderson, E.S., and Nathenson, M.B. *Using Student Feedback to Improve Learning Materials.* London: Croom Helm, Ltd., 1980.

Markle, S.M. Empirical testing of programs. In Lange, P.C. (Editor), *Programmed Instruction.* 66th NSSE Yearbook, Part 2. Chicago: National Society for Study of Education, 1967.

Melton, R.F. Course evaluation at The Open University: A case study. *British Journal of Educational Technology,* 1977, *8,* 97-102.

Melton, R.F. Item analysis at The Open University: A case study. *British Journal of Educational Technology,* 1978, *9,* 111-130.

Parlett, M., and Hamilton, D. Evaluation as illumination. In Tawney, D. (Editor), *Curriculum Evaluation Today: Trends and Implications.* A Schools Council Publication. London: Macmillan Education, Ltd., 1976, 84-101.

Schutz, R.E. The nature of educational development. *Journal of Research and Development in Education,* 1970, *2,* 39-64.

Scriven, M. The methodology of evaluation. In Tyler, R.W., Gagné, R.M., and Scriven, M. (Editors), *Perspectives of Curriculum Evaluation.* AERA Monograph on Curriculum Evaluation, No. 1. Chicago: Rand McNally, 1967, 39-83.

Steadman, S. Techniques of evaluation. In Tawney, D. (Editor), *Curriculum Evaluation Today: Trends and Implications.* A Schools Council Publication. London: Macmillan Education, Ltd., 1976, 55-83.

Thiagarajan, S. Learner verification and revision: What, who, when, and how? *Audiovisual Instruction,* 1976, January, 18-19.

Part IV

Basic Skills Required for Course Development

In order to carry out the course development procedures described in PART III, additional skills are likely to be required. This part of the book is concerned with providing sufficient knowledge and skills to ensure that course teams so wishing can adopt a fairly rigorous approach to the process of course development. However, in saying this, it is recognized that not all course teams will wish to approach the development process with the same degree of rigor. The point to recognize here is that the effort put into the development of a course is likely to depend to a large extent on the resources that can be made available in terms of personnel, time, and financing, and that in turn the provision of such resources is likely to depend on other factors, such as the life expectancy of the course, the number of students likely to be affected by it, and the expected impact of the course on students and other interested parties. In other words, course teams must decide for themselves to what extent they should adopt the techniques described. Nevertheless, if such decisions are to be made on an informed basis, with course teams recognizing the weaknesses likely to arise from less rigorous approaches, then it is considered essential that course teams at least be conversant with the contents of this part of the book, regardless of the degree to which they subsequently adopt the techniques described. Bearing the above points in mind, readers should find that this part of the book provides them with sufficient knowledge and skills to undertake course development with reasonable confidence. The knowledge and skills referred to are in fact discussed here within four chapters, as described below.

Chapter 8 is concerned primarily with *the development of domain-descriptions,* taking note of the way in which a specific domain-description may be used to generate alternative forms of tests to measure student mastery of the related objective. It is noted that since a unit of instruction may cover a number of objectives, several domain-descriptions may be required to generate alternative forms of any given unit test.

Chapter 9 discusses techniques that may be used in *analyzing and developing unit tests,* regardless of whether these are in the form of alternative final tests (to be responded to on completion of the unit of study) or in the form of self-assessment questions within a unit (to be responded to while studying the unit). Since the techniques described may be used to help identify weaknesses in test items, they may be used in turn to help identify weaknesses in domain-descriptions that have been used in generating the related items.

It follows that *Chapters 8* and *9* highlight an iterative process in which domain-descriptions are used to generate related tests, and in which the analysis of the tests leads to subsequent modification of the related domain-descriptions.

In looking at ways of analyzing and developing tests (in *Chapter 9*), note is taken of how basically the same process may be used to help evaluate not only the tests and related domain-descriptions, but also the related instruction. However, this is not the only way in which instruction may be evaluated, and *Chapter 10* discusses complementary techniques of evaluation based on the use of questionnaires for *monitoring student perceptions of, and attitudes towards, instruction.*

Finally, *Chapter 11* is concerned with *the interpretation of unit test scores,* bearing in mind that a unit test provides no more than an estimate of a student's competence with regard to the unit as a whole.

Chapter 8

The Development of Domain-Descriptions

This chapter begins (*Section 1*) by looking at *the nature of domain-referenced objectives,* note being made of the characteristics of simple domain-descriptions and the way in which they might be used to help generate related domain-referenced tests. It then goes on (*Section 2*) to consider different techniques that may be used for *developing domain-descriptions.* It follows automatically that in developing domain-descriptions, one must give careful thought to the types of items (multiple-choice, essay type, etc.) that are to be included in the domain, and the chapter concludes (*Section 3*) with a brief discussion of factors that need to be taken into account in considering *different item types.*

1. The Nature of Domain-Referenced Objectives

The basic characteristics of domain-referenced objectives have already been discussed in PART II of this book, in considering the way in which such objectives might be used in different types of instructional models. The intent here is not to repeat, or elaborate on, this discussion, but to provide readers with additional insights into the nature of domain-referenced objectives that may help them in generating such objectives for themselves.

The nature of domain-referenced objectives in fact emerges clearly if we look at the nature of the background from which they have emerged. The section therefore begins (*Section 1.1*) by looking at *the background* from which educational and behavioral objectives emerged, and then goes on (*Section 1.2*) to look more closely at the *basic characteristics of behavioral objectives.* The reason for doing this is that domain-referenced objectives might be perceived as a special form of behavioral objective, and insights into the latter provide a greater understanding of the nature of domain-referenced objectives. This becomes clearer from the subsequent discussion (*Section 1.3*) concerning the *characteristics of domain-referenced objectives*, where note is taken of the way in which the design of domain-referenced objectives might be described as improving on that of behavioral objectives.

1.1. The Background

The need for educational objectives to be expressed as clearly and unambiguously as possible was the subject of much discussion even in the early part of this century, with researchers such as Search (1901), Thorndike (1911), Burck (1913), and Bobbitt (1918) contributing significantly to the debate. However, the idea of expressing such objectives in terms of "behaviors to be achieved by students" did not emerge until much later. Tyler's (1934) contributions to the debate were a significant milestone in the development of the concept of behavioral objectives. In a clear exposition of why educational objectives might be usefully expressed in behavioral terms, Tyler argued that:

> "Each objective must be defined in terms which clarify the kind of behavior which (a) course should help to develop among the students...This helps to make clear how one can tell when the objective is being attained, since those who are reaching the objective will be characterized by the behavior specified..."

These ideas were subsequently placed in a broader perspective by Skinner (1957), who argued that:

> "(The) concepts and methods which have emerged from the analysis of behavior ... are the most appropriate to the study of what has traditionally been called the human mind."

Despite these early beginnings, the behavioral objectives movement did not have a wide effect on educational practice until the 1960s. As Popham (1969) reports, at that time there was a "swelling of interest and activity in instructional objectives," with "educators, in large numbers, beginning to think rigorously regarding the issues involved in specifying educational goals." A number of factors are likely to have contributed to this rapid growth in interest. In particular, the literature was continuing to grow, bringing with it an increased understanding of behavioral objectives, while Mager's (1962) classic book on *Preparing Instructional Objectives* provided considerable impetus to the movement by making the concept of behavioral objectives comprehensible to most educators.

1.2. Basic Characteristics of Behavioral Objectives

Mager (1962) argued that if we are to be able to measure the acquisition of knowledge, we must have some outward manifestation of its existence, and we should look for this in student behavior. With this in mind, he went on to describe how objectives might be expressed in terms of behavior, suggesting that a behavioral objective should contain three basic elements. These he identified as including statements of:
- the behavior to be observed,
- the conditions under which the behavior should be observed, and
- the level of performance considered acceptable as an indication of achievement of the objective.

An example of a behavioral objective is quoted below to illustrate these characteristics.

"Given the names of the concepts listed below (Figure 16) and a list of definitions, the student should be able to identify correct definitions of at least 80 percent of the concepts within a period of five minutes without referring to related instructional material."

It may be noted that the behavior to be observed is that "the student should be able to identify correct definitions" of the different concepts. The conditions under which the behavior is to be observed are the student must be "given the names of the concepts listed," and that he or she must answer "without referring to related instructional material." The level of performance required to indicate mastery of the objective is that "the student should be able to identify correct definitions of at least 80 percent of the concepts within a period of five minutes."

Mager argues that such objectives should not only indicate what is expected of the student, but also should indicate how mastery of the objective might be measured. In other words, the objective

Figure 16

*List of Concepts to Be
Defined According to Stated Objective*

R and D Budgets

R and D Goals

Scientific Merit

Nitrogen Fixation

Eutrophication

Extrinsic Criteria

Intrinsic Criteria

---

should identify test items that might be used to measure achievement of the objective. Thus, in the example above, one should provide students with a list of definitions from which to identify the correct ones, and one should not attempt to measure the objective by asking students to define the listed concepts in their own words. The point here is that the test item(s) required to measure achievement of the objective should not require a higher or lower level of performance than that stated in the objective. The logic behind this is that if the test item demands a higher level of performance, failure to master the test item will not necessarily indicate failure to achieve the stated objective. Conversely, if the test item demands a lower level of performance, mastery of the test item will not necessarily imply mastery of the objective. The relationship between objective and test item envisaged by Mager was one which enabled the measurer to relate student success or

The Development of Domain-Descriptions

failure on a test item to success or failure in an attempt to master a related objective.

Although researchers such as Walbesser (1970), Briggs and Gagné (1974), the author (Melton, 1976), and others have attempted to make behavioral objectives more explicit by identifying additional elements to which attention might be paid in developing statements of objectives, the related objectives still reflect the same *basic elements* as those described by Mager.

1.3. Characteristics of Domain-Referenced Objectives

Much has been learned about the strengths and weaknesses of behavioral objectives since the 1960s, and the findings have been well summarized in major reviews by Walbesser and Eisenberg (1972), Duchastel and Merrill (1973), Macdonald-Ross (1973), Barth (1974), and Melton (1978).

Needless to say, behavioral objectives have their weaknesses as well as strengths, and one of the greatest weaknesses is what Macdonald-Ross (1973) describes as the specificity problem, that is, the fact that "if you have only a few general objectives they are easy to remember and handle, but too vague and ambiguous (to be helpful), but if you try to eliminate the ambiguity by splitting down the objectives and by qualifying the conditions of performance, then the list becomes impossibly long." The domain-referenced objective is seen as largely overcoming this apparently intractable problem. The way in which it achieves this is probably best illustrated in the first instance by looking at how a fairly explicit behavioral objective might be clarified by referencing it to a domain of test items, that is, by converting it to a domain-referenced objective. The example in Figure 17 should help illustrate the point.

It will be noted that the objective to be achieved is expressed in fairly explicit behavioral terms, namely that:

> "Given any ten pairs of two-digit numbers, you should be able to compute the product of at least nine out of ten pairs correctly within a period of five minutes."

At first glance, it would appear that the ten pairs of numbers used to measure student achievement of the objective might be selected

Figure 17

A Simple Domain-Description

Objective

Given any ten pairs of two-digit numbers, you should be able to compute the product of at least nine out of ten pairs correctly within a period of five minutes.

Sample Test Items

12x11 =	(11) (15) =
16x13 =	(18) (14) =
17x18 =	13 times 16 =
14.12 =	19 multiplied by 19 =
10.10 =	the product of 15 and 11 =

Item Characteristics

1. Test items to measure mastery of the objective will be selected at random from a matrix containing all possible pairs of two-digit numbers, that is, from a matrix of 8,100 possible items.

2. Each test will contain the six item formats that are included in the above sample, and the formats used will be distributed in the same manner between test items.

The Development of Domain-Descriptions

from a domain of 8,100 different pair combinations (assuming that the reverse presentation of any given pair of numbers produces two different combinations). In fact, the domain of possible items from which selection is possible may be considerably greater than this. Thus, in the example in Figure 17, the sample test items include six alternative forms of presentation, and from the description of the item characteristics, it is clear that the domain from which selection is made contains 48,600 items.

Not all domains can be described in such simple terms, particularly if the objective is stated in much broader terms than those in the example discussed. Nevertheless, the principle remains the same, namely that of clarifying the objective by means of a sample of items drawn from the domain together with a description of the characteristics of items within the domain. The approach, in fact, permits objectives to be stated in much broader terms than is the case with conventional behavioral objectives, since sample items and domain-descriptions may be used to provide necessary clarification. However, if objectives are expressed in relatively broad terms, related domain-descriptions still need to provide essential clarification, and these are likely to contain much more detail than that found in the simple example illustrated (Figure 17). To present such detail to students might be confusing and counter-productive, and the strategy adopted within all the instructional models discussed in this book is simply to provide students with a statement of the objective itself together with a sample of items (self-assessment questions) drawn from the related domain. The view taken here is that the sample of items not only identifies the characteristics of the domain, but also provides a clear indication of the characteristics of the equivalent final test which will be used to measure students' performance with regard to the stated objective. Whether or not students should be provided with full domain-descriptions, however, may be a matter for further debate and research.

2. Developing Domain-Descriptions

The effort put into the development of domain-descriptions and related tests will tend to depend on the resources available for this purpose. Nevertheless, even where resources are limited, it is suggested that there is much to be gained from undertaking the development work in stages, as described below, rather than in a single "one-time" effort.

During the first stage, it is suggested that course team members should develop relatively simple domain-descriptions for each specified objective in the unit of instruction for which they are responsible. The intent should be to produce domain-descriptions with the same basic characteristics as those of the description illustrated in Figure 17. To do this, course team members should complete three basic tasks with regard to each objective, that is, they should:

- State the objective in behavioral terms, recognizing that the statement may be in broader terms than those normally associated with behavioral objectives, so long as the related domain-description provides a clear indication of what students should be able to do.
- Identify the characteristics of items that may be included in the domain to measure student mastery of the objective, recognizing that the domain so described defines the objective.
- Produce a sample of items that are representative of those found in the domain, and which thus illustrate the characteristics of items within the domain.

For obvious reasons, this approach is usually described as an 'amplified objective' approach to domain-description.

Once simple domain-descriptions have been produced, these should be used to help generate alternative forms of tests not only for each individual objective, but also for each unit as a whole. The tests should then be subjected to student testing, and Chapter 9 describes how item analysis procedures might be used during the "group try-out" stage of student testing to help identify weaknesses in the tests, and hence in the related domain-descriptions.

The next step (or stage) is to use the feedback collected to help improve the domain-descriptions, and to use the refined descriptions to generate further test items—replacing items that have already been identified as having weaknesses. (Where particularly

The Development of Domain-Descriptions

rigorous tests are to be developed, the whole process of testing and development may be repeated several times.)

In recommending that domain-descriptions be developed in stages, one of the main intents is to avoid unnecessary expenditure of effort in clarifying the characteristics of a domain before the acceptability of the domain has been ascertained. The point is that feedback—for example, from the "group try-out" stage—may suggest the need for some objectives to be substantially modified, and it would appear to be unwise to put too much effort into the development of related domains prior to such student testing.

At this point, it may be helpful to look at an example of a rather more elaborate domain-description, and the description found in Figure 18 is included for this purpose. At first glance, it may appear that the format of this description is not the same as that used for the domain-description in Figure 17, but closer inspection will show that the two have essentially the same basic characteristics. Thus, comparing the description in Figure 18 with that in Figure 17, it may be noted that the "general description" corresponds to the statement of the "objective," the "sample item" to the "sample test items," and the "stimulus and response attributes" to the "item characteristics." Of course, the degree of detail in the two descriptions is very different, but this depends in part on the generality of the stated objective and on the judgment of the individual as to the extent to which this needs to be clarified.

Finally, it should be noted that the "amplified objective" approach described is not the only approach to developing domain-descriptions, and readers interested in developing rigorous tests, either for wide-scale use on a national basis or for research purposes, should review a variety of other approaches that have been developed. These include the linguistic transformation approaches developed by Bormuth (1970) and Anderson (1972), the somewhat similar sentence-mapping, or facet-design, approach developed by Guttman (1969), and the item shell, or item form, type of approach developed by Hively *et al.* (1973).

Figure 18

A Domain-Description of an 'Amplified Objective'

An illustrative set of criterion-referenced test specifications: job interview procedures

General description

Having read a description of a job interview in which the applicant may make one of several specified types of errors in appearance, conduct, or preparation, the student will select the error made or indicate that no error was made.

Sample item

Directions: Read the description of each job interview below. If the applicant makes an error in interview behavior, mark the letter of the response alternative that matches the error described. If no error was made, mark "e."

> Anita arrives five minutes early for an interview for a trainee job in floral design and sales. She wears a white dress with long, full sleeves and shoes with high heels. She brings a portfolio of her work as a design major in high school and briefly points out the designs she feels are most closely related to floristry. She answers the interviewer's questions in a brief, courteous manner and indicates her willingness to perform all aspects of the florist's trade, including scrubbing floors, washing buckets, and disposing of spoiled flowers.
>
> What is Anita's error?
>
> (a) lack of punctuality
> (b) inappropriate dress
> (c) irrelevant materials presented
> (d) inappropriate attitude
> (e) no error was made

Stimulus attributes

1. Each item will consist of a fictitious description of 100 words or less dealing with a named person's job interview, followed by that person's name inserted into the question, "What is ....'s error?"

2. The description will include the type of job being applied for and illustrations of at least four of the following behavioral factors that may influence an impression of an applicant:

(a) Punctuality–arrival at or within a reasonable time before the specified interview time. Arrival after the specified time, or arrival more than ½ hour early will be considered lack of punctuality, as both may inconvenience the interviewer.

(b) Appropriateness of dress– dress which is neat, clean, and practical for the type of job being applied for. If one expects that an interview may include a demonstration of

Figure 18 (Continued)

skills, one's clothing must not interfere with such a demonstration. Extremes such as very high heels, low cut dresses, very tight pants, etc., are almost always inappropriate. Appropriateness of dress also includes such personal grooming items as length of fingernails, length and style of hair, etc., which are inappropriate only if they are likely to interfere with the work involved in the job being applied for (e.g., long fingernails on a secretarial applicant).

(c) General courtesy—pleasantness and politeness to all individuals encountered before, during, and after the interview.

(d) Frankness—honesty and directness in answer to personal or experience-related questions. False answers, misleading answers, attempts to change the subject, or attempts to rationalize answers will be considered lack of frankness.

(e) Careful thought to answers—brief, clear, well-thought-out answers to problems posed by interviewer. Excessive wordiness, self-contradiction, disorganized answers, and answers that do nothing more than reiterate the problem will be considered evidence of lack of careful thought to answers.

(f) Appropriateness of attitude—interest and enthusiasm displayed toward all aspects of job, but without pushiness or opinionatedness. Interest and enthusiasm may be indicated by simply stating their presence (e.g., "John appears very interested in the techniques demonstrated") or by a direct or indirect quotation on the part of the applicant expressing enthusiasm or interest (e.g., "Of course I don't mind emptying buckets, I want to learn all about the business"). Pushiness and opinionatedness may be indicated by attempts to tell the interviewer how the business should be run, boasting about superiority of knowledge or ability (as opposed to offering to demonstrate ability), sarcastic comments, attempts to bully interviewer, and similar actions. General lack of enthusiasm (indicated by description or quotation), complaints about specific aspects of the job, or the presence of any of the indications of pushiness or opinionatedness will be considered inappropriate attitude.

(g) Relevance of materials presented—direct and obvious relationship to job being applied for of any education or experience-related materials brought to interview. Examples of appropriate materials are a typing award for a secretarial applicant, or a portfolio of works from a high school design course for an applicant in any art- or design-related field. Examples of inappropriate materials are a tennis award for an engineering applicant, or a record of offices held in high school for a janitorial applicant. The relevance or irrelevance of such materials may be made more obvious by describing the applicant's mode of presentation (e.g., "She brings a portfolio of her work as a design major in high school and briefly points out the designs she feels are most closely related to floristry"), or by indicating the purpose of the applicant in bringing the material (e.g., "John, who is applying for a job as an engineer, brings a letter of recommendation from his previous employer (who runs a hamburger stand) to show his reliability and industriousness").

(h) Specific and realistic goals—applicants' ability to explain their purpose for applying for the job (to start a career, earn money for college, etc.) and what working conditions, salary, and rate of advancement they expect. Inability to answer specific questions dealing with these issues (e.g., "What salary do you expect?" "I don't know. What did you plan to pay?") or working conditions, salary, or advancement expectations that are exceptionally high or low for the job being applied for (e.g., plans to be vice-president of company within two years of being hired as a secretary, or asking only

Figure 18 (Continued)

$2.50 per/hour for work requiring a graduate degree or highly specialized training), will be considered lack of specific and realistic goals.

3. The interview description may illustrate completely correct behavior, or one of the behavioral factors illustrated may exemplify erroneous behavior, whereas the rest of the description exemplifies correct behavior. No more than 20 percent of the test items will exemplify completely correct behavior.

4. The description may include direct quotation of the interviewer and/or the interviewee, as well as a description of their actions and conversation.

5. If several descriptions are used in a test, the names given to interviewers will be evenly divided between male and female, and will include some names characteristic of the most common ethnic groups in the population to be tested. The name to be used with a given job will be chosen at random so that discrimination cannot be made on the basis of sex or ethnic group.

6. The readability of the descriptions will be no higher than tenth-grade level.

Response attributes

1. The students will mark on their answer sheets the letter that corresponds to the error made by the job applicant (if any) or the statement that "no error was made."

2. There will be five alternatives, consisting of the correct response and four distractors. The options will include the response "no error was made" along with four of the following behavior factors: lack of punctuality, inappropriate dress, lack of general courtesy, lack of frankness, lack of careful thought to answers, inappropriate attitude, irrelevant materials presented, and lack of specific and realistic goals. The four behavioral factors chosen will correspond to four of the factors illustrated in the interview description and will include that factor (if any) in which an error is illustrated.

3. The correct response will be that alternative that correctly names the error illustrated in the description of the interview description, or, in the event that no error was illustrated, that alternative that states "no error was made."

Reprinted from Popham, W.J. *Criterion-Referenced Measurement* (First Edition), Copyright © 1978, pp. 132-135, by permission of Prentice-Hall, Inc., Englewood Cliffs, New Jersey.

3. Different Item Types

In developing domain-descriptions, course team members need to consider not only what objective is to be measured in each case, but also what type of items (multiple-choice, short answer, etc.) are most likely to be appropriate for measuring the objective. The rule to follow is that if an objective strongly suggests the use of a particular type of item, then that item type should be used. For example, if an objective requires students to be able to synthesize given information, then it may be decided that this cannot be measured satisfactorily with conventional forms of objective items (such as multiple-choice, matching, or short answer questions) and that essay type items (extended or restricted) are more appropriate for this purpose. However, in most cases, it is likely that a range of alternative forms of item types may be used, and in such cases it is suggested that objective item types (multiple-choice questions in particular) be preferred due to the degree of objectivity that may be brought to bear, both in scoring responses and in analyzing items for weaknesses. Where essay items are preferred, it is suggested that these be broken down as far as possible into a number of related parts. This not only makes it possible to score each item with greater objectivity, but also it makes it easier to use item analysis to help identify weaknesses in items.

Much has already been written in the literature about the characteristics of, and the rules for producing, the different types of items referred to above, and many readers will be familiar with standard texts on the subject. There is no attempt here to repeat what has already been covered in the literature. However, for readers who wish to review the related item writing literature more carefully, articles by Wesman (1971) and Coffman (1971) on objective type and essay items may be recommended as providing particularly comprehensive reviews of the respective topics.

References

Anderson, R.C. How to construct achievement tests to assess

comprehension. *Review of Educational Research*, 1972, *42*, 145-170.

Barth, R.J. A selected annotated bibliography on behavioral objectives in the English language arts (elementary and secondary). ERIC: ED 102580, 1974.

Bobbitt, F. *The Curriculum*. Boston: Houghton Mifflin Co., 1918.

Bormuth, J.R. *On the Theory of Achievement Test Items*. Chicago: University of Chicago Press, 1970.

Briggs, L.J., and Gagné, R.M. *Principles of Instructional Design*. New York: Holt, Rinehart, and Winston, 1974.

Burck, F. Lock-step schooling and a remedy; the fundamental evils and handicaps of class instruction; and a report of the progress in the construction of an individual system. Monograph Series A. San Francisco: State Normal School, 1913.

Coffman, W.E. Essay examinations. In Thorndike, R.L. (Editor), *Educational Measurement*. Washington, DC: American Council on Education, 1971, 271-302.

Duchastel, P.C., and Merrill, P.F. The effect of behavioral objectives on learning: A review of empirical studies. *Review of Educational Research*, 1973, *43*, 53-70.

Guttman, L. Integration of test design and analysis. *Proceedings of the 1969 Invitational Conference on Testing Problems*. Princeton: Educational Testing Service, 1969.

Hively, W., Maxwell, G., Rabehl, G., Sension, D., and Lundin, S. *Domain-Referenced Curriculum Evaluation: Technical Handbook and a Case Study from the Minnemast Project*. CSE Monograph Series in Evaluation, No. 1. Los Angeles: Center for the Study of Evaluation, University of California, 1973.

Macdonald-Ross, M. Behavioral objectives—a critical review. *Instructional Science*, 1973, *2*, 1-52.

Mager, R.F. *Preparing Instructional Objectives*. Palo Alto, California: Fearon, 1962.

Melton, R.F. The role of objectives. In *Management in Education*, An Open University Course. Milton Keynes: Open University, 1976.

Melton, R.F. Resolution of conflicting claims concerning the effect of behavioral objectives on student learning. *Review of Educational Research*, 1978, *48*, 291-302.

Popham, W.J. Objectives and instruction. In Stake *et al.* (Editors), *Instructional Objectives*. American Educational Research Association Monograph Series on Curriculum Evaluation. Chicago: Rand McNally and Co., 1969.

Search, P.W. *An Ideal School, or Looking Forward.* New York: Appleton and Co., 1901.

Skinner, B.F. *Verbal Behavior.* New York: Appleton-Century-Crofts, 1957.

Thorndike, E.L. *Animal Intelligence.* New York: Macmillan, 1911.

Tyler, R.W. *Constructing Achievement Tests.* Columbus: Ohio State University, 1934.

Walbesser, H.H. *Constructing Behavioral Objectives.* Maryland, U.S.A.: Bureau of Educational Research and Field Services, University of Maryland, 1970.

Walbesser, H.H., and Eisenberg, T.A. A review of research on behavioral objectives and learning hierarchies. ERIC: ED 059900, 1972.

Wesman, A.G. Writing the test item. In Thorndike, R.L. (Editor), *Educational Measurement.* Washington, DC: American Council on Education, 1971, 81-129.

Chapter 9

Analyzing and Developing Unit Tests

This chapter is concerned primarily with identifying and describing techniques that might usefully be adopted to help develop and improve alternative forms of any given unit test, and to help ensure that alternative forms of the same test provide effectively the same estimate of a student's ability.

The extent to which course teams will be able to adopt the techniques described will depend as always on a variety of factors, with resource considerations being not the least of these. However, in making decisions concerning this, course teams must be aware of the type of problems that are likely to arise if tests are inadequately developed. The point to bear in mind is that alternative forms of each unit test are used with all the instructional models described in this book to identify standards that students are expected to achieve, and to determine whether students are ready to move on from one unit to the next. If such tests provide unreliable measures of student performance, then students are quite likely to be incorrectly classified as having achieved, or having failed to achieve, the desired performance levels, and the implications of such misclassification need to be kept constantly in mind. What, for example, are the implications of permitting students to proceed to further units of study if they have not acquired the necessary prerequisites? What is the likely effect on students of being incorrectly advised to undertake remedial studies if they have in fact achieved sufficient mastery of the unit concerned? How will student attitudes towards a course be affected if they feel that different forms of the same unit test often require different levels of performance, and as such are often unfair? Needless to say, tests will never be perfect, and related problems will always arise, but at least the extent of such problems may be reduced by paying careful attention to the needs of test development.

With the above factors in mind, the chapter begins (*Section 1*) by describing a *student testing strategy* which has been designed to illustrate how different forms of given unit tests may be analyzed to identify weaknesses in test items and related domain-descriptions.

The strategy is designed in a manner which ensures that each alternative form of each unit test is responded to under two quite different sets of conditions as far as study of the related unit of instruction is concerned. Under the first set of conditions, students are given a limited period of time in which to complete an initial study of the unit, and are advised to attempt to study all aspects of the content to some extent in the time available, rather than to study a few aspects thoroughly. The time prescribed is deliberately limited so that students of average ability might be expected to achieve related unit test scores in the region of 50 to 60 percent of the maximum possible, with group scores being fairly *normally distributed* about this mean. Under the second set of conditions, students are advised to study the related unit thoroughly with a view to mastering all the objectives identified, and they are advised to determine for themselves how long they need for this purpose. Only when they feel they have mastered the stated objectives are they asked to respond to a related unit test. It is expected that under these second conditions students will tend to achieve a fairly high level of mastery of objectives and that the related test scores will tend to be *strongly skewed*, with a large proportion of students achieving scores fairly close to the maximum possible.

The advantage of the strategy is that it permits analysis of each alternative form of unit test from two quite different points of view. Thus, *analysis of normal score distributions* may be primarily used to help identify weaknesses in the quality and consistency of items within each alternative test form, while *analysis of skewed score distributions* may be primarily used to

Analyzing and Developing Unit Tests

help identify factors affecting student mastery of specified objectives and related test items, and both modes of analysis are described in some detail (in *Sections 2* and *3,* respectively).

The chapter concludes (*Section 4*) with a discussion of the way in which the *equivalence of alternative forms of any given test* may be established such that the score on one form of test may be compared with scores on any of the alternative forms.

1. Student Testing Strategy

The strategy described is intended primarily to illustrate how different modes of analysis of score distributions may be used to help identify weaknesses in tests and thus to provide guidance concerning their improvement. Needless to say, the detailed requirements of any strategy will depend on the number of alternative test forms to be developed, and the strategy is therefore described with reference to a specific situation requiring the development of four alternative forms of each unit test: one for student self-assessment purposes and three alternative forms for the final assessment of students with regard to each unit. The strategy is in fact illustrated in diagrammatic form in Figure 19 in as far as it relates to a given unit of instruction. As will be seen from the diagram, the particular strategy described depends on the availability of four alternative forms (A, B, C, and D) of each unit test, and these may be produced in the first instance with the help of domain-descriptions, as already described in the foregoing chapter. Within the strategy, students are divided at random into four equal groups, with students in each group studying the same unit of instruction on an individualized basis before responding to different forms of the unit test. As illustrated in the diagram, the design of the strategy is such that the same four alternative forms of the unit test may be used for both self-assessment and final assessment purposes, without any group of students being required to respond to the same form of the test for both purposes.

Students are advised in the first instance to spend a prescribed, and limited, period of time on an initial study of the unit, covering all aspects to some extent rather than concentrating on a few. At the end of the prescribed period, students are asked to respond to

Figure 19

*A Procedure for Evaluating Four Alternative Forms
(A, B, C, and D) of a Criterion-Referenced Test Using
Four Equivalent Student Groups (1, 2, 3, and 4)*

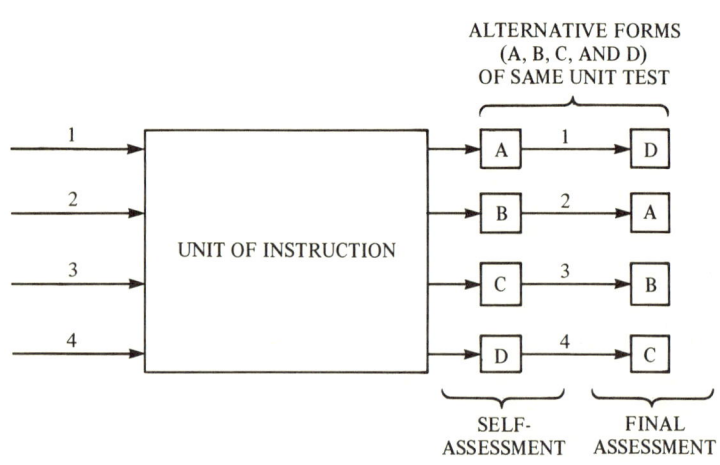

one of the alternative forms of the unit test which has been provided for self-assessment purposes. Student performances with regard to each alternative form of test are recorded for subsequent analysis (as described in Section 2), while students are provided with immediate feedback concerning weaknesses and are given guidance concerning remedial studies required. Students are in fact advised at this stage to pursue their further study of the unit with a view to mastering all the specified objectives, taking whatever time they consider necessary for this purpose. Only when they feel individually ready are they asked to demonstrate their mastery of the unit by responding to an alternative form of the unit test provided for final assessment purposes.

Under the above conditions, one might expect the scores on each alternative form of unit test used for self-assessment purposes to be well distributed, if the prescribed time limit has been carefully chosen, while in contrast one might expect the related scores emerging from the final assessment of students to be highly skewed, with most students demonstrating a high level of mastery of related objectives. Needless to say, the different types of scores have to be analyzed from different viewpoints, and a few comments here on each mode of analysis may help place the more detailed discussions (in Sections 2 and 3) in a clearer perspective.

In analyzing the scores emerging from the final assessment of students, the prime concern is to note to what extent students have been able to master specific objectives and related test items. Where the performance of a group with regard to a particular item, or group of related items (an objective), is relatively poor, course teams should search for possible explanations. It may well be that there are weaknesses in particular test items and related domain-descriptions that need to be rectified, but it must be remembered that these are not the only possible causes of poor performances. Thus, it may be that there are weaknesses in related instruction: explanations may have been ambiguous or inadequate, incorrect assumptions may have been made concerning existing student knowledge, inappropriate performance levels may have been specified, and so on. All such possible causes need to be explored. Inevitably, the weaknesses identified will sometimes reside in test items and at other times in related instruction.

In analyzing scores emerging from the self-assessment of students, high performance levels are not expected, and attention is in fact focused on the way in which each alternative form of test ranks student performances relative to one another. Basically, it is assumed that, since the test items within a given form of test all relate to the same unit of instruction, they should individually tend to rank students in much the same way as the related form of test as a whole. In other words, it is assumed that in any given alternative form of test there should be a reasonable correlation between item scores and test scores, and that where this is not the case, course teams should examine related test items, domain-descriptions, and related aspects of instruction for possible explanations.

As far as test development is concerned, the strategy is designed to help identify weaknesses in test items and related domain-descriptions. Where such weaknesses are identified, the feedback collected may be used to help improve test items and related domain-descriptions, with the latter being used to help generate replacement items. This is not the only way in which poor items might be replaced, and it is useful to consider how a slightly modified strategy could help generate replacement items on a more reliable basis. Let us imagine that we still wish to produce four alternative forms of each unit test for subsequent usage. If we start by generating eight forms of each unit test in the first instance, these may be analyzed by means of the same basic strategy. However, in this case, the four best alternative forms of each test may be selected for further development, with weak items in the selected tests being replaced by good items (with known item characteristics) taken from the rejected tests. In this respect, item analysis statistics (as described in the next section) are particularly helpful in identifying the relative qualities of tests and related items.

Needless to say, the type of student testing strategy adopted is likely to depend on a number of factors, such as the number of alternative forms of each unit test to be developed, the degree of reliability required in the tests developed, and the extent to which an extensive development program is feasible and justifiable in the existing circumstances. However, although individual strategies may vary, it is not difficult to design these in a manner which can take full advantage of the two modes of analysis referred to, and these are now described with particular reference to the type of statistics that may be used advantageously in analyzing the related test scores.

2. Analysis of Normal Score Distributions

Since the scores emerging from the self-assessment of students, in the strategy described, may be expected to be fairly normally distributed, the related scores from each of the alternative forms of a unit test may be analyzed with the help of conventional, norm-referenced, item analysis statistics, with only very limited qualifications being required concerning their usage. The statistics

Analyzing and Developing Unit Tests

described here for analyzing the self-assessment scores may, therefore, also be used in analyzing any normal distribution of scores, and were in fact developed for such usage. A variety of related statistics exists, and they are therefore discussed here under the headings of *item statistics (Section 2.1), cell statistics (Section 2.2),* and *test statistics (Section 2.3),* according to whether they relate to items within a test, parts of items (or cells), or to the test as a whole.

2.1. Item Statistics

Two of the most commonly used statistics in item analysis are the discrimination and facility indices. (The term facility index is used here—and in The Open University in general—in preference to the term difficulty index, although the two are defined in the literature in precisely the same way.)

The discrimination index measures the correlation between student scores on an item and those on the related test as a whole, and may have values ranging from plus one to minus one. Where one can assume a degree of homogeneity between items in a test, one might expect a reasonable correlation between individual items and the test as a whole, and any relatively low index is likely to be viewed as a matter of concern. Thus, it may be noted that factors such as student guessing of the correct response to a multiple-choice question could result in an index close to zero being recorded, while the keying (marking) of an incorrect alternative as the correct response could lead to a negative index.

The facility index for an item is simply the mean score achieved by students on the item expressed as a percentage of the maximum possible item score. Where an item is a multiple-choice item with only one correct response (that is, a binary item with either a correct or incorrect form of response), then the facility index actually indicates the percentage of students providing the correct response. The term facility index is preferred here to that of difficulty index because of the simplicity of interpretation. Thus, an item with a high facility index is simply one that is easy for students to answer, while one with a lower index is more difficult.

There is, in fact, a close relationship between the two above indices, and it is not difficult to see that in a norm-referenced test, which ranks students in order of ability with regard to one another, that there can be very little correlation between an item score and test score if the item concerned is answered correctly by all students or by none. In other words, items of extreme facility are unlikely to discriminate between students, and the related discrimination indices for such items will tend to approach zero. It is in fact possible to demonstrate mathematically that the maximum discrimination index of an item is related to its facility index (Moss, 1974), and the theoretical relationship is illustrated in graphical form in Figure 20. The main point to note is that items of high facility are unlikely to discriminate well between students, while good discrimination is more likely to be achieved with items in the middle facility range. This should explain why care was taken in the student testing strategy to prescribe a time limit for the initial period of study, which would result in students on average achieving scores in the region of 50 to 60 percent of the maximum possible on the self-assessment tests.

Normally, in developing norm-referenced tests which are primarily designed to discriminate between students, items of extreme facility tend to be removed from the tests simply because of their lack of discriminating power. However, this policy cannot be automatically adopted in analyzing the self-assessment scores emerging from the student testing strategy. The point is that in developing criterion-referenced tests, as is the case here, the prime concern is with measuring student mastery of specified objectives. If students perform well, related items will have high facility indices and hence depressed discrimination indices, but this on its own cannot justify removal of the items from the test. In other words, in analyzing the self-assessment scores, low discrimination indices should be carefully noted, as they may be indicators of weaknesses in test items, domain-descriptions, or related instruction. However, they should not be used as an automatic mechanism for accepting or rejecting related test items.

2.2. Cell Statistics

Cell statistics, like item statistics, may be used to help identify

Figure 20

Theoretical Variation of Discrimination Index (r) with Facility Index (f)

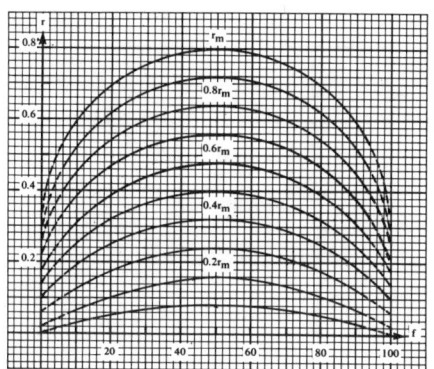

r_m = Maximum value of discrimination index (r) for any given value of facility index (f).

weaknesses both in test items and in related instruction. However, because cell statistics refer to more specific parts of test items, they tend to be more precise indicators of weaknesses.

Cell statistics are generally associated with multiple-choice items, and typically include statistics which record the frequency of student responses to the various alternative responses possible, while they may also include statistics which identify the type of students giving a particular response. An example of cell statistics for a multiple-choice question is included in Figure 21. It is worth noting that although the item statistics (the low discrimination index in particular) are helpful in that they suggest there is some form of anomaly, the cell statistics are more precise in helping pinpoint this. Thus, it may be noted that although the majority of students (56 percent) identified the response keyed as correct (i.e., alternative E), a substantial proportion of students (28 percent)

Figure 21

*Example of Item and Cell Statistics
for a Multiple-Choice Test Item*

ITEM	FACILITY INDEX	DISCRIMINATION INDEX	ALTERNATIVE / CELL STATISTIC	A	B	C	D	E	F	DON'T KNOW	TECH. ERROR
X1	56%	0.14	STATUS*	N	N	N	N	B	N		
			RESPONSE %	2	0	1	11	56	28	1	0
			MEAN SCORE ON TEST	66	40	60	71	73	83	65	68

*| N = INCORRECT RESPONSE |
| B = CORRECT/BEST RESPONSE |

not only selected alternative F, but the students concerned were amongst the most able of those tested (with mean test scores of 83 percent compared with mean test scores of 73 percent for those identifying the keyed response). Clearly, cell statistics provide test developers with more precise guidance than item statistics in the search for anomalies.

2.3. Test Statistics

Remembering that a score on a test is no more than an estimate of a student's true level of performance, it is particularly helpful to have some measure which provides an indication of the reliability of each test in making such estimates. One of the commonest measures used for this purpose with norm-referenced tests is the measure of internal test consistency, originally developed by Kuder and Richardson (1973). Basically, this measures the degree to which items within a given test are consistent in measuring the same overall ability. Applied to the scores emerging from the self-assessment of students in the student testing strategy described, this measure of internal consistency may provide a useful basis for comparing different forms of the same unit test with one another, and may also be used to determine whether modifications to tests actually lead to improvements in reliability.

Apart from calculating reliability indices for tests, it is also useful to calculate means and standard deviations for the related scores. In the case of alternative forms of a given test, the mean scores are particularly helpful in identifying any variation in standards between alternative forms. Standard deviations are equally useful in that they help determine whether observed variations in standards are significant or not, while they also provide a useful indication of the extent to which student performances on any given test vary.

Readers intending to undertake the item analysis of tests for themselves may wish to read much more about the subject before undertaking the task for the first time. Guilford's (1973) text on *Fundamental Statistics in Psychology and Education* provides a good starting point with a very helpful discussion of item analysis in general and reliability in particular. For further reading, Henrysson's (1971) article on "Gathering, Analyzing, and Using Data on Test Items" is to be particularly recommended, while readers may also be interested in an article on item analysis by the author (Melton, 1978), which describes and defines a variety of indices that are used in analyzing tests at The Open University.

3. Analysis of Skewed Score Distributions

It has already been noted that in analyzing the scores emerging from the final assessment process in the student testing strategy, the prime concern is to determine to what extent students have been able to master the specified objectives and related test items. It follows that facility indices (as already defined) have a particularly useful role to play in the analysis of related test scores, for they may be used to monitor group performance levels with regard to individual items and groups of items (or more specifically with regard to objectives). Where performance levels are noted to be relatively poor, course teams need to search for possible explanations, and cell statistics (as already described) may be used advantageously to facilitate the search. Mean test scores may also be used (although median and other percentile scores are preferred) to help identify variations in standards, not only between alternative forms of the same unit test, but also between tests related to different units of instruction.

At this point, it should be noted that there is no suggestion that discrimination indices or internal consistency indices should be used in analyzing the final assessment scores. This is because the two indices are defined with specific reference to normal score distributions, and their use is limited here to analyzing such distributions. This does not create a problem, for the student testing strategy was designed with this in mind. Thus, the whole question of item consistency (from the point of view of both item discrimination and internal test consistency) is looked at within the strategy through the analysis of scores emerging from the self-assessment process.

Although specific suggestions are made here as to how skewed distributions of scores might usefully be analyzed, it should not be forgotten that the whole student testing strategy (based on the analysis of both the self-assessment and final assessment scores) is concerned with the analysis of such scores and the related criterion-referenced tests. Nor should it be forgotten that this is not the only possible strategy for analyzing and developing such tests. Readers interested in learning more about alternative strategies will find that Klein and Kosecoff's (1973) article on "Issues and Procedures in the Development of Criterion-Referenced Tests" provides both a useful and readable introduction to the subject. For those wishing to look much more deeply into the subject, two texts may be particularly recommended. These are Martuza's (1977) book on *Applying Norm-Referenced and Criterion-Referenced Measurement in Education,* and Popham's (1978) book on *Criterion-Referenced Measurement.*

4. Equivalence of Alternative Forms of Any Given Test

Since the alternative forms of unit tests developed will be used ultimately to make decisions concerning whether or not students are ready to progress from one unit to another, it is highly desirable that the decisions made with regard to any given unit of instruction be basically the same, regardless of the alternative form of test used. To achieve this, one needs to be able to equate scores on any given form of a unit test to scores on any alternative form of the same test, and the intent here is to look briefly at how this might be realized.

The student testing strategy already described (and illustrated in Figure 19) might usefully be adopted for this purpose, so long as this is done at a point in time when no further changes are to be made to the tests that have been developed. (In other words, although the strategy may be used during the "group try-out" stage for analyzing and developing alternative forms of unit tests, the earliest point in time at which it may be adopted for the present purposes is likely to be the "field testing" stage.) Although basically the same strategy might be adopted, prime interest would be focused on the scores emerging from the self-assessment process, for these scores are likely to be well distributed, making relative comparisons easier to make. Assuming that scores are collected on each of the alternative forms of each unit test during the self-assessment process, all that is required is to equate the scores on each form of the unit test concerned to a percentile ranking of students within the related student group. So long as the different student groups may be described as equivalent to one another, the scores on the alternative forms of the test may also be described as being equivalent if they have the same percentile ranking.

Needless to say, the effort put into equating scores on alternative test forms will depend, as always, on a variety of factors. Inevitably, some course teams will wish to adopt less rigorous procedures, and some may be content to rely purely on subjective comparisons. In contrast, others may wish to consider more rigorous approaches, and for such readers, Angoff's (1971) article on "Scales, Norms, and Equivalent Scores" is to be highly recommended as providing an excellent review of alternative methods of equating test scores.

References

Angoff, W.H. Scales, norms, and equivalent scores. In Thorndike, R.L. (Editor), *Educational Measurement.* Washington, DC: American Council on Education, 1971, 508-600.

Guilford, J.P. *Fundamental Statistics in Psychology and Education.* New York: McGraw-Hill Book Company, 1973, 396-460.

Henrysson, S. Gathering, analyzing, and using data on test items. In Thorndike, R.L. (Editor), *Educational Measurement.* Washington, DC: American Council on Education, 1971, 130-159.

Klein, S.P., and Kosecoff, J. Issues and procedures in the development of criterion-referenced tests. *ERIC TM Report 26.* Princeton: ERIC Clearinghouse on Tests, Measurement, and Evaluation, Educational Testing Service, 1973.

Kuder, G.F., and Richardson, M.W. The theory of the estimation of test reliability. *Psychometrika*, 1973, *2*, 151-160.

Martuza, V.R. *Applying Norm-Referenced and Criterion-Referenced Measurement in Education.* Boston, Massachusetts: Allyn and Bacon, Inc., 1977.

Melton, R.F. Item analysis at The Open University: A case study. *British Journal of Educational Technology,* 1978, *9,* 111-130.

Moss, A.G. A Method of Decoupling Item Discrimination Index from Facility Index. Milton Keynes: Institute of Educational Technology, Open University, 1974.

Popham, W.J. *Criterion-Referenced Measurement.* Englewood Cliffs, New Jersey: Prentice-Hall, Inc., 1978.

Chapter 10

Monitoring Student Perceptions and Attitudes

We have already discussed in some detail (Chapter 7) the type of strategies that course teams might usefully adopt in evaluating comprehensive (full-draft) forms of instructional materials, and have taken careful note of the way in which tests and questionnaires may be used advantageously in the evaluation process described. The intent in this chapter, therefore, is not so much to elaborate on this process, but rather to describe different types of questionnaires that may be used within it. Nevertheless, before discussing different types of questionnaires, it is useful to remind ourselves of the basic elements of the evaluation strategy to be served, taking note of the types of perceptions and attitudes to be monitored and the reasons for such measurements. Similarly, it is helpful in conclusion to add a few words of caution about the way in which questionnaire findings might be used to provide guidance for the subsequent modification and development of materials.

With the above points in mind, the chapter begins (*Section 1*) with a brief review of *the role of questionnaires within the evaluation process*. It then goes on (*Section 2*) to look at the *different types of questionnaires* that may be used to advantage within the process, and finally (*Section 3*) concludes by taking note of factors that need to be taken into account in *interpreting data from questionnaires*.

1. The Role of Questionnaires Within the Evaluation Process

In the evaluation strategy already described (Chapter 7), it was assumed that (where objectives have already been stated for instruction) it is logical to begin the evaluation process by taking careful note of the extent to which students are able to achieve the stated objectives. Where student performance with regard to mastering a particular objective is relatively poor, it was considered equally logical that course teams should attempt to identify possible causes.

We have already taken note (Chapter 9) of how tests may be used to monitor student performance with regard to units of instruction in general and domain-referenced objectives in particular, and have taken note of the way in which item analysis may be used to help identify weaknesses in test items and related domain-descriptions. In fact, it is clear that poor student performance with regard to a particular objective may often be attributed (in light of item analysis) to weaknesses in test items or related domain-descriptions. However, a variety of other possible causes do exist, and, where poor student performance cannot be attributed completely to weaknesses in related test items, course teams need to ask themselves questions such as the following:

- Was the objective concerned expressed in reasonably clear terms? Did it provide students with appropriate guidance? Was it seen to be helpful?
- Were students adequately motivated towards achieving the objective?
- Did students perceive the objective to be important and relevant to their needs? Did the materials developed pay sufficient attention to making students aware of the relevance and importance of the stated objective?
- Did students perceive the objective to be achievable in the existing learning conditions? Was sufficient attention paid in designing the instruction to the fact that students have different abilities and different achievement potentials? Was the performance level specified realistic in the circumstances?
- Were there weaknesses in instruction which made it difficult for students to achieve the objective concerned? Did some concepts and principles need to be explained in greater detail? Were unjustified assumptions made concerning student knowledge prior to the instruction?

In so far as questionnaires may be used to measure student perceptions of, and attitudes towards, instruction, they have a particularly important role to play in helping course teams to seek answers to questions such as those indicated above. Thus, they may be used to help determine student attitudes (motivations) towards achieving specified objectives, to monitor student perceptions of the clarity, importance, relevance, and achievability of stated objectives, and to identify problems perceived by students in related instruction, such as problems in understanding particular terms, concepts, or principles. A variety of different types of questionnaires may be used to help monitor such attitudes and perceptions, and these are discussed in the following section.

2. Different Types of Questionnaires

The intent here is to describe a number of different types of question formats that may be used in monitoring student perceptions and attitudes, and to take note of the varying advantages of each.

The first format referred to (*Section 2.1*) is described as *a basic, bipolar format*, since each question posed requires students to respond with reference to a bipolar adjective. Thus, students may be asked, for example, to indicate the degree to which they perceive specific aspects of instruction to be "interesting-uninteresting" or "informative-uninformative," and so on. *Different types of bipolar format* are then described (*Section 2.2*), with note being taken of the advantages of each. This leads to a discussion of the advantages of using a modified form of bipolar format, which is described here as *a unipolar format* (*Section 2.3*). As the name implies, this type of format requires students to respond to each question with reference to a unipolar adjective. For example, instead of bipolar questions asking students to indicate the extent to which they perceive different concepts as being "difficult-easy" to understand, a unipolar question might ask students to identify those concepts (included among a list of concepts provided) which were "particularly difficult" to understand. Needless to say, these are not the only formats that could be adopted within questionnaires, and the final comments (*Section*

2.4) are intended to place the types of questionnaires considered more clearly *in perspective.*

2.1. A Basic, Bipolar Format

A basic, bipolar type of format is widely used in questionnaires, and simply requires students to respond to each particular question with reference to a bipolar adjective. The format is illustrated in question 1, Figure 22. Although the question referred to is concerned with determining the extent to which students feel motivated towards achieving a particular objective, it could equally have been concerned with measuring student perceptions of a wide variety of different aspects of instruction. In the question illustrated, students are asked to respond with reference to a five-point bipolar scale, but the scale could have had, say, three or seven points, the number depending on the sensitivity of response considered feasible and desirable. The response of a group as a whole may be indicated simply by recording the percentage of students responding at each point on the scale. Alternatively, and often more conveniently, a mean score and standard deviation may be determined to indicate, respectively, the average student response and the distribution of the responses within the group.

Although the actual distribution of responses may be of interest in themselves, it is difficult to determine in isolation what action should, or should not, be taken in light of a particular pattern of responses. For example, what mean score should be seen as a matter for concern requiring remedial action by the course team? Such decisions are more easily made if comparisons are made between group responses to precisely the same question, when this is asked with regard to different objectives. Thus, concern may be expressed if the mean score, indicating student motivation towards achieving a particular objective, falls well below that recorded for most other objectives, and course teams might usefully attempt to determine why motivation is so much less in such instances. Bearing in mind the desirability of making such comparisons, it is logical to present questions within a format which helps both evaluators and students to make appropriate comparisons, and

Figure 22

A Basic, Bipolar Question Format

Q.1. TO WHAT EXTENT DO YOU FEEL MOTIVATED, AT THIS POINT IN TIME, TOWARDS ACHIEVING OBJECTIVE X IN UNIT Y?

	VERY STRONGLY ← → VERY WEAKLY
	+2 +1 0 -1 -2

(TICK *THE ONE* RESPONSE WHICH *MOST* APPROPRIATELY REFLECTS YOUR FEELINGS)

Q.2. TO WHAT EXTENT DO YOU FEEL MOTIVATED, AT THIS POINT IN TIME, TOWARDS ACHIEVING EACH OF THE FOLLOWING OBJECTIVES IN UNIT Y:

	VERY STRONGLY ← → VERY WEAKLY
A. OBJECTIVE 1?	+2 +1 0 -1 -2
B. OBJECTIVE 2?	+2 +1 0 -1 -2
C. OBJECTIVE 3?	+2 +1 0 -1 -2
D. OBJECTIVE 4?	+2 +1 0 -1 -2
E. OBJECTIVE 5?	+2 +1 0 -1 -2

(TICK *THE ONE* RESPONSE WITH REGARD TO EACH OBJECTIVE WHICH *MOST* APPROPRIATELY REFLECTS YOUR FEELINGS) question 2, Figure 22, illustrates the type of format that might be used for this purpose.

2.2. Different Types of Bipolar Format

The type of basic, bipolar format so far described is essentially a variation of, or a derivation from, the Semantic Differential type of question format that was developed by Osgood, Suci, and Tannenbaum (1957) to measure student attitudes towards "objects" such as people, institutions, laws, and so on. The same format may be used within education to measure student attitudes towards (and student perceptions of) different parts of instruction, such as units, sections of units, media, strategies, objectives, and so on, and is illustrated within this latter context in question 1, Figure 23. Typically, the question referred to focuses on a specific "object"—in this case an objective—viewing it from a variety of different viewpoints. The question referred to is in fact designed to measure student perceptions of the importance, achievability, and relevance of the objective concerned.

Once again, it may be added that although student perceptions of a given "object" may be of interest in themselves, in general in evaluating instruction, it is often more useful to make comparisons between "objects." For example, student perceptions of a number of different objectives could usefully be compared by addressing question 1 (Figure 23) to students with reference to a number of different objectives. However, comparisons are often more easily made, both by students and evaluators, if the question format is modified to permit the objectives to be compared separately with regard to each of the perceptions in turn. Question 2 (Figure 23) illustrates the type of format that could be used for this purpose, and it should be clear that three such questions (comparing the objectives separately in terms of perceived importance, achievability, and relevance) would be required to perform the same function as question 1.

The type of bipolar questions illustrated here may be used to make comparisons not only between objectives but between many different aspects of instruction (such as between units, sections of units, principles, concepts, and so on). Similarly, comparisons may

Figure 23

Different Types of Bipolar Format

VERY IMPORTANT ←——— VERY UNIMPORTANT +2 +1 0 -1 -2 VERY ACHIEVABLE ←——— VERY UNACHIEVABLE +2 +1 0 -1 -2 VERY RELEVANT ←——— VERY IRRELEVANT +2 +1 0 -1 -2	Q.1. TO WHAT EXTENT, AT THIS POINT IN TIME, DO YOU PERCEIVE MASTERY OF OBJECTIVE X IN UNIT Y TO BE: A. IMPORTANT TO YOUR UNDERSTANDING OF THE UNIT AS A WHOLE? B. ACHIEVABLE UNDER THE GIVEN LEARNING CONDITIONS? C. RELEVANT TO YOUR PERSONAL INTERESTS? (TICK *THE MOST* APPROPRIATE RESPONSE *FOR EACH PERCEPTION*)
VERY IMPORTANT ←——— VERY UNIMPORTANT +2 +1 0 -1 -2 +2 +1 0 -1 -2 +2 +1 0 -1 -2 +2 +1 0 -1 -2 +2 +1 0 -1 -2	Q.2. TO WHAT EXTENT, AT THIS POINT IN TIME, DO YOU PERCEIVE MASTERY OF EACH OF THE FOLLOWING OBJECTIVES IN UNIT Y TO BE IMPORTANT TO YOUR UNDERSTANDING OF THE UNIT AS A WHOLE? A. OBJECTIVE 1 B. OBJECTIVE 2 C. OBJECTIVE 3 D. OBJECTIVE 4 E. OBJECTIVE 5 (TICK *THE MOST* APPROPRIATE RESPONSE *FOR EACH OBJECTIVE*)

be made with reference to a wide variety of different perceptions (such as with reference to student perceptions of difficulties, ambiguities, lack of clarity, readability, and so on, as well as with reference to perceptions of relevance, importance, and achievability). Information may be collected, therefore, at a variety of different levels. For example, information may be collected at what may be described as a "macro-level" by making comparisons between units, blocks of units, and courses, while it may be collected at a more "micro-level" by making comparisons between parts of units, objectives, adjunct aids, principles, concepts, and terms. Both types of information are useful, although they tend to be useful in different ways. Thus, information collected at a macro-level tends to be more useful in identifying broad problem areas that need to be given attention as a matter of priority, but it is not usually sufficiently specific to provide guidance concerning what needs to be done. Such guidance is better provided by information collected at a micro-level, since this tends to pinpoint problems more precisely, and as such provides clearer guidance concerning what needs to be done.

It is in fact important to recognize that if course teams are to be provided with sufficient guidance to help them improve materials, much information needs to be collected at a micro-level, and this means that a wide variety of questions needs to be addressed to students concerning specific aspects of instruction. Unfortunately, increasing the number of questions asked, in order to increase the information collected, also increases the burden placed on students, and this needs to be controlled if students are to cooperate in providing feedback. One way of achieving this, without reducing the coverage required, is by making it simpler for students to respond to effectively the same questions, and the unipolar format described below was designed with this requirement clearly in mind.

2.3. A Unipolar Format

The relationship between unipolar and bipolar formats is explained here with reference to questions 1 and 2 in Figure 24. Both questions referred to are designed for the same purpose,

Figure 24

Bipolar and Unipolar Formats for Effectively the Same Question

Q.1. TO WHAT EXTENT DID YOU HAVE DIFFICULTY IN ACQUIRING AN UNDERSTANDING OF THE FOLLOWING TERMS, CONCEPTS, AND PRINCIPLES:

VERY MUCH ←———————→ VERY LITTLE

	-2	-1	0	+1	+2
HETEROTROPHE?	-2	-1	0	+1	+2
AUTOTROPHE?	-2	-1	0	+1	+2
FOOD CHAINS AND WEBS?	-2	-1	0	+1	+2
ENERGY FLOW?	-2	-1	0	+1	+2
CLIMATIC FACTORS?	-2	-1	0	+1	+2
EDAPHIC FACTORS?	-2	-1	0	+1	+2
MORTALITY?	-2	-1	0	+1	+2
FECUNDITY?	-2	-1	0	+1	+2
SURVIVORSHIP CURVE?	-2	-1	0	+1	+2
LOGISTIC CURVE?	-2	-1	0	+1	+2
KEY FACTOR ANALYSIS?	-2	-1	0	+1	+2

(TICK THE MOST APPROPRIATE RESPONSE FOR *EACH TERM, CONCEPT, OR PRINCIPLE*)

Q.2. DID YOU HAVE MUCH, OR VERY MUCH, DIFFICULTY IN ACQUIRING AN UNDERSTANDING OF ANY OF THE FOLLOWING TERMS, CONCEPTS, OR PRINCIPLES:

- HETEROTROPHE? ☐
- AUTOTROPHE? ☐
- FOOD CHAINS AND WEBS? ☐
- ENERGY FLOW? ☐
- CLIMATIC FACTORS? ☐
- EDAPHIC FACTORS? ☐
- MORTALITY? ☐
- FECUNDITY? ☐
- SURVIVORSHIP CURVE? ☐
- LOGISTIC CURVE? ☐
- KEY FACTOR ANALYSIS? ☐

(PLACE A *TICK* IN THE BOX ALONGSIDE *ANY TERM, CONCEPT, OR PRINCIPLE* WHERE YOU HAD MUCH, OR VERY MUCH, DIFFICULTY IN ACQUIRING THE NECESSARY UNDERSTANDING) namely to enable comparisons to be made between the terms, concepts, and principles listed, with the comparisons being made in terms of the difficulties which students perceive themselves as encountering in acquiring an understanding of each term, concept, or principle.

Using question 1, comparisons would normally be made by noting the average response of the student group (i.e., by noting the mean group score) with regard to each term, concept, or principle. However, similar comparisons could be made (using the same question) simply by noting the percentage of students indicating that they had "much difficulty" or "very much difficulty" in acquiring an understanding of each of the terms, concepts, and principles listed. Thus, one would expect the variation in percentage responses recorded to generally identify the same relative weaknesses as the variation in mean scores emerging from the related bipolar format. However, one would expect the variation in percentage responses to provide a somewhat less reliable and less sensitive measure than the variation in mean scores. Recognizing this limitation, it is nevertheless noted that if the responses to be monitored are limited to a unipolar characteristic (in this case to "much difficulty" or "very much difficulty"), then the question may be addressed to students in a simplified form which can be responded to more quickly and easily, and this is the form illustrated in question 2. Despite slight variation in wording, it should be recognized that question 2 addresses itself to effectively the same problem as question 1, and that analysis of responses to question 2 should identify relative difficulties in the same way as analysis of limited responses (in the -1 and -2 categories) to question 1.

The unipolar format is in fact seen as providing a particularly useful way of making a wide variety of comparisons between many specific elements of instruction (terms, concepts, etc.) in terms of a variety of different student perceptions (perceived difficulties, ambiguities, etc.). It may even be used to make comparisons between relationships (such as those between aims and instruction, comparisons being made in terms of perceived relevance, helpfulness, and so on). In other words, very much the same type of comparisons may be made with both the unipolar and bipolar formats. However, care should be taken in determining the terms to be used in a unipolar format, since a slight variation in wording (e.g., in choosing to use the term "particular difficulty" rather than "difficulty") may affect the sensitivity of the question to variations in perceptions.

2.4. In Perspective

In describing the different types of format, the intent has been to describe simple, and useful, ways of monitoring student perceptions of, and attitudes towards, instruction. It is not suggested that these are the only formats that may be used for this purpose, nor is this the only purpose for which questionnaires may be designed. For example, questionnaires may be designed for the collection of factual data. However, much has already been written in the literature about the more general aspects of questionnaire design, development, and usage, and readers wishing to learn more about the subject should have little difficulty in finding relevant texts. Nevertheless, two texts are recommended here for possible further reading, namely *Survey Methods in Social Investigation* by Moser and Kalton (1971) and *Data Collection Procedures* by Byner, Oppenheim, and Hammersley (1979).

3. Interpreting Data from Questionnaires

In monitoring student perceptions of different aspects of instruction, it should not be assumed automatically that if an obvious weakness is perceived in a particular aspect of instruction, that this must be the cause of any poor performance that may have been observed on related objectives. In general, several factors are likely to affect student performance, and some are likely to be more critical than others. An example might usefully illustrate the point.

Let us imagine that during the evaluation of a course it is noted that student performances on one particular unit are much poorer than for all other units. Let us also imagine that in comparing the units with one another it is noted that students perceive the unit to be very poorly structured in comparison with the others. In light of such coincidental data, a course team might contemplate a careful restructuring of the unit. However, before putting a great deal of time and effort into such a task, it would be wise to remember that other factors might be equally—or more critically—responsible for the poor performances observed. After all, it would be most unfortunate to put a great deal of effort into restructuring the unit to find out that this had only a marginal impact on student performances. For example, if students perceived the objectives as having very little relevance to their particular needs, and if this emerged as a critical factor affecting student learning, it is quite possible that restructuring the unit would have a very marginal impact on related student learning. Clearly, careful consideration should be given not only to identifying perceived weaknesses in instruction, but also to determining the relationships between such weaknesses and related student performances.

It is in fact possible to use multivariate analysis techniques to help examine the relationships between student perceptions and student learning, and readers interested in doing this should find Kerlinger and Pedhazur's (1973) book on *Multiple Regression in Behavioral Research* a comprehensive and useful reference. Those interested in looking more closely at ways of using such techniques for examining cause-and-effect relationships may also be interested to read an article by the author (Melton, 1979) on "The Effect of Behavioral Objectives on Student Perception of Instructional Material and Hence on Related Student Learning." The main advantage of such multivariate techniques is that they may be used to help identify causes of poor performance with greater reliability, and therefore may help reduce the degree of subjectivity involved in determining what action should be taken (concerning further development of materials) in light of data collected.

References

Byner, J., Oppenheim, A.N., and Hammersley, M. Data collection procedures. In Block 4 of The Open University course, DE304, on *Research Methods in Education and the Social Sciences.* Milton Keynes: Open University Press, 1979.

Kerlinger, F.N., and Pedhazur, E.J. *Multiple Regression in Behavioral Research.* New York: Holt, Rinehart, and Winston, 1973.

Melton, R.F. The effect of behavioral objectives on student perception of instructional material and hence on related student learning. A paper presented to the Congress of the European Association for Research and Development in Higher Education at Klagenfurt, Austria, 1979.

Moser, C., and Kalton, A. *Survey Methods in Social Investigation.* London: Heinemann Educational Books, Ltd., 1971.

Osgood, C.E., Suci, G.J., and Tannenbaum, P.H. *The Measurement of Meaning.* Urbana: University of Illinois Press, 1957.

Chapter 11

The Interpretation of Unit Test Scores

Once tests and instructional materials have been fully developed in light of evaluative feedback, the materials may be used for instructional purposes with a fair degree of confidence. Even so, care still has to be taken in using unit tests for decision-making purposes, for it must be recognized that a unit test is no more than a sample of items drawn from a much larger domain of items, and a student's score on a unit test is simply an estimate of his or her competency (or true performance level) with regard to the domain (or unit) as a whole.

With the above factors in mind, this chapter is concerned with looking at how one might go about determining whether or not a student has achieved a particular level of competency with regard to a domain (or unit), given the student's related unit test score. The question is in fact discussed in two stages: the first (*Section 1*) being concerned with factors that need to be taken into account in the first instance in *identifying the true performance level desired*, and the second (*Section 2*) being concerned with *estimating the student's competency* (or true level of performance) from related unit test scores.

1. Identifying the True Performance Level Desired

It has already been noted, in discussing the specification of unit objectives, that as far as possible the objectives should be seen to be not only relevant and important but also achievable, so that students might be expected to achieve high levels of performance in responding to related domain-referenced tests. One of the reasons for paying attention to feasibility as well as desirability of stated objectives is to avoid, as far as possible, the type of situation where a substantial number of students find themselves unable to master specified objectives. Under such conditions, there is always the risk that, during the course of instruction, teachers will accept partial levels of domain mastery (e.g., 80 percent, 70 percent, and so on), and one then has the problem of subsequent instruction building on assumptions (concerning acquired knowledge, skills, abilities, interests, etc.) that are no longer valid—a common problem in most teaching situations. Thus, in specifying objectives, what has to be borne in mind is that the items within the related domain generally represent a desired level of performance with regard to a continuum of ability, and the level of performance required may be varied by modifying the items within the domain. However, once the level of items within the domain has been established, it is highly desirable that students achieve high levels of performance with regard to the domain, since it is much easier to make inferences about acquired knowledge when performance levels with regard to the domain are high (say, 90 percent or more) than when they are relatively low (say, 70 percent or less).

Very much the same point may be made with regard to the unit as a whole, if it is remembered that within any given unit of instruction (as described in this book) the domains related to specific objectives are combined together to produce a much larger unit domain, so that samples of items drawn from the domain may be used as alternative forms of unit tests to measure student competency with regard to the unit domain (that is, with regard to the unit as a whole). Once again, it is much easier to make valid assumptions concerning the knowledge and skills that have been acquired in studying a unit, if students are required to achieve high levels of performance with regard to the unit domain.

Having said this, it must be recognized that however carefully instruction may have been developed, field testing may suggest that it is unreasonable to expect students to achieve complete mastery of unit domains, and course teams may decide to identify desired performance levels that fall short of complete mastery. This is acceptable so long as the implications of accepting reduced levels of true performance are clearly recognized, and so long as subsequent instruction is designed to take this into account.

2. Estimating the Student's Competency

Once a desired performance level has been specified with regard to a unit domain, the task ahead is to determine what scores on related unit tests suggest that students have achieved the desired level of competency.

There are in fact two clear risks that are taken in estimating a student's competency with regard to a domain on the basis of an observed, domain-referenced score. The first is that of making a false positive error (also described as a Type 1 error), that is, the error of assigning a student to a mastery category when his or her true competency level places him or her in a non-mastery category. The second risk is that of making a false negative error (also described as a Type 2 error), that is, the error of assigning a student to a non-mastery category when his or her true competency level places him or her in a mastery category. Needless to say, it is highly desirable that such errors be reduced to a minimum, for these are likely to create a number of related problems. For example, false positive errors may easily give rise to subsequent student learning problems, while false negative errors may create psychological problems for students. With such factors in mind, a number of statistical approaches have been developed to identify the probability of such errors being made in categorizing a student on the basis of given test scores.

One of the most widely adopted approaches is based on the use of Bayesian methods, and is designed to determine the probability of a student possessing a desired competency level given varying observed scores on domain-referenced tests of varying length. Novick and Lewis (1974) have made a particularly useful contribution to this approach, not only developing tables to identify the probability of students having achieved specified competency levels (given related observed scores on tests of varying length), but also indicating how the probabilities determined may be related to score distributions on the related domain-referenced test. For example, the tables indicate the probability of a student having achieved a competency level of 0.80 or more when he or she is able to respond correctly to ten out of 12 items on a related test. Where student scores on the test are assumed to be uniformly distributed, the probability of the score indicating the competency level has been achieved is only 50 percent. However, where scores on the test are assumed to be skewed such that 75 percent of students achieve scores at, or above, the 80 percent level, then the probability of the same score indicating that the competency level has been achieved increases to 75 percent.

The main disadvantage of the above approach in interpreting unit test scores is that it takes virtually no account of the variations (such as in reliability) that inevitably occur between alternative forms of the same test, since probabilities are related simply to observed scores and related test length. Nevertheless, it is one of the most promising approaches that has so far been developed, and from a statistical point of view it is particularly relevant for use in interpreting unit test scores.

Needless to say, alternative statistical approaches do exist for interpreting domain-referenced test scores, and these are reviewed in articles by Millman (1973), Meskauskas (1976), and Hambleton, Swaminathan, Algina, and Coulson (1978). However, before adopting any alternative approach, it is suggested that course teams seek psychometric advice. The main point to bear in mind is that different approaches tend to make different assumptions, and it is important to ensure that these hold with regard to the unit domain and related unit tests before the approach is used to help interpret unit test scores. In particular, in considering any alternative approach, there is a need to take careful note of the assumptions that are made concerning the homogeneity of items within the domain, and to take similar note of the type of inferences that are to be made concerning student competencies.

References

Hambleton, R.K., Swaminathan, H., Algina, J., and Coulson, D.B.

Criterion-referenced testing and measurement: A review of technical issues and developments. *Review of Educational Research*, 1978, *48*, 1-47.

Meskauskas, J.A. Evaluation models for criterion-referenced testing: Views regarding mastery and standard setting. *Review of Educational Research*, 1976, *46*, 133-158.

Millman, J. Passing scores and test lengths for domain-referenced measures. *Review of Educational Research*, 1973, *43*, 205-216.

Novick, M.R., and Lewis, C. Prescribing test length for criterion-referenced measurement. In Harris, C.W., Alkin, M.C., and Popham, W.J. (Editors), *Problems in Criterion-Referenced Measurement*. CSE Monograph Series in Evaluation, No. 3. Los Angeles: Center for the Study of Evaluation, University of California, 1974.

In Conclusion

In discussing the various aspects of course design and development within sequential parts of this book, we have progressively considered more and more specific aspects of related concepts and techniques. It is therefore useful in conclusion to look back at the process of course design and development as a whole, highlighting important facets that can all too easily disappear from sight beneath the details presented. This is done in this final chapter in reviewing the main arguments in support of *the need for models* (*Section 1*) and in looking once again at the *course models* and *the instructional materials development process* (*Sections 2* and *3*, respectively) that have already been discussed in detail within this book. However, in doing this, the intent is not to summarize in detail what has already been said, but rather to place each aspect discussed more clearly in perspective.

1. The Need for Models

Having discussed different models (and the related development process) in so much detail, readers may take for granted that models are an essential part of instructional development. However, not all developers will of necessity be convinced of this, and it is useful to begin by reminding ourselves of some of the reasons for choosing to use models in the manner suggested in this book.

One of the main reasons is that in developing instructional materials it is all too easy to focus attention on the content of what is to be taught and to pay very limited attention to how best to facilitate student learning. The models discussed in this book address themselves to precisely this problem by focusing attention on different ways of presenting instruction to students and by highlighting the educational principles underlying each mode of presentation. As such, they not only provide course teams with a choice of a number of broad strategies for facilitating student learning, but they also encourage more open debate of related philosophies. They also open up adopted strategies (in the form of models) to wider inspection, and encourage researchers and instructional developers to subject such strategies to careful analysis, using the findings to help develop and improve related models.

Models also have the advantage of focusing course team attention on aspects of instruction that need to be closely interrelated in the materials to be developed, and hence help focus attention on the importance of related stages within the development process itself. For example, in choosing to adopt any of the models discussed in this book, the attention of course team members would be drawn to the importance of the relationships to be realized within each unit between advance organizers, unit content, domain-referenced objectives, self-assessment questions, and final unit tests. In turn, this would help highlight the relevance and importance of related stages in the development process that are designed to ensure that such relationships are given careful attention at appropriate points in time in developing related materials.

2. Course Models

In looking once again at course models, the intent is not to review specific models that have already been discussed, but rather to place these models in a broader perspective.

With this in mind, it may be useful to begin by noting that all the models discussed in this book adopt a criterion-referenced approach to student learning; that is, an approach in which criteria to be achieved are expressed in terms of desired performance levels on related unit tests, with students being required to achieve these levels of performance in order to gain any credit for what they have learned. At first glance, the approach might appear to be rather rigorous and inflexible, particularly if compared with a more conventional approach, in which student performance levels are simply recorded, before the group as a whole moves on to

In Conclusion

further units of study. In fact, such a comparison is oversimplistic and misleading, for the type of criterion-referenced approach described in this book is more flexible in a number of respects than the conventional approach. Thus, in the criterion-referenced approach, students are individually free to determine for themselves how long they need for the study of a unit; they respond to unit tests when they feel that they are adequately prepared for them; and they are free to repeat the tests as often as necessary (even three or four times, if desired) in order to achieve the desired level of performance. In contrast, in the more conventional type of situation, students (regardless of the degree to which they vary in ability) are typically given a limited period of time in which to complete the study of a particular unit, or topic, and are usually expected to respond to related tests at fixed points in time, which are the same for all students. The only advantage offered in terms of flexibility in the more conventional situation is that students may proceed to further units of study regardless of the level of performance achieved with regard to the given unit of study. This would appear to be a very dubious advantage, if the expectation of subsequent success is low for inadequately prepared students.

In considering the appropriateness of different course models, note needs to be taken of the extent to which each reflects well-organized principles of learning, and the models discussed in this book have already been reviewed with this in mind. In doing this, it has already been noted that no model is seen as offering an ideal, or complete, prescription for the presentation of instruction. Rather, each model is seen as providing a broad, well-defined framework for the presentation of instruction, with course teams free to develop their own individual strategies within the constraints of the broad framework. Such strategies may vary within a given model, not only from course to course, but also from unit to unit within a given course. Needless to say, the strategies adopted within the constraints of a given model may also be designed to reflect further principles of learning.

In reviewing different course models with a view to adoption, it follows that a course team not only needs to take note of the extent to which each model reflects various principles of learning, but it has to bear in mind the type of strategies that might be adopted within the constraints of any chosen model. However, these are not the only factors that need to be taken into account. Thus, there is also a need to take note of the resources that are likely to be required (in terms of personnel, time, and finance) in order to produce materials conforming to the requirements of any preferred model. Needless to say, the realization of resources is likely to depend on whether or not these can be justified in the circumstances, and this in turn is likely to depend on such factors as the purposes of the course, the size of the student population likely to be affected by it, and the expected impact of the course on students and other interested parties. Clearly, a variety of interrelated factors needs to be taken into account in considering the appropriateness of different types of models.

3. The Instructional Materials Development Process

Just as it is useful to look once again at course models in order to place these more clearly in perspective, so it is equally useful to look back at the instructional materials development process, particularly since there is a major difference between that described and more conventional approaches. Thus, in describing conventional, objective approaches to instructional development, it is generally suggested that objectives be specified in fairly precise terms at the beginning of the process, and that these should then be used to provide guidance concerning the instruction to be developed. In practice, it is not usually .as simple as this. Objectives do not usually emerge in such a simple manner, and more often than not perceived objectives are modified and changed as development proceeds, even if broad aims remain the same. The point is that throughout any instructional development process, thinking is usually clarified, and refined, as development proceeds, and it would be most unfortunate not to encourage such development and innovation in thinking.

The instructional materials development process described in this book (and summarized in Figure 25) is designed to encourage innovative thinking within broad frames of reference, so that new

In Conclusion

Figure 25

Outline of the Instructional Materials Development Process

Phase 1

—Determination of broad course aims based on an analysis of student needs, taking note of the variation in needs of students with different interests and abilities.

Phase 2

—Determination of broad instructional strategies for achieving course aims, including choice of course model to be adopted.

—Identification of broad aims to be achieved in individual units, and determination of responsibilities (such as those of unit authorship) to be undertaken by individual course team members.

—Development of unit outlines (say four to five pages of manuscript each) providing a clearer statement of the aims to be achieved within each unit and the strategies envisaged for achieving them.

Phase 3

—Preparation of first full-draft presentation, including statements of objectives, but excluding assessment materials.

—Course team evaluation of first drafts.

—Preparation of second full-draft presentation, including domain-referenced objectives and all related assessment materials.

—Student testing of materials with at least a 'group try-out' stage of testing. (Adoption of 'field-testing' and 'individual try-out' stages likely to depend on existing circumstances.)

—Finalization of materials to conform to requirements of the chosen course model.

---

ideas can be accepted without disruptive effects on the work of the team as a whole. Thus, the process moves progressively forward initially obtaining agreement on broad course aims and then on more and more specific aims, with the stated aims providing a broad, and increasingly refined, frame of reference to guide the work of development at every stage in the process. Thus, in the early stages of the process, the broad aims are sufficient to make broad strategy decisions concerning the type of course model, but more specific unit strategies are not determined until later on in the process when the unit aims and objectives have been further clarified. In fact, domain-referenced objectives are not finalized in every detail until the very end of the process, since changes to test items and related domain-descriptions in the final stages of student testing inevitably modify objectives that are defined with regard to the related domains. The process might be best described as an iterative one, in that thinking at each stage in the process is likely to be refined in light of developments at the next stage. A continuing process of evaluation tends to reinforce the iterative nature of the process by ensuring that development at each stage takes careful note of feedback received.

Where to Now?

Hopefully this final chapter has helped to place the process of course design and development more clearly in perspective, although a fuller appreciation of the finer points may not be realized until one becomes fully involved in the development of course materials using the techniques described in this book. Hopefully, the book should provide all the guidance one needs to go ahead with confidence in developing instructional materials for courses.

Subject Index

ADVANCE ORGANIZERS
Characteristics of, 20-1
Concept of, 11
Development of, 101-4
Use of, 24-7

AIMS
Achievability of, 73-4
Assumed Knowledge, 90-1
Definition of, 21
Derivation of, 63-79, 90-1
   Iterative Hierarchical Approach, 65, 67-8
   Simple Hierarchical Approach, 65-7
Different Types of, 68-74
   According to Ability, 73-4, 89-90
   According to Importance and Relevance, 72-4, 92-3
   Affective, 72-3
   Cognitive, 70-2
   Goals, 50
   Importance of, 72-4, 92-3
   Knowledge Acquired, 70
   Means of Achievement, 81-97
   Relationships Among, 65-8
   Relevance of, 72-4, 92-3

DESIGN OF INSTRUCTION (See MODELS)

DEVELOPMENT OF INSTRUCTIONAL MATERIALS (See INSTRUCTIONAL MATERIALS DEVELOPMENT PROCESS)

EVALUATION
  Analysis of Tests (Also see **ITEM ANALYSIS**)
    Domain-Descriptions, 124-5
    Domain-Referenced Objectives, 104-5, 123-8
    Domain-Referenced Tests, 133-146
    Equivalence of Alternative Forms, 145-6
  Assumptions Underlying Instruction, 90-1, 108
  Continuous Process of Evaluation, 60-1
  Course Team Evaluation, 103-4
  Intrinsic Evaluation, 103
  Pay-Off Evaluation, 103
  Staff Perceptions of Instruction, 111-2
  Student Attitudes Towards Instruction
    Analysis of Attitudes, 147-9
    Motivation Towards Objectives, 111
  Student Needs
    Analysis of Needs, 63-5, 74-9
    Responding to Needs, 73-9
  Student Perceptions of Instruction
    Analysis of Perceptions, 110-1, 147-9
    Open-Ended Inquiry, 110-2
    Relationship to Performance, 158
    Strongly Guided Inquiry, 110-2
    Use of Questionnaires, 64, 147-158
  Student Performances on Tests
    Analysis of Test Scores (See **ITEM ANALYSIS**)
    Factors Affecting Performance, 108-110
    Measurement of Performance, 107-8
    Relationship to Perceptions, 158
  Student Testing of Instruction
    Developmental Testing, 105
    Field Testing, 112-3
    Group Try-Out, 106-7
    Overview of Student Testing, 147-9
    Validation Testing, 105
  Use of Multivariate Analysis Techniques, 158

Subject Index

INSTRUCTIONAL MATERIALS DEVELOPMENT PROCESS
  Development of
    Advance Organizers (Also see related aspects of **ADVANCE ORGANIZERS**), 101-3
    Aims and Objectives (Also see related aspects of **AIMS** and **OBJECTIVES**), 63-79, 90-1
    Domain-Referenced Objectives (Also see related aspects of **OBJECTIVES**), 104-5, 123-8
    Domain-Referenced Tests (Also see related aspects of **TESTS**), 104-5, 123-8, 133-146
    Frames of Reference, 59-61, 79, 81-2, 96-7
    Initial Drafts, 101-5
    Outlines, 90-7
    Summaries, 28
  Evaluation as a Parallel Process (Also see related aspects of **EVALUATION**), 60-1
  Phases of Development Process
    Phase 1: Identification of Course Aims, 63-79
    Phase 2: Outlining the Means of Achieving Aims, 81-97
    Phase 3: Progressive Development and Evaluation of Materials, 99-113
  Strategies of Development
    Determination of Media (See **MEDIA SELECTION**)
    Determination of Sequence (See **SEQUENCING OF INSTRUCTION**)
    Selection of Methods (See **METHODS OF INSTRUCTION** and **MODELS**)

ITEM ANALYSIS
  Analysis of Normal Score Distributions, 138-143
  Analysis of Skewed Score Distributions, 143-4
  Cell Statistics, 140-2
  Item Statistics
    Difficulty Index (See Facility Index)
    Discrimination Index, 139-140
    Facility Index, 139-140

Reliability
  Internal Consistency, 142-3
  Use of Item Analysis, 110, 133-144

MEDIA SELECTION AND FACTORS AFFECTING SELECTION
  Acceptability of Media, 95-6
  Method of Instruction, 94
  Senses Used, 93
  Sequence of Instruction, 94
  Student Ability, 96
    Enactive Learning, 96
    Iconic Learning, 96
    Symbolic Learning, 96

METHODS OF INSTRUCTION (Also see MODELS)
  Discovery Approach, 91-2
  Use of Case Studies, 92-3

MODELS
  Basic Characteristics
    Achievability of Learning, 73-4
    Active Involvement, 53, 91-2
    Anxiety Control, 50-1
    Cognitive Feedback, 49-51, 91-2
    Core Learning, 38-42, 89
    Drive Conditions (See Motivation)
    Goal Setting, 51-3
    Freedom of Choice (See Goal Setting)
    Importance of Learning, 72-4
    Learning with Understanding, 48-9, 72
    Motivation, 50-4
    Optional Learning, 38-46, 89
    Organization of Knowledge, 48-9
    Processing of Information, 72
    Profiles, 34, 39, 41
    Redundancy of Information, 72
    Relevance of Learning, 72-4
    Remedial Learning, 32, 49-50
    Retention of Knowledge, 34

Subject Index 177

   Basic Characteristics (Continued)
     Reward System, 50
     Section of Instruction, 18-24
     Self-Pacing, 33-4, 50-1
     Structure of Content, 21, 48-9
     Student Choice, 41-2, 51-3
     Summaries, 28
     Unit of Instruction, 24-8
     Varying Learner Abilities, 50-1, 73-7
   Course and Unit Models
     Branched Model, 39-41
     Keller Plan, 34-6
     Limited Time Models, 31-2, 42-6, 51
     Personalized System of Instruction (See Keller Plan)
     Refined Linear Model, 37-9
     Simple Linear Model, 32-7
     Unit Model, 17-29
     Unlimited Time Models, 31-2, 42-6, 51
     Variable Route Models, 41-2
   Models in Perspective, 168-170
   Need for Models, 5-12, 167-8
   Selection of Course Models, 89-90
   Use of Models, 7-8

OBJECTIVES
   Amplified Objectives, 125-8
   Assumed Knowledge (See related aspect of **AIMS**)
   Behavioral Objectives
     Characteristics of, 119-121
     Concept of, 118-9
     Effect on Student Learning, 9-10
     Location of, 9-10
   Definition of, 21
   Derivation of (See related aspect of **AIMS**)
   Different Types of (See related aspect of **AIMS**)
   Domain-Descriptions
     Characteristics of, 21-2, 118-123

Domain-Descriptions (Continued)
  Development of, 123-8
  Different Item Types, 129
  Evaluation of, 124-5
  Response Attributes, 125
  Stimuli Attributes, 125
Domain-Referenced Objectives
  Characteristics of, 21-2, 118-123
  Concept of, 10
  Development of, 104-5, 123-8
  Effect on Student Learning, 22-4
  Location of, 22-3
  Purpose of, 22-3
Importance of (See related aspect of **AIMS**)
Means of Achievement (See related aspect of **AIMS**)
Relevance of (See related aspect of **AIMS**)
Taxonomies of, 70-3

PRINCIPLES OF LEARNING, 54-6

QUESTIONNAIRES
  Different Types
    Bipolar Formats, 150-4
    Unipolar Formats, 154-7
  Interpreting Data, 157-8
    Multivariate Analysis Techniques, 158
    Perceptions and Performance, 158
  Use of Questionnaires, 64, 147-158

SEQUENCING OF INSTRUCTION
  Backward Chaining Approach, 86
  Forward Chaining Approach, 86
  Hierarchical Approach, 82-5
  Progressive Differentiation Approach, 85, 101-3
  Spiral Approach, 85

TESTS
Alternative Forms of Tests
Development of, 104-5, 124-5, 135-8
Equivalence of, 112-3, 145-6
Use of, 32, 35
Domain-Descriptions for Tests
Characteristics of, 21-2, 118-123
Development of, 123-8
Evaluation of, 124-5
Domain-Referenced Tests
Analysis of, 133-146
Characteristics of, 23-4
Desired Performance Levels, 161-3
Development of, 133-146
Different Item Types, 129
Estimation of Student Competency, 163-4
Interpretation of Scores, 161-4
Observed Scores, 161-4
True Performance Levels, 161-4
Use of, 23-4
Final Assessment Materials
Development of, 104-5
Interpretation of Scores, 161-4
Use of, 17, 23-4
Self-Assessment Materials
Development of, 104-5
Use of, 17, 23-4
Teachers' Assessment Materials (See Final Assessment Materials)

Author Index

AAAS Commission on Science Education, 92
Algina, J., 10, 164
Allen, M.K., 49
Anderson, R.C., 125
Angoff, W.H., 24, 32, 34, 112, 145
Ausubel, D.P., 11, 20, 82, 85, 101
Baker, E.L., 106
Barth, R.J., 121
Berlyne, D.E., 92
Bloom, B.S., 71, 73
Bobbitt, F., 118
Bormuth, J.R., 125
Bower, G.H., 47, 48, 49, 50, 51, 53, 54, 91
Briggs, L.J., 84, 93, 121
Bruner, J.S., 72, 85, 96
Burck, F., 118
Byner, J., 157
Castaneda, A., 51
Coffman, W.E., 129
Corey, J.R., 36
Coulson, D.B., 10, 164
Duchastel, P.C., 121
Eisenberg, T.A., 121
Gagne, R.M., 71, 82, 83, 84, 93, 121
Gilbert, T.F., 86, 106
Glaser, R., 10
Guilford, J.P., 143
Guttman, L., 125
Hambleton, R.K., 10, 164

Hamilton, D., 106
Hammersley, M., 157
Heidt, E.V., 93
Henderson, E.S., 106
Henrysson, S., 143
Hilgard, E.R., 47, 48, 49, 50, 51, 53, 54, 91
Hively, W., 125
Hoberock, L.L., 36, 39
Husek, T.R., 10
Kalton, A., 157
Keller, F.S., 9, 32, 39
Kerlinger, F.N., 158
Klein, S.P., 144
Kosecoff, J., 144
Krathwohl, R.D., 65, 73
Kuder, G.F., 142
Lawrence, W.G., 60
Lewis, C., 163
Liebert, R., 49
Lynn, R., 51
McCandless, B.R., 51
McMichael, J.S., 36
MacDermot, H.G., 36
MacDonald-Ross, M., 121
Mager, R.F., 9, 11, 21, 119
Markle, S.M., 105
Marton, F., 72
Martuza, V.R., 144
Masia, B.B., 73
Melton, R.F., 9, 13, 22, 29, 30, 46, 100, 107, 121, 143, 158
Merrill, P.F., 121
Meskauskas, J.A., 10, 164
Millman, J., 164
Moser, C., 157
Moss, A.G., 140
Nathenson, M.B., 106
Novick, M.R., 163

Author Index

Oppenheim, A.N., 157
Osgood, C.E., 152
Parlett, M., 106
Pask, G., 70
Payne, D.A., 65
Pedhazur, E.J., 158
Popham, W.J., 10, 118, 128, 144
Richardson, M.W., 142
Rogers, C., 72, 92
Sahakian, W.S., 54
Schutz, R.E., 99
Scott, B.C.E., 70
Scriven, M., 61, 103
Search, P.W., 118
Sheppard, W.C., 36
Sherman, J.G., 9, 35, 36
Skinner, B.F., 92, 118
Steadman, S., 107
Stotland, E., 50, 72, 73, 74, 92
Suci, G.J., 152
Swaminathan, H., 164
Tannenbaum, P.H., 152
Thiagarajan, S., 105
Thorndike, E.L., 118
Tyler, R.W., 63, 118
Walbesser, H.H., 121
Wesman, A.G., 129
Young, I., 60